Danny Rolling
Serial Killer

INTERVIEWS

By Sondra London

Danny Rolling
Serial Killer

INTERVIEWS

By Sondra London

Table of Contents

Sondra London with Anthony Meoli

A Sturdy Effigy

On October 28, 2020, criminologist Anthony Meoli gave Sondra London an interview about Danny Rolling.

Photo © Anthony Meoli

Sondra   Tell us about your background as a criminologist.

Meoli   I hold four degrees. My degrees include a Bachelor of Science in Criminal Justice from Penn State University, a law school from John Marshall Law School and two Master's degrees in Forensic Psychology and Clinical Mental Health Counseling. However, at the time I was writing Danny, my background was primarily in criminology and law.

London   Well, I know you have interviewed some other serial killers, but had any of those interviews been accomplished before you met Danny?

Meoli   When I met Danny, I had interviewed many people through written correspondence, but not in person. That was in 2003. Danny was not the first inmate I had interviewed, because I had actually worked inside a prison for a year. I had already interviewed nearly a thousand inmates, including hundreds of murderers, but Danny was the first serial killer that I spent six hours with – face to face.

London   So you had not only the academic background, but that time you spent working full-time in a prison. How long did you spend doing that?

Meoli   I spent from late 1998 to the end of 1999 at the Fulton County Prison in Atlanta, Georgia, which as many people say, is the "most dangerous jail in America." But I don't know, when you worked there, it did not seem so bad.

London   Then what was it, that particularly attracted you to want to know more about Danny Rolling? Of course, day in and day out, we have new crimes and personalities. But what was it about Danny in particular that made you say, I want to get to know this guy?

2

Meoli   I had seen his case profiled on an investigative reports show at the time and I realized my home was physically close to the prison. I was living in Atlanta, GA, so Gainesville, FL was not that far from me – about six hours to drive. So I could actually drive and go visit the crime scenes to fully understand the case, insofar as the geography of it. That is what drove me to go down there before I contacted him, because I wanted to be familiar with the three sites and crime scenes, understand the movements that he made, and that helped me when contacting him.

London   You went to that wooded area behind Archer Road?

Meoli   Yes, I did visit that area. Unfortunately, many of the places have either been changed or moved. But some of the scenes are very much like they were back in 1990, even today.

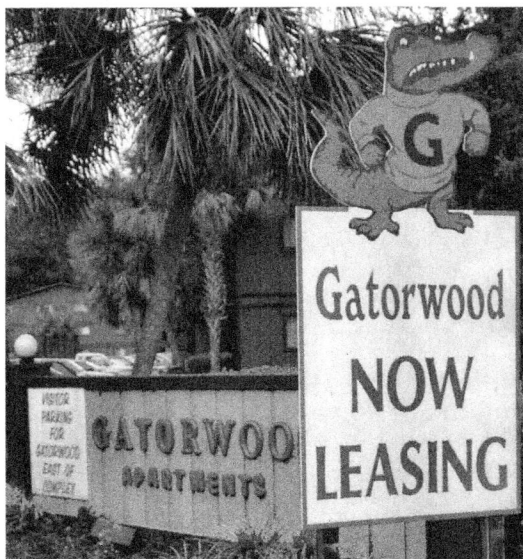

Photo © Sondra London

London   Well, the apartment buildings were still there, the Gatorwood. This is a little side note here, Glen Rogers' brother Clay told me that he had camped out in Archer Woods, and he said it was a hot spot for hobos.

Meoli   Yes, but it didn't look like the safest place to be. And today it's probably even worse. Danny wasn't there all that long. But I cannot imagine living there for weeks on end.

Meoli   So what drove me to get involved in Danny's case was learning what happened directly from the source – the graphic nature of the crimes. His case struck me as something different. I've read a lot of books in my studies, but nothing that was a ten on a one-to-ten scale of the gravity of what was done to those victims in Gainesville. That's what compelled me to want to know why someone would do this.

London   I'll tell you how Danny first caught my interest. I was in New York City when the crimes happened. So, I read about the case in York City newspapers. But what really caught my interest was when I saw him on TV singing in court. And I said, what kind of nut is this?

Meoli   Well, I don't know if it was a nervous thing for Danny, but he seemed to break out into song for some reason at inappropriate times. I don't know if that was something in his personality, because it was not something you would typically see from a defendant in court.

London   It's a way to change the subject, if the drift of things is going in a direction that might threaten some stronghold you're protecting. Other people would change the subject other ways. And Danny might do other things as well, but you notice from corresponding with him, that he does that with

4

graphics in his letters. I think that is the same tendency as his versifying and his singing. It emanates from the same trait. He's writing along in language and words, then he just bursts out in a picture, right?

Meoli   Right. With him, there were often some incongruent drawings, like he would start off a letter to me, and he would make my name "Anthony" into a gruesome character, but then the content of the letter would be friendly. So the "*A*" might be a skull and the "*Y*" might be a knife. And then everything else in the letter would be normal, and he would act like it was no big deal for me to see that. But, he knew, obviously, I was looking at it.

London   Well, I would imagine that at that point, he was consciously gifting you with valuable artwork. Because when I first encountered Danny, he had no idea that he was an artist at all. And I had to tell him, these things that you keep sending me, you're an artist, you need to sign your work and date it. And then, boy, did he ever take that to heart. And ever after that, everything he did, he signed and dated religiously. And I had tell him, this stuff that you are sending me is valuable. It is valuable because it's rare. And it needs to stay rare. So that was my instruction to him. By the time you met him, he was self-aware of the things he was sending people having value. And I think he probably put the creepy, scary stuff in there because it was the trademark killer imagery, right?

8-15-2003

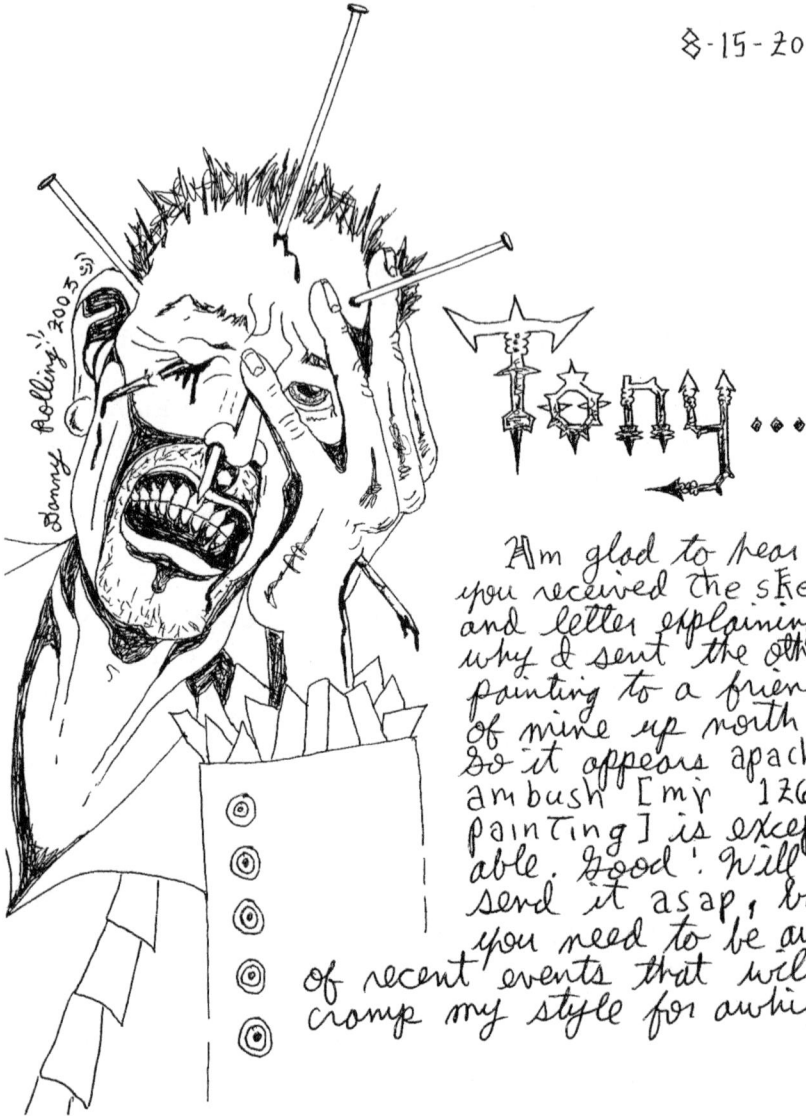

Drawing by Danny Rolling © Anthony Meoli

Meoli   Right. I think there is something to that. He knew
we weren't expecting flowers. He thought a skull
would be more marketable, or more along the lines
of what the, "Gainesville Ripper" would produce.

London   Exactly. And then you've got your roles. You were
          not there as a buddy-buddy. You were there as a
          criminologist.

Meoli   Right.

London   I remember when Danny was rebutting various the
          things that were being said about him, and how
          some were saying he was gay. And he wrote back to
          me in his letter, all-caps and bold, *"NO HOMO!"* He
          was very emphatic about that. So, I think, to relate
          to a guy in a mutually respectful way, he wouldn't
          want to be too adorable and cute and cuddly-
          kittens.

Meoli   No, I agree. He was very, I don't want to say
          "macho," but he presented this image as being one
          of strength. When it related to how he would
          converse in letters, he always used powerful words
          like *formidable* and *strong*.

London   About himself? Or was it just words he used a lot?

Meoli   It was words he used. Even after our visit, in the
          first letter that I got a few days later, because
          again, I was only one state away, he wrote, *"You
          present a sturdy effigy in person."* I thought that
          was really unique way of describing our visit.

London   Yeah, I don't think he knew what the word effigy
          means.

Meoli   No, but he liked big words, even if they were often
          misspelled, and he would tend to use bigger words
          with me. It seemed that was his way of trying to
          say, Hey, I'm educated, and I want you to
          understand that, or I'm well-read and I want you to
          respect that. Either way, he came across as fairly
          intelligent in person, so that was never really an

issue. But it seemed like something he struggled with when he would write.

London   Why don't you walk us through your visit with Danny Rolling?

Meoli   At the time, Death Row at Union Correctional Center was a little bit different than it is today. There was a little less security in some respects, and I didn't know exactly what to expect on Death Row with regards to Danny, because he was such a high-profile inmate. But when I got there, they checked me in. This was before the handprint technology had been developed. It was just a number code on a card. They logged my name in, I went through the security thing, they made sure I didn't have my keys on me or any metal, and I walked the long way around to get to Death Row. They buzzed me in two more doors, and I was the first person in the room that day.

London   Were there other Death Row visitors in your group?

Meoli   There were, but I was the first person to sit down and tell the deputy who I was there to see. And I was just waiting, because they would have the inmate put on white pants to designate they were having visitation. It depends on what year it was and whatever the warden was doing, but at the time, they would wear an orange top and white pants, to denote visitation. There were three rows of round tables and I was dead center in the middle. The way it worked was depending on whoever came in the room, they went and got the inmate, because often visitors would come in sporadically, so they wouldn't just dress out an inmate until their visitor was sitting there.

London   I see.

Meoli   So I was just sitting there all alone with the deputy when all of a sudden Danny appeared behind the door. It surprised me because it was just Danny, myself, and the deputy. I was surprised because I thought they would keep him in leg irons or hand irons. I don't know how they did it, but they took everything off of him. He was completely free of restraints. He didn't have any leg irons. He didn't have anything on his hands. And then I got up because he was sort of like waving to me. We didn't really know, this was before email pictures were being sent. We had each seen other in some photographed copies, but it's weird to see somebody in person.

London   Well, you were the only people there, right?

Meoli   Right. So, all that stuff comes together, and now we're face to face and I stand up to greet him as he comes out the door, and he shakes my hand, and that was the weirdest thing. And I've heard this from other people who have interviewed him as well. He shook my hand, and I've never felt such a strong grip. I'm a pretty strong guy. At the time, I was probably 185 pounds, five-foot-nine, and Danny is about six-three and lanky. But I didn't expect the strength he had in his hand. It seemed to almost crush my hand. I tried to match his handshake–

London   Right, now you're in an arm-wrestling match with a serial killer.

Meoli   It's this weird guy-code thing, you shake a guy's hand as firmly as he shakes yours. And it happens in a matter of a split second. Some guys have a firm handshake, some guys have a soft handshake. But Danny's was a crushing handshake, like something I've never really felt even to this day, seventeen years later.

London   What message was he sending you by doing that?

Meoli   The oddest thing about the message is I did not
          sense he was sending me a message. There are
          some guys who you could see them, their brow gets
          all frowned when they're shaking hands. This was
          just his natural style. And at this very moment, I
          can recall how hard my hand was being held. You
          don't forget things like that.

London   You know, Tony, you can have all the strength in
          the world, but it's up to you to apply it.

Meoli   I agree.

London   And he chose to apply it. Was he putting you in
          your place? Was he dominating you?

Meoli   Maybe there was some attempt to intimidate factor
          because he was physically five to six inches taller
          than me. And he had a big firm handshake. He
          wanted to see how I reacted, and I didn't really
          react in a negative way. I didn't pull back. Because,
          frankly, he could have just strangled me right
          there. By the time somebody got to me, he could
          have been on top of me, because there was nothing
          holding his arms back, and the guard was several
          few feet away. He probably could have strangled me
          to death, I mean he wouldn't, but he could have. He
          could have been on top of me in seconds.

London   How long did he maintain that vise grip on you?
          Was it longer or was it just a brief shake and let go?

Meoli   No, no, no. It was just a firm handshake. Two,
          three, four seconds tops. And it wasn't like he held
          it and just crushed it. It was like, here's your
          handshake, but very firm. So firm I will remember
          it for the rest of my life.

London   Let's go back to that letter you talked about, where he inscribed your name with such aggressive imagery and then was so friendly. So the handshake is like the aggressive heading. In other words, he's establishing that he's in character as a serial killer on Death Row. So after he made his point with that impressive grip, then the rest of it was similar, in that he was very friendly and cordial.

Meoli   He was cordial for the entire six hours. And again, because I got there very early, I was the first person there. I knew from different people who had been there, if you get there early, you'll get in early. And so, visitation began at nine o'clock sharp, and I was in the room already. They were allowed visitation till three, sometimes three-thirty. So we went the full six hours, maybe longer. But he was never at any time overtly aggressive or overbearing. He was always listening to me and answering my questions. Yeah, there's a few times where I purposely bothered him to see if this would change his demeanor. And that's where I saw the real Danny pop up a little bit.

London   Oh, no. You must tell me about that.

Meoli   Well, it was a little disturbing. We had gone back and forth about Ted Bundy in his letters, and he always got upset about me mentioning Ted Bundy in connection with the name him. It wasn't that I was comparing crimes, it was just the question of why certain people ended up in Florida, like Bundy and himself.

London   Right! That is fascinating question.

Meoli   I insinuated the migration of serial killers, and I mentioned a few people who had traveled the country and ended up on Florida's Death Row.

London   Glen Rogers had done the same thing. Here are three guys who could have gone anywhere. Why Florida? That was my question.

Meoli   Why Florida? Well, I asked him that question during our visit, because I had asked it in a letter. So, it wasn't like it was something new. I asked him, is there a rationale for your actions? You could've gone west. You went east. We believe that the three happened in Louisiana and nothing in between, we believe, and then he gets to Florida, and we have the five more murders in Florida, for a total of eight. But my question to him was, why would you migrate to a state where you know there's a death penalty?

London   Right. Where they do not play.

Meoli   They don't play around.

London   Florida will kill you.

Meoli   Back in the early nineties, Florida was known, if you kill here, you will be killed here. They knew that. And yet I was fascinated, was this an internal thought, like you knew you'd be on Death Row, that you would be executed. Danny got very upset by that line of questioning. I mean, he didn't get up and walk out or anything, but he was visibly upset that I had talked about it again in our visit.

London   I wonder, were you were ever aware of any interaction between Danny Rolling and Glen Rogers?

Meoli   As far as inmate-to-inmate?

London   Yeah.

Meoli   I know that Glen was not a big fan of Danny's bravado, if you will, about murder. He had heard enough about it, so to say, because Danny apparently talked about murder all the time, and a lot of the guys didn't like it. He talked about some pretty disturbing stuff. People think, well, you're on Death Row, so what's the problem? But not everybody on Death Row likes hearing about murder, and we know there's a hierarchy. Young women are not so bad. Teenagers –

London   Then we come to the "short eyes."

Meoli   Right, "short eyes" gets them right around like eleven, twelve or so. And then you get into the pedophile range, which is below ten. This is where inmates are usually on a different wing of the prison.

London   You're in big trouble.

Meoli   So if you killed a bunch of 25-year-olds, you're all right on Death Row.

London   Gerard John Schaefer was very particular as to what I might call his victims. He had two murder victims who were seventeen and eighteen, and I had to call them young women. Not girls. Not even teenagers. Once the killer has to live in prison, those kids graduate to being women.

Meoli   I always found it interesting that with Ted Bundy, Kimberly Leach was only 12, and yet nobody really attached any kind of negative connotation to her murder. Now believe it or not, this is a weird story. One of my best high school friends, Kimberli Lee – her father back before they moved to New Jersey, where I lived, they lived in Florida in the 1970's. They owned a bar that Ted Bundy had been in right after Kimberly Leach's murder. He came into the

bar and asked if he could use the bathroom, but he
went into the female bathroom. Her father thought
this was odd, because he had told him where the
bathroom was located. When Bundy came out, he
was a little disheveled. He wanted directions to go
to this small town, which his father also found
strange, because most people asked him how to get
to Jacksonville or some larger city like that. So
after Bundy left, her father went into the bathroom.
He was like, "Why was this guy in the girls'
bathroom?" When he went inside the bathroom he
found this little round earring that wasn't there
before. And that was really strange. So a few days
later, when they were looking for the murderer of
Kimberly Leach, they put Ted Bundy's picture up
and sure enough, when they found her body, she
only had one earring. And it matched the one Ted
Bundy had left in that bathroom. Whether it was
accidental, or on purpose, nobody really knows. But
I do know that, for some reason or other, Ted
Bundy never really took heat in prison for killing a
12-year-old girl.

London   Did Danny ever say or write to you anything about
          Gemini telling him where to go?

Meoli   We had sort of left that in the letters, that my
          personal belief was Danny backwards is Ennad. It
          makes sense. I don't really fight with inmates who
          have a, quote, alter ego or whatever they want to
          call it. Because the Danny who sat across from me
          for six hours was not the one that the victim saw.
          The Danny I saw was composed, he was intelligent,
          he was at times thought-provoking. But he wasn't
          that premeditated murderer persona, lying in wait
          for me to get home, so he could kill me. I got to see
          the Danny Rolling who most people probably saw
          for most of his life. And as with most of the serial
          killers I have either talked to or visited, they
          present in such a different way because they're not

in the thrall of the things that brought them to prison. They are just there as a human being talking one-on-one in a very friendly setting. We were talking over cinnamon buns and Cokes to start the morning off. And what did strike me was Danny had a ton to eat when we were there.

London   Oh God bless him. It was probably nervousness and also the flavors of the junk food compared to the flavorlessness of the prison fare.

Meoli   I forget what the limit was at the time, but it was mostly in singles. I think it was like thirty or forty dollars that you could bring into the prison, because they would check for how much money you could have. You could have quarters in see-through bag, and they inspected it all before you went in. But right away Danny asked me, "Would you mind if we got a soda and some things?" We went up to the window, and the inmate had the window halfway open. Danny was like, "Can I get two sodas and two Snickers... and M&Ms?" In the six hours were there, he must have consumed over 3000 calories.

London   Was it all sweets? Or did you have hot dogs or stuff like that?

Meoli   Yes. We had a cheeseburger from the machine. You know, the kind where it just swings around, and you order by number and then microwave it. We had a cinnamon bun and multiple candy bars plus at least four Cokes. One of the techniques I like to use is, giving mu inmates lot of carbohydrates early in the morning. Because then there's a lag in the afternoon where they get a little tired and then they're more likely to let down their guard and just talk. There is the getting used to each other period. Then the delivery, the understanding that you don't have to be afraid of his emotions. This is who he is.

Getting over some of the initial reservations I had
about asking him things. There is a small
microphone above our heads of course. Well, there's
a little microphone on the ceiling. Apparently, you
can't really see it but the inmates believed it was
there. Danny was always wary of how loud we were
talking.

Photo © Anthony Meoli

London   Wasn't he already condemned to death?

Meoli   He was already condemned to death, but there were
certain things that if we were going to talk about,
he would do a motion like this, *<pointing to ceiling
with thumb>.* This was three or four hours into our
interview, and I didn't quite understand, and I
looked up and he was like *<pointing>,* and then we
did request to move.

London   Was he fighting an appeal?

Meoli   This was in 2003, three years before his death.
Danny was always fighting something, filing

something, whether or not it was anything worthwhile, but I don't believe there were any active appeals that would have stopped his execution at the time of our visit. But, at the time, he hadn't really admitted to the three Grissom murders. And I wanted to get some information directly from Danny, since I was face to face with him. I knew was probably the last time I would have the chance.

London   Well, it was the first time.

Meoli   Right, it was the first time. But I also realized the odds of me getting back there were going to be slim. So it took me a little time. It wasn't like I instantly was going to ask him these questions, but this was like hour four that I slowly had worked him into it. You know, I'm comfortable with you, you're comfortable with me, so now I want to ask you some tougher questions. We were talking in the third person at this time, as Danny liked to do. I would say something to the effect, "I wasn't quite sure if the person could have possibly gone upstairs knowing someone was downstairs, and have done what they did upstairs, without the person downstairs waking up."

London   Scene number one.

Meoli   Right, scene number one. So, he goes, "No, that is how it happened." He said, "The person was probably able to get into the apartment and not awaken the person, because he was a very experienced burglar. He was able to disable the person upstairs fairly quickly."

London   According to his written account, simultaneously putting the duct tape on her mouth with his left hand and stabbing her in the heart with his right hand.

Meoli   That was his method to get in, using his burglar tool, which was a simple screwdriver. It was not something he struggled with; he was very good at doing that. He was also good at being quiet, for a six-foot-three man. I had been inside that apartment at least twice.

London   How did you get in?

Meoli   Luckily, the first time I went down there before I saw Danny, I had asked to see an apartment. The apartment manager asked if I wanted to rent there as a student or a graduate student, I guess because I was 32. I said, "I'm just interested in what the apartments look like." So the manager took me to the apartment. She said, this apartment does have a bad reputation; and I acted like I didn't know anything about it. She opened the door, and it was the exact apartment the first two victims had been murdered in. I was shocked that this was what they were using to show people how the apartments looked – but who would know? They didn't allow anybody to rent it, because it was their "show apartment." And about a year later, when I went to visit Danny, I went back to that crime scene again. And sure enough, I was able to get into that apartment the same way. It was interesting to see what Danny saw that night and how he came in from the back of the woods, if you will. It's a weird apartment because you have to go up the stairs to get into the back door, which faces the woods. But, after breaking in, he would have had to come in at a 45 degree angle from the door and not awaken Christina Powell, who was downstairs on the couch sleeping, and then head upstairs to do what he did. After walking the scene myself, I found it very interesting to hear Danny go over his take on what happened. He talked about it like, the person would have been an experienced burglar, sort of patting himself on the back, if you will, to be able to quietly enter the apartment and murder the victim upstairs very quickly, so she couldn't make a sound.

Photo © Sondra London

London   Doesn't that sound like a maneuver that was practiced? It just seems too professional to be the first and only time he ever did that.

Meoli   I think he may have even been inside that apartment before, to become familiar with the layout. Because remember, it's dark, and it's easy to bump into something and wake somebody up. Danny did lay in wait at the second murder scene, so it wouldn't have been a stretch for me to think that he may have familiarized himself with that apartment too. The entrance was perfect for him. It allowed him cover of night, because he was in the back of the apartment complex. It was easy to break

19

into, so it was ideal. It contained two females, which was a gruesome fantasy for him. He was able to sexually assault and murder two females in the same apartment, with one downstairs still sleeping, while he did fairly unspeakable things to the victim upstairs.

London   Well, I'll be the devil's advocate and pretend it was me, and I do bump into something, and I look at the girl to see if she woke up, and she didn't, so then I figure, well, she's sound asleep, she's going to stay asleep. It might have gone into his calculus of how sound asleep she was. It might happen, but never rise to the level of being worth mentioning.

Meoli   It definitely could be within the realm of possibility.

London   Well, it's just a thought.

Meoli   He did many other things that were needless. He was gruesome in what he did, taking a chunk out of Sonya Larson's left thigh with his knife. It was almost like he was starting to practice with his knife – post mortem. When I saw the crime scene photos at the Alachua County Courthouse, I was shocked at what he did to her. It went so far beyond what was needed for murder. It was even beyond overkill.

London   That's the point – beyond murder. So, let's pretend you're just a thug. And some guy betrays you. So, you kill him. Okay, your problem has been eliminated. Next thing on your to-do list is get the hell out of there. If you want to get away with murder. Now, when you see a case where the person has committed the murder and they stay there, then it's not about the murders. There's something more going on there. That's the extraordinary part of all of Danny's murders, the postmortem lingering at the crime scene. In the case of Christa Hoyt, if what he told me was true, he actually left and came back. There has to be a very compelling reason to come back to a murder scene.

Meoli   Danny had always stressed that fact. He had this need to explain the reason to go back. But getting back to the first murder, if we're to believe that this is the first Florida murder, because the Shreveport, LA murders had already happened the year previous. But if this is the very first Florida murder, with the graphic nature of what he had just done, if that were me, I would have thought, wow, I can't believe I just did that! And maybe I'd say I can't believe I just did that and got away with it without her roommate waking up. Maybe it would be more shocking if I just leave. What if she wakes up in the morning and goes to find her roommate, and her roommate looks the way she did. I mean, she would be like, "How could this have happened?" Mind blown? Obviously Danny's DNA would still have been there. But to then to go downstairs, risk further capture because you are there even longer, and then do the same thing to the other victim. He then cleaned the victims, and in some grotesque way, then posed the victims. Posing a victim is, again, unnecessary postmortem action, which only happens in about one to two percent of all serial killing cases. It's extremely rare. When you see the posing of a victim, police should immediately realize that more murders are going to occur – or have occurred and they jut have not found the victim(s) yet.

London   That's an interesting statistic.

Meoli   Jack Trawick, an Alabama serial killer, told me about one of his victims that was found behind a church. And he said, everybody wanted to find some crazy satanic or religious reason for it. "But for me, it was just the closest place, and I figured there'd be nobody behind the church because it was a Monday. So that's where I put the body." Jack said, "If you want to learn about murder, 99.9% of the time, the reason is convenience. You want to get rid of the body and get out of there as soon as possible." I took that to heart, because looking at crime scenes years later, I would always keep in mind what Jack said to me: Don't build your case based on where the body is found, because maybe the body was just put there simply because it was convenient.

London   And the obverse of that exact same thing is, don't dwell so hard on decoding the victimology. They go into, why did he kill girls with their hair parted in the middle? It's not a fashion preference, it's opportunity. Victims are selected because they're vulnerable. You could take the exact same person, put them in a different setting, and the serial killer would not even notice them. It's the circumstance. You know, no one knows where they are. No one's around, the place is deserted. They are befuddled, they're clueless. It's not because they part their hair in the middle. It's not like he would bypass five girls with curly hair and then follow this one girl around until she entered a setting where she was now rendered vulnerable. He feels like killing, so he looks for the first opportunity, like Pee Wee Gaskins and his Coastal Kills, right? Just trolling for vulnerable victims of any description.

Meoli   People will say the hair color is similar. Well, more girls are brunette than blonde, and far less yet are redheads. So, you're going to see more brown-haired girls murdered simply because there are more of them. You don't always want to get too deep into the specifics of how someone looks just, while ignoring the overall population.

London   They went into that with Glen Rogers, they said he had a thing for redheads, so I took photos of all his known victims and just sampled the hair color and lined up the samples. They were not even close to the same.

Meoli   No, they weren't. I don't know where they come up with that stuff.

London   It's an artifact created by people who want to make a better story.

Meoli   Right, and who are not actually deeply involved in a case enough to do exactly what you did. These are the kinds of things that I look for, those little nuances. Danny said, "and then the person would have gone downstairs and done a similar thing to the other victim."

London   That's exactly the way Ted Bundy talked to Stephen Michaud.

Meoli   Right. He didn't say I or me. It was always "that person would have, or the person who did that would have," which allows him a little bit more leeway because he could fantasize the case and not take blame for it by saying it that way.

London   Well, remember, murder can be quite traumatic, and if the killer has been traumatized, then trauma is attached to recalling it. If they allow themselves to go there again, then they will be disturbed. And they're trying to cooperate with an interview. So, they want to be able to give you the answers you want, so they try to handle them with protective techniques, in such a way that they can maintain without falling into a post-traumatic flashback that overwhelms them. And there goes your interview. You're just trying to ask questions, and you have to become a psychotherapist. So I think that there's a good reason for him to keep his murder experience at arm's length.

Meoli Right. And there's some self preservation necessary because regardless of how tough they are, it's difficult to live with what they've done. And people always say, how can you possibly talk to these murderers week after week, month after month? I'm like, I don't always talk to them about murder. I say, in fact, I rarely do. The reason they do talk to me is because I don't talk about that. We've gone over the graphic nature early on in our relationship, and this goes for inmates who I've talked to for two decades. We've gotten past what they did, the reasons the why the who, what, when, where and how. But they don't want to regurgitate the worst thing that they've done in their life over and over again. So I think the reason why they relate to me, and call me again and again, is because they know I won't be asking them about murder, and I'm there to just listen. And sometimes they'll tell me something that's new or they'll say, hey, something else happened in my childhood, that I just wanted you to know about. And that's the kind of stuff that I'm there for. And I learned that it's not even healthy for me, to constantly be talking about gruesome murders in every single phone call. That's not healthy for anybody.

London That's right.

Meoli How many phone calls do you expect me to take, to hear about killing somebody? If I'm talking to an inmate every week, taking their collect calls for a decade, most likely I haven't talked to him about murder for the past nine years. I mean, you do have your Phillip Carl Jablonskis, the serial killers who enjoy regurgitating all the gory details, and sometimes making up stuff just to relieve their boredom, or to see if it upsets you. But those people are relatively few and far between.

24

London   Well, that's one of the symptoms they list under the diagnosis of sadism, deriving pleasure from causing not just pain but even discomfort, or disgust. It can be a manifestation of the same syndrome that put them where they are.

Meoli   I talked to Lee Boyd Malvo, and I talked to Jablonski, and I talked to Bianchi, and I talked to Orr, and I talked to all these different types of individuals who did everything from arson to serial murder. And people think it's easy to just ask these questions and get these answers. But it takes quite some time for them to get comfortable with you. People don't realize what goes into it. They say, you just interviewed Malvo for an hour, and you got all this information. Yeah, but the questions I asked him were extremely specific and detailed. He was revealing a childhood suicide attempt, and that would not have come out, had we not had a hundred phone calls previously. We were able to break that ice gradually, over a long time, and so answering that type of question was easy because we had already covered it.

London   People can be so foolish. They look at what you've done, they look at what I've done, and they think, well, I can do that, too. And then while the perp's being walked across the yard, the reporter from the little local newspaper runs up and sticks a mike in their face, yelling "Why'd you do it?" like the answer is going to be forthcoming. Like that's not a person, it's an Answer Machine. You pop in your quarters and out come your answers. On ice.

Meoli   Exactly.

London   Now you can provoke someone into responding to anything. Walk up to them and yell: Why did you do it! You might get an answer. But I guarantee you it's not the real answer to the question. If you do

25

want to know the real answers, you have to give a lot – in terms of sweat equity, in terms of your own time and attention, and you have to invest a lot before any questions you ask are going to produce anything significant. Otherwise it's just stimulus and response. And what value is that level of interaction? But that's as far as most of these ambitious journalists are willing to go.

Meoli   You have to be willing to almost climb inside the serial killer's own mind for a prolonged amount of time and live there, if you're going to truly get to know him. And that is very uncomfortable to do. Like with Danny Rolling, writing to him every week, and going to visit him, slowly coming to understanding him and his mindset. It's a disturbing way to live. And what you did with Danny, I know I've said this a thousand times. It's depressing, it's scary, it produces anxiety. But in order to tell the story that you told, you have to be willing to crawl inside their skin. And not everybody is willing to get that close to them, to pull out that story.

London   Good for them, Good for them. May they be happy and healthy and live long and prosper. But they are not going to do anything of value without making that kind of in-depth sacrifice. And when you devote your time and attention to any endeavor, you have to calculate profit versus loss, risk versus benefits. The time that you spend on this, you're not able to spend doing anything else. So you have to calculate how much you've lost from not investing that same time and energy in another project. And be that as it may, did we finish talking about your visit with Danny? I've interrupted you too many times.

Meoli   No, it's okay. One question I asked him, because he really hadn't admitted as much to me as he had to you, so I wanted to know from Danny himself, sitting right in front of me, and watch his reactions. I wanted to see if he would admit to the Grissom murders, the three victims in Louisiana in 1989. And so I asked him, "Would the person be responsible for eight murders?" Saying to Danny, "There are not five but eight murders." And I'll never forget this. He thought about it for a second, then he said, "Well, if the person did what they did in Florida, they would tap their finger five times." And then he explained, "If the person in Louisiana did what they did, they would tap their finger three times". I didn't fully understand what he meant. Then he sort of laid back in his chair and he went like this. <*Slowly raps the metal table slowly eight times while looking at me.*> It sent a chill down my spine. As he was looking at me, and I will swear to this day – I thought his eyes turned black. Because his eyes were so blue, as you know, it was odd. When some people get excited, their pupils can grow larger and they get really big – making the eyes appear to darken. In my mind he was experiencing this phenomenon because his eyes went from blue to black. I didn't see any of the blue, his whole iris appeared almost black. I had spoken to all sorts of people while I was Atlanta, and there were some serious gang killers in the Fulton County jail. But this was the first time I felt this shiver down my spine. It seemed like Danny was looking through me, not at me. It was at that very moment I think I did saw what his victims saw before they were killed.

London   You saw something real in his eyes.

Meoli   Yes.

London   That echoes my experience with getting Gerard John Schaefer to talk. I had been playing games with him for over a year about whether he was a serial killer or not, and on this one visit I confronted him frankly, demanding an explanation of why he was telling me one story, and then sending newspaper editors letters telling them the direct opposite story. They can't both be true, I said, I don't understand. Either you are lying here or you're lying there. And Schaefer leaned forward. He put his face right up close to mine, and through those clunky prison glasses, he peered deep into my eyes. And he said in an undertone: You don't understand, because you're not a serial killer. And after all the words that had passed back and forth, finally something real happened there with the eyes. And it's like you said, in a prison visit you are limited to what you can say verbally. So that's why you get these messages that can't be spoken.

Meoli   But here's the thing. As much as I want to translate that story to you, and as much as you can understand it, probably better than anyone else regarding Danny Rolling, I can't ever capture that moment, I can only feel it again, and I can only try to explain it.

London   It's not something you can present on the witness stand. It's like, do you believe what he said? And you'd be like, Yes, I believe it. Then they'd go, why? And the only thing you could say would be, because I looked into his eyes. And you know that dog won't hunt. But you are not going to get the death-stare chills like that unless there's something real behind it.

Meoli   Yes, you could feel it.

London   I wonder if maybe his pupils dilated because he was mortally invested in knowing your reaction. He had given you a weapon that you might turn on him. And I think that finding out how you were gonna handle this was foremost in his mind. He was trying to take in as much information as he could about you, because he had just crossed a critical line. Do you remember how you reacted?

Meoli   I remember it felt like he was looking more through me than at me, and the chill that ran through me was delayed a little, because I was trying hard to maintain my cool, if you will. I was very much in the moment, but when he did that tapping.

London   That was high drama right there, that was pure Danny.

Meoli   Yeah, it was very dramatic. His fingers were only an inch or two off the table. And he was just going *<tap, tap, tap>* and I can still hear it in my ear. To this day, it just keeps ringing. And yes, he definitely wanted to elicit a response for me. He wanted to see what my reaction would be.

London   Yes. And what was it? Did you continue talking about Grissom, or did you just move on?

Meoli   Well, I had already upset him about Ted Bundy earlier in the day. I had pushed a few buttons by that point, and I had actually gotten the story of the Gainesville five, if you will, and this was about four hours in. I just felt like he had told me enough, and I didn't want to push him any further. He had slumped back in his seat, and now we were at the furthest distance apart than we had been before. We model behavior, when I lean towards you, if you are in tune, you will lean towards me. If Danny was going to continue to lean back, we'd just be too far apart to continue that conversation. So, I left it alone after that point. I got the information I needed. I believe in my heart that he was admitting to those murders. I had to bring him back a little bit, so I left it alone so that we could continue on for the next two hours.

London   Okay, so this is what you could not have known.
          Danny had sworn that his confession to the
          Shreveport murders was my story. It belong to me.
          He said he owed it to me for all the suffering I went
          through for standing by him. He had written that
          story for me years before. And I refused to release it
          because of the abuse I had taken for publishing the
          confessions to the Gainesville murders, and all the
          horrors that were brought down on me from all
          sides, for what Danny and I both considered to be
          our best effort at doing the right thing. I didn't ask
          him to send it to me. He just sent it on his own
          volition. And after I had it in hand, we did
          correspond about it in several letters, and that's
          where he wrote me and said you can do anything
          you want with it. He promised me, this story is
          yours. You make your own choices. So in 2003
          Danny was well aware that I had still not published
          the story, and he was honorable enough to respect
          the promises he made to me. Danny continued to
          keep his word, all the way to his execution. At the
          very last minute, all he would ever give was a very
          bare admission of guilt. When it came to the kind of
          details that he gave me about the Gainesville
          murders in *The Making of a Serial Killer,* he would
          never give that to anyone else ever again. And the
          promise he had made to me was something he
          couldn't tell you. He couldn't just frankly say,
          "That's Sondra's story, leave it alone." Because even
          that admission would violate our confidentiality,
          giving notice that the confession did exist and was
          in fact in my hands. Right?

Meoli   Yes. And without saying more, it ended there. It
          ended with a bang, so to say, and that was it. There
          was nothing about Julie, nothing about her son or
          her father, no details. The number of victims was all
          I got. You got the rest.

Drawing by Danny Rolling © Sondra London

London   I was just reading a letter that Danny wrote early in
1993. I had said to him, someone told me that the
number five is very important to you. And he wrote
back, "Well, I suppose it is. But what if I told you
the numbers is actually eight?" And then he drew a
portrait from a photo of me peering out from
behind a tree, that he embellished with all these
curious figures in the creases of the bark. And then
he wrote to me that the number of his victims could
be found in that tree. So I wrote back, yeah I see the
five. He says, that's great, but that's not it, leading
me to search again and finding the figure eight in

there as well as the five; and then I realized he had put a three near the five. So he was using that number thing as early as 1993, as an encrypted way to let me know what was involved in his story, without getting in trouble for it.

Meoli   I never got really a chance to ask you this, and you would know better than anybody. Do you believe that those first two victims were accidental? Because allegedly he was seen on a video camera in a Walmart at the same time as they were, and again, I don't know if this is actually true.

London   Oh yeah, that did happen, and the sales tickets were admitted into evidence. The girls were there within minutes of when Danny bought some of his supplies at a different cash register. So I did ask him, did he see those girls at the store, and he said no, it was just a coincidence.

Meoli   Yes, he told me it was a coincidence, too. And I am still not sure I believe that.

London   Oh, I believe it. Because if he saw them there, he'd be romanticizing it, going on about how beautiful they were, the captured butterflies who must die, he would want me to know exactly why and how he followed them. Telling all that detail would be interesting to him.

Meoli   So you think its pure coincidence?

London   Yeah, sure. Everyone goes to Walmart, they're both in the same area. It happens. There's no motivation for him to freely admit all those criminal acts and then lie about something this inconsequential. I tested his veracity constantly and I did not find him to be a liar, at least when it came to me. He was on notice from the very beginning that if I ever caught him in a lie that would be the last he would hear from me. I kept him on constant threat of abandonment, if he lied to me, disrespected me, or gave anyone else the story he promised me. On direct questioning, he said he did not see them at the Walmart, and there is no evidence to the contrary. So I'm satisfied with that. And I also think many of those alleged sightings that were written up in police reports were not of him. He also went drinking at the Bennigan's where Taboada worked, but he told me he never noticed Taboada there or had any interactions with anyone like that, and that he didn't know Taboada was in the apartment when he went looking for someone to murder.

Meoli   There was a lot of hysteria going on.

London   And I don't hold this case up as an example of great law enforcement at all. There were Keystone Kops falling all over each other and it was nothing to be proud of. The way they trampled over the civil rights of law-abiding Floridians is a shame. And the way they shook down Ed Humphrey, they're lucky he didn't sue, because that boy was a schizophrenic off his meds. I read the transcript of everything he said. It made no sense at all. It did not conform with the forensics. He said he did things at the crime scenes that were never done. He reported supernatural delusions. And then, receipts were produced proving he was not even in Gainesville at the times of the three crimes. And still, the authorities freely defamed him. Even after Danny Rolling was charged, there were still factions who held on to the idea that Humphrey was his accomplice. Do you know that artist Mike Diana?

Meoli   No.

London   Back in the nineties he was putting out a zine called *Boiled Angel,* in which he gleefully used his artwork to commit blasphemy, among other deadly sins. And when these gruesome murders happened, someone pointed the police at him. They shook him down and got blood tests on him – just because somebody disapproved of his cartoons. It was ridiculous. And the whole time, they had the real perpetrator sitting there in jail. And they had the tape, the evidence where he says, "I'm Danny Harold Rolling." And then he winds it up with "Whelp, there's something I gotta go do." That, of course, being murder. They had the tape but they didn't listen to it for two years. Some of them were also involved in the Aileen Wuornos case, and you know they accepted money for their stories of that. Remember, they were both in the same county jail in Ocala, Wuornos and Rolling.

Meoli   With Christa Hoyt's murder, whether or not he did or did not lose his wallet and have to go back, nobody really knows. Because only Danny knows whether that's made up or whether Gemini made him go back. Like you said, why would you re-enter a horrific crime scene that's chock-full of forensic evidence that the perpetrator was there.

London   There has to be a very compelling reason.

Meoli   He's so graphic as he's talking about removing her head and what he did to her. And as if that were not enough, to move the bookcase – he even sort of laughs at her head falling on the floor, and how he had to reposition it –

London   Yeah, that's a knee-slapper, Danny.

Anthony   And then posing the headless body like *The Thinker*. I saw that in the crime scene photos. It was like nothing I've ever seen. To think that he was willing to go that far, whether or not Gemini made him do it, I think some people just have that in them for that moment. And maybe it's a protective mechanism to say "Gemini" was responsible; to say I didn't do it, it's "Gemini" who did it. Maybe it's just easier for him to sleep at night. But those photos of the Christa Hoyt murder, I'll never forget them.

Drawing by Danny Rolling © Anthony Meoli

London   I was mostly disturbed by the Manual Taboada photos.

Meoli   Somebody said, how could you possibly look at those crime scene photos? I'm like, you just make a request and you go to the Alachua County Courthouse. Oddly enough, the records are kept in the same room number as the first murder.

London   Oh, I didn't notice that.

Meoli   The apartment number from Scene One is the same room number where the records are kept, which is a very strange phenomenon. The clerk brought the books. There are two big books, with about 200 color photos, and the clerk was sitting to my right. He said, I don't even wanna look at that book. I've seen it once, and I don't need to see it again. I asked him, how many people have looked at it? And he said, I think you're about 150th person to ever look at that book, including law enforcement. You sign your name in the registry, and then you sit in the room with him keeping an eye on you, so you don't take any of the photos. He gave me pretty much the leeway I wanted. There was no real time limit that day. He probably figured I'd flip through one page and then be done. But I was going page by page and was there for over half an hour.

London   Were you allowed to take photographs?

Meoli   No, no photographs were allowed. But you're right, I have to admit there were some really shocking images in Manny's scene. There was blood on all five walls.

London   The ceiling.

Meoli   Yeah, all four walls and the ceiling. But when you read your book where he jumps on top of Manny and thrusts the knife in and then he rears it back, all that blood spatter starts to make sense.

London   Flinging.

Meoli   Yes. You're talking about a brutal weapon that is designed to cut into almost anything. And he's attacking somebody who's not awake, who just is barely awakening to the knife going through him. That scene was really brutal. I think the reason for that was Danny had to protect himself from a big, strong man.

London   He got more physical, right?

Meoli   Right. He had to get more physical, to just to make sure he didn't lose control of the knife, so the guy didn't turn it on him, because he didn't know exactly how much damage he had inflicted right away. But the side of Manny's face was cut and there were so many stab wounds. It was a very frenzied killing.

London   You can tell there was a fierce fight.

Meoli   Right. I think he over-fought Manny because this was a big 220-pound football player, not a hundred-twenty-pound female. I think Danny overestimated what he needed to do to immobilize him. And then once he got on top of him, he got into a frenzy, and over-killed him.

London   The crime scene photos were just shocking.

Meoli   What was your take on his first attempted murder?

London   You mean his father?

Meoli   No, no, I'm talking about that jogger.

Drawing by Danny Rolling © Anthony Meoli

Sondra   Oh, from the story called "Close Call." I see Danny
as a rapist. He was comfortable with rape and he
was trembling on the edge of murder, but he was
not ready for it. I think in writing the story, he did
a good job of helping us to be there with him as he
caught himself doing something that was not
congruent with his own idea of who he was. The
murderous mind that emerged from Danny was not
in tune with his central ego; it was *ego-dystonic.*
You know, Danny never expressed the slightest bit
of remorse over rape to me. He never backed off
from it, so he owned rape and he owned armed
robbery. I'd say all that behavior came from the
Ennad side of Danny. He had made room within his
ego for Ennad. So even though Ennad was all that
Danny was not, he was still within the boundaries
of who Danny knew himself to be, so you could call
the Ennad state of mind *ego-syntonic;* in an
harmonic relation with his central ego. The
Danny/Ennad split was an unstable and
uncontrollable condition, but it was a workable
configuration that carried Danny through his years
of crime and confinement. Emotionally, Danny
would never grow up. But by behaving as Ennad, he
could participate in adult behavior. He was a stand-
up convict who could walk the yard like a man. But
when it came to murder, upon that occasion he lets
us see that he was scared. Murder was out of
bounds from who he sensed himself to be. And there
was that other time, too, when he was raping a
woman and there was a baby by her. And the baby
smiled at Danny so sweetly it reminded him of his
own daughter. And it was just so inappropriate to
what he was doing, it just spoiled the mood,
completely. And when he lost his mojo, he snapped
back to his right mind. I think that's similar to
when he heard the water tinkling with the jogger.
He was using that knife as a force multiplier, to
project the threat of his brute power and to focus

his malicious will. But I don't think he attempted to murder her. He was just there to rape, she surprised him by putting up a resistance, and he was well into the frenzy of fighting with her when something sensory broke his focus; he came to his senses and regained his self-control before he actually tried to murder her. I was very gratified with the job Danny did in writing this story. He was able to set aside who he was at the time: a confessed killer. And take himself back to who he had been at the time in his life when the homicidal impulse was threatening to overwhelm his resistance to it. But I'd like to know what you make of his psychological diagnoses. You've seen what the psychiatrists put on the record. You've made your own personal observations. So what are your clinical impressions? What does Anthony Meoli have to say?

Meoli   You really put me on the spot as far as a clinical diagnosis.

London   That's okay. <*Laughs*> That's why I'm here.

Meoli   I think he had several things that went on underneath the dissociation. I think he had a major depressive disorder, as an underlying condition. I saw that in his letters and his artwork. He chronically had depression, at least in my experience, and again, I'm just an armchair clinician on this at the moment. So when he gets to Gainesville, he's still bringing along his depression, his years of failure, the way his father abused him, and his mother really didn't do anything to dissuade his father. She just sort of let things happen. Danny had almost killed his father, as you know. We're talking about the mindset he brings to these murders, and all of these factors were in play. I would say there's definitely a degree of psychosis. I do think there's a splitting of Danny. We do see fracture between the Danny that we knew and the

Danny who says, "I have to go now, there's something I got to do," as he infamously says on his tape. He's almost leaving that Danny behind as he leaves the camp site. He definitely presents with psychotic features. And I think there is some mania with Danny. There's a certain manic nature to him. He would shift his focus entirely on one thing; well, his artwork is a prime example. Even the way he created a piece of artwork was overkill.

London   Grandiosity is one of the attributes of mania.

Meoli   Right. And we saw how he explained how he did a piece of art. He didn't just draw it. He would draw a piece, and then you would see the obverse of it. And then he would trace over that, and he would get that image, and then redo the same thing three times that he didn't have to do, on the most simple of drawings. People didn't realize that for Danny, a simple sketch was a four-stage process, so you were actually seeing the mirror image of what he was drawing, because he had flipped the image and then drawn over that real heavily, and then put that onto a new piece of paper, and then drawn over that again. Danny did things, that were in many ways, completely unnecessary. But, he found this compelling need to do them. I found that to be a definite component of his psychological makeup.

London   That's interesting. I never thought of that. What jumps out at me is the neediness of the borderline personality. The splitting and the fear of abandonment. The behavior that permeates every aspect of Danny's life, including every crime he ever did, and even just meeting him on the street, is the violation of boundaries. You see it so many times in the police records and investigative reports. You'll have investigators, detectives, and prosecution psychiatrists interviewing him. They're trying to find him guilty of crimes, they are not there on a social call. And you'll see Danny trying to befriend them, chat them up, ask them, where you from? And going, yeah, I like being there, too. If there was a boundary, he was likely to cross it. Escaping from prison is an obvious example of it. Voyeurism, B&E, burglary and robbery. Rape, of course. Violating boundaries throughout every part of his personality. Even when he shook your hand so hard, that's a mild form of defying convention. When I extend my hand to you, I trust you not to grip the hell out of it and hurt me. That's just violating the basic social contract.

Meoli   I would go with psychosis. As organized as they might appear, his murders were still somewhat disorganized. You have the hallmarks of psychosis. You have aggression, agitation, hostility, and with those, you have disorganized behavior. You have confusion, you have delusions, you have nightmares, which Danny suffered from for most of his life. And that continued even when he was in prison. Other inmates used to say they would not even want to be near him, with the stuff he would say at night. And then depression is a part of psychosis as well. I honestly think Danny was truly psychotic, with a lifelong struggle with depression. Some of his self-hatred stemmed from the fact he never could make his father proud. And every boy wants to make his father proud. Danny never lived up to expectations. He failed at school. He failed out of the military. He got to the point he almost killed his father, which is the ultimate failure for a son. He takes this self-hatred, and he wants to put the horror of his life onto someone else who is going to have a much better life than he did.

This is aggravating!

step 1

First sketch

The original rough drawing or sketch

Bravo

I placed This first sketch over The second blank page And rubbed the pencil on the back of this one... Printed it backwards on the second.

Drawing by Danny Rolling © Sondra London

Second sketch

step 2

1. Lengthened The wirgs

2. worked on the face & hands

Turred it over And on the third blank it AgAin bAckwArds.

rubbed the pencil pAge... printed

Drawing by Danny Rolling © Sondra London

Third drawing

step 3
refired it And
rubbed it on the
Fourth And final
print...O.k.

Drawing by Danny Rolling © Sondra London

Fourth drawing
Final print.

Step 4

by D.R. 11-13-92

Drawing by Danny Rolling © Sondra London

Sondra   That's it, that's why he was a serial killer instead of a simple homicide. Because what he was attacking was society itself. His victims were emblematic of being cherished. He was always on the outside, looking at a normal family life with his face pressed up against the window. He killed perfect strangers because he thought they had a life he would never have. There's a really creepy boundary violation Danny did, as he was building up to murder. He said, who knows how many times I've broken and entered into a house and just lingered there for hours, while the people were there. And he said they never knew he had been there. Violating their space just to get a feeling of belonging; of course that was spurious, but that's why he said he did it.

Meoli   Along with psychosis you have detachment, even a detachment of the self.

London   Depersonalization.

Meoli   When it comes to Ennad and Gemini, it's not that I dismiss those as being fake. But he didn't have multiple personality disorder, because of the rarity of that diagnosis. Additionally, you would need more personalities than what he had, negating that clinical diagnosis. But in psychosis, we have someone stepping out of themselves in a way that what Danny says actually makes sense. He's trying to put a name to it, so whether it's Ennad or Gemini, or if they are one and the same, that makes sense to me as psychosis. Danny explained one crucial thing to me, that I took away with me forever. I asked him, if the person who did this kept ratcheting up their behavior, how could that person do it? He said, that person who does that, every time they do it, they would lose a part of their soul. By the time they had committed multiple crimes, they had no soul left. So that made it easy for them

47

to escalate what they were doing. And that would explain why the second and third Gainesville crime scenes were so gruesome. Because by that point, there was nothing left of Danny. He could feel nothing. So as gruesome as it was, he was trying to feel something inside himself.

London   If he was undergoing a desensitization then he would want to amp up the sensory input.

Meoli   You probably know this better than anyone on the planet, but Danny had difficulty expressing love in a way that made sense.

London   Hah! Wow, that's a really good way to put it.

Meoli   It is disturbing that someone would have to go to that extent to feel something, but for someone who is psychotic it makes perfect sense.

London   Now, we haven't used the word psychopath. I believe a psychopath is numb not only to the suffering of others, but to their own suffering. Just take Clay Rogers, for example. I dealt with him for that documentary "My Brother the Serial Killer" for over the two years. And during that time, he suffered three head injuries serious enough to require hospitalization. He was mugged, he was knifed, and he never expressed any suffering. He just shrugged off everything that hurt him. So he didn't feel his own pain. And he was as pure a psychopath as I've ever known when it came to his indifference towards other people.

Meoli   When you're talking about Danny Rolling, it's difficult to avoid psychopathy because he had trouble with the law his whole life. A psychopath doesn't respect authority figures, and Danny struggled with authority figures, starting with own father. Manipulating and hurting others, he checks that box as well. He also had a tendency to lie. Even when he confessed, he did it through Bobby Lewis.

London   Okay, but that's not lying.

Meoli   No, but he was having difficulty saying it himself.

London   That was not psychological, it was because of his obligation to me. Because he was threatened that he better not give that story to the State. They'd already used FOIA requests to put thousands of pages of our correspondence in the public record and that way they were taking my story away from me. I was fit to be tied. I said, don't you dare put your story on the public record. So that's the hidden hand at work there. They tricked Danny to think that if he would take responsibility for these murders, they would allow visitation with me. Of course, that was just a typical cop trick. They got their admissions of guilt, via Bobby Lewis, then they released defamatory lies about me to the media. They said I was banned from all Florida prisons because I had used false pretenses to get in to see Danny. And that's not possible, because Ed Dix with the FDLE called me and said, "Would you like to see Danny? Come on in." "But it's not visiting day, and I don't have permission." "It's okay, we'll get you in on a special pass." Now, I don't know what a special pass is, nobody ever handed me any paper or form. I never heard of any such thing as a special pass, but that's exactly what he told me. And the Department of Corrections released a statement. "We can't let her back in," they told the Associated Press. "Next time she might bring a gun or a bomb." That statement went out over the wire, all over the world. This gave plausible deniability to the FDLE as to their role in bringing me in for that one visit behind glass, just to coerce Danny's confessions. It was coercion, holding out a false hope of visitation to gain his cooperation. And he insisted I cooperate as well. "You, me, and the FDLE, babe," was how he put it.

Meoli Well, the one thing about psychopathy, Danny checks almost every box, but a psychopath allegedly does not know right from wrong. This is where a psychopathic diagnosis for Rolling fails.

London The key to right and wrong for Danny is in a scripture he pointed out to me, it's the seventh chapter of Romans, where the suffering soul describes knowing right from wrong and yet doing the wrong anyway. And the other side of the M'Naughton test is when you fail to appreciate the nature and consequences of your actions. And I have multiple written statements from Danny to the effect he wanted to be caught and he wanted to be executed for his crimes. He required me to cooperate with the FDLE to ensure his execution. So he knew he had done wrong, and he not only knew the consequences, he affirmatively sought to engage them. And he made me an intimate part of that process. But getting back to your point about psychopathy, I did notice some psychopathic traits in Danny, but lying was not one of them. Danny was not a compulsive liar like Clay Rogers, Glen Rogers, and some of the other psychopaths we both know.

London Okay, so let's talk about artwork. First, correct me if I'm wrong, but I believe you are the owner of the world's most comprehensive Danny Rolling artwork collection.

Meoli I do have quite a few pieces.

London Yes, well, you don't know anyone who has more, do you?

Meoli Probably not. No.

Portrait of Meoli by Lee Boyd Malvo © Anthony Meoli

London   So the prosecution rests. *<Laughs>* Tag, you're it.
         Has Danny ever made any portrait of you?

Meoli   Hmm, I'm trying to think back. I never asked him
         to. I don't think he would have said no, but I just
         never requested one. I'm trying to think, because I
         do have several serial killers who did do my portrait
         including Lee Boyd Malvo, Elmer Wayne Henley
         and Glen Rogers.

London   I know, I asked that question because I'm fascinated
         by Malvo's art, and one of the first things that
         impressed me was this drawing he did of you. I just
         thought it was brilliant. Intuitive talent.

Meoli   Malvo, Rogers and Henley and a whole bunch of
         guys have done my portrait.

London   And you didn't ask Danny?

51

Meoli   No, I never did ask Danny, but I'll tell you what. I
           am probably the last person to ever send him
           canvases, because in 2005 Florida had banned him
           from using the acrylic paint that he was using to
           create his artwork.

London   Absolutely disgusting. We used to call those Rolling
           Rules. They were obviously aimed at him.

Meoli   I used to get him the eight by ten and sixteen by
           twenty canvas sheets. I'd order them and they
           would ship directly to him. He did all of his artwork
           on them. I just supplied his art supplies. But then
           one time I sent a bunch of art supplies through
           Dick Blick. The warden wrote to me and said "Mr.
           Rolling is no longer allowed to accept such items.
           They have been returned back to Dick Blick." So the
           last pieces of art that Danny ever completed were
           watercolors, completed in late 2005 on through to
           his death in 2006. Watercolors were the only kind
           of paint he was allowed to have. I have one
           watercolor from 2006, which was the last year he
           was alive. So it was one of the final pieces he did.

London   Did Danny do any self-portraits for you?

Meoli   Like you said earlier, like there's always a face or
           something in the artwork that's more than the
           artwork, and you don't see it right away.

London   Sending messages.

Meoli   Yeah, there's lots of faces in the artwork that I
           have, and I often did the same thing you did, I
           would look for the number five or the number eight.
           And count, are there eight victims in this particular
           composition or are there more? Is he signifying
           something that maybe none of us knows? He liked
           to have this power in his art, and women were often
           a sexual subject in his artwork. Not like some serial

killers. I've seen a lot of serial killers who draw sadomasochistic kind of stuff. It wasn't that with Danny, insomuch as he revered the female form. But like you said, Danny was a rapist. There's no doubt Danny raped more people than he killed. We just don't know the number.

London   Well, he wasn't taking names. He did write up plenty for the book, so that's enough to give you the general idea.

KiLLER ART

Logo © Sondra London

Meoli   So I've always tried to get artwork from my inmate contacts, because it's another medium that allows me access into their psychology. If you look at Picasso or if you look at Dali, you'll be like, these guys were probably serial killers. Because some of their stuff is pretty disturbing.

London   A lot of people are intimidated and overwhelmed by writing and by trying to be verbal, and they have barriers that can't be surmounted. In that case, drawing pictures can allow the transmission of important information. I worked with the serial killer Ottis Toole. As you know, he's illiterate, and so I am the one who got him started drawing. I had to get some kind of dialog going with him and he couldn't write. In fact, that's how I coined the term, "Killer Art." I had finished *Killer Fiction* with Schaefer, so when I put out a catalog of Toole's drawings under the Media Queen imprimatur, I called it *Killer Art* to link it to the book.

Anthony Right.

London Well, Toole was always drawing these faces with these huge Dumbo ears. At that time, I was working with Joel Norris, who authored that book *Serial Killers: The Growing Menace*. And he had some training in art therapy. So when Norris went through the drawings Toole had done for me, he suggested, maybe they yelled a lot in the home, but that was tentative. So when we got a chance to meet Toole and interview him in prison, we asked him why the ears were so big. It was a dramatic moment, because he could not speak, and he just barely mumbled. I had to say, excuse me? And he spoke up. "They're handles," he said. They used them for sexual abuse, to hold the child by the ears. And that was the only way that Toole was able to ease into actually talking about the things that had been done to him, his own sexual abuse. He could sit there and just go la-la-la about all the vicious things he had done, nonchalant as can be. But when it came to what he had suffered, he could not speak of it, and it took over a year before he could speak freely of being violated. And that was the breakthrough, when he drew kids whose ears were being used as handles.

Meoli That's interesting.

London It goes to the importance of things you can't say openly: body language, gestures like pointing up at surveillance, or tapping out a message about murder. All forms of data that go beyond the verbal, I think, are extremely important.

Drawing by Ottis Toole © Sondra London

Meoli   Oh, I agree. But not everybody does, because I've
         shown artwork at some forensic seminars, and I've
         had people say, "Why would you send Danny
         Rolling money to do artwork?" I reply, because it's
         very revealing as to his personality, I said, and they
         don't have these supplies, so in order for them to
         draw for me, I've got to either send them money, or
         pay the vendor to send the supplies to them, and
         then pay the shipping for them to send the artwork
         back to me. In order for me to give you this artwork
         to critique, that's what is involved. At least you
         have the ability to critique it. But if it weren't for
         me stepping out so far to get to know someone, you
         wouldn't have the art to critique.

London   That's such a good point.

Meoli   And I said, look at what therapists do with children.
         When children are struggling to tell their story,
         they say draw something for me.

London   That's right.

Meoli   Because it's more comfortable for them to draw Mommy beating Daddy or Daddy beating Mommy than it is for them to say it in so many words.

London   It's more comfortable for a troubled adult, too. I follow the practice of asking my correspondents to draw a house, a tree, and a person. Because that's a psychological test, it's called the *House-Tree-Person* test, or HTP. Each one of these is symbolic of the self. I have a portfolio of these drawings.

Meoli   I had Glen Rogers do a whole battery of tests. Granted, it wasn't in the kind of psychological medium that people are supposed to have, but I sent him a Rorschach test. He gave me his answers. I always think it's interesting to know, is what they see congruent with what somebody else would see? Is the image two witches over a fire? Or is it something else that that most people would not say? The Rorschach test has been taken way too far in psychology. You present somebody with a blot, and you ask them, tell me what it is. And you decipher whether or not it is logical. If I show you a blot that looks like a butterfly and you say, that's a decapitated head, and that's the scalp. That's not a normal answer. That's way off the beaten path. The average person would say, it's a butterfly or it's a bird.

London   That would be unremarkable, right?

Meoli   Right, that's an unremarkable or normal response. But when somebody goes off and says something crazy, then it is worth noting.

London   Oh look, that's Poland, and you see over here, this is Russia and they are at war, the Polish are winning, but you can see that the Russians are plotting something.

Watercolor by Danny Rolling © Anthony Meoli

Meoli   Right. I think sometimes we go a little too crazy
with having all these rules, like you need to be
seated at a 45 degree angle and they need to have

their back to you, and you need to be in a perfect room. No, you don't. You just need to have somebody tell you what their thoughts are off the cuff. Even if we do get a little batty with these psychological tests, I still think they are useful. Like you said, like if you tell them to draw a person and they come back with two people, and one of them is doing a sexual act against the other, that's not what you asked for – so we would note that response as abnormal.

London   Anything that they put in that goes over and above what you asked for gets double importance, like when I told John Schaefer to draw a house, he drew a house all right, and then he put a bush next to it and a little cat peering out from under the bush. And no one asked him to draw that cat, but for him, the picture was not complete without it. I never asked Schaefer about the kitty; it's just a curious anomaly. But it is interesting that Rolling's own "House" was built from different-colored rocks.

In *Killer Fiction,* I had described the metaphor Schaefer had used to explain to me what it was like to be a serial killer, in reply to my telling him I didn't understand how he could behave one way and then the opposite. He spoke slowly and thoughtfully.

> "What I tell you... is inconsistent... because the experience itself... is inconsistent."
> I thought about that for a moment and finally shrugged. "You're right. I don't understand. You've got to explain it."
> He leaned back, sighed, sipped his coffee. Groping for words and finding them by fits and starts, he finally came up with an analogy. "It's like... I'm throwing rocks at your window... and you're trying to figure

out where the rocks are coming from... and you can't... because they're all different colors. But you see... they're different colors... because they're all coming... from different places."

"Ah! I see." For some reason, that imagery made perfect sense to me, as it elucidates the striking inconsistencies in the serial killer's psyche.

The discrete and rigid contrasting elements symbolize the fragmentation of the personality into an uneasy amalgam of diverse components. With this type of personality, every truth conceals its equal and opposite, just as a perky smile masks a simmering rage — except when the mask slips, and the madness flares.

Drawing by G.J. Schaefer © Sondra London

London   I consulted with a clinical psychologist who was conversant with the HTP test, and I found his interpretation of the Rolling "House" highly relevant. He pointed out how elaborate Rolling has made the entryway into his home. The landscaping, with its looming bushes, takes up a great deal of our attention. And this is consistent with his concern with putting up an effigy of the Danny Rolling he wants to be, that he can use to mask the failed and flawed man he knew himself to be, behind that many-colored stone wall. It's like we were talking about earlier, with the homicide, when you're not done yet. Anything that you're doing at a crime scene after you've finished ending the life of the victim is highly significant. And in the Rolling case, investigators who viewed his crime scenes said they were staged to send a message. I asked Danny so many times, I said, you went to all this trouble to interfere with the remains because you had a message to send. So what was it? And he's like, I don't know, ask Gemini. And I'm like, no, you ask Gemini!

Meoli   Yes, you are closer to him, right?

London   Yeah, I know! Well, he did say he wanted to prove that Evil is real; it walks the Earth like a natural man. That is kind of abstract to me. So he didn't have a message in so many words. I guess if you couldn't interpret the crime scene, he would just have to re-enact it all over again.

Meoli   Danny is contradictory in some of the things he did, in that he would overkill, and then clean the body. But he would have to know his semen would be inside the body after committing the sexual act.

London   He put his semen on a paper towel and left it on the counter.

by Danny Rolling
12-18-94

Drawing by Danny Rolling © Sondra London

Meoli   So he takes the time to use duct tape to incapacitate them. Then removes the tape. He would keep the tape when he left. It's not in the trash anywhere. He kept it somewhere. Yet he made a mistake like that, where it's something so obvious. He even left cleaning solution between the victims' legs. And you have to ask, why did he do some of these things?

London   Well, I would say, because he was phasing in and out of different ego-states. Because in his excited condition, he was highly unstable. Yeah, he would be conscious in a certain way, and then something would trigger him, and he'd be conscious in a different way. So he is sitting in the same room. But when he looks around he sees something completely different than he saw a minute ago. He takes his cue from that and he's off on another track.

London
The most sickening thing that I ever heard about Danny Rolling was when he stabbed Sonja Larson to death. And then he whispered in her ear, I'll be back for you after you're dead. And I was like, Danny, you didn't need to do that. I mean, you did your murder. You got off, right? That was what you were there to do, murder. Then what the hell was that all about? While she was dying? And then after he killed Christina Powell, he came back upstairs. And he says, she was too bloody to rape. Well, who's to blame for that, Danny? This was your creation. You put a lot of energy into making this gruesome mess. You did exactly what you wanted to do. Now, what have you got? To me, that was just the most disgusting thing Danny Rolling ever did. And that's what I told him.

11-02-2003

Drawing by Danny Rolling © Anthony Meoli

Meoli   When I read *The Making of a Serial Killer*, probably
        1998, I was shocked at the graphic nature of what
        Danny had said, because it was so real, there was
        no filter. It was so graphic. I thought, maybe
        Sondra should have edited out this part. This is a
        bit too much. But then, as I thought about it, it
        made sense. To release the details, exactly as they
        were stated, is important. If you want to know the
        real story, you have to know the whole story – even
        if you don't enjoy reading it, the truth matters.

London If you want to show what the human mind is
        capable of doing, if you want to show what the
        criminal mind is capable of conceiving, you need to
        keep it real. Our sensibilities have been shaped by
        the dynamics of the entertainment business.
        Shakespeare was never satisfied until he left the
        stage littered with corpses. And the crowd loved it.
        They screamed for more. Most rituals deal with
        matters of life and death, and it was ever thus, the
        world over. We had Greek tragedy five centuries
        before Christ, and Sanskrit theater has been traced
        back at least that far. The urgency of life and death
        conflict heightens the drama and excites the crowd.
        But while entertaining us, they are training us to
        expect life to be like that.

London So what is the best Rolling artwork you own?

Meoli   I have one piece of art that Danny called his
        masterpiece. He sent me the pre-paint sketch. And
        then he sent the painting, and then he sent three
        long letters explaining what it meant. He was like,
        this is my masterpiece of masterpieces. And it's got
        all these crazy stuff: a ram and a wizard, angels and
        a ghost holding a skull. You want to see it?

Drawing by Danny Rolling © Anthony Meoli

London   Sure, bring it on!

Danny Rolling's Rooftop View

By Sondra London

We try to understand things by connecting dots to make a picture. Whether it makes sense depends upon the dots you connect. And yet, for one reason or another, there are often dots we don't see, and that can lead to misinterpretation. Once you do see them, the puzzling aspects of your picture are resolved, the picture appears, and it makes perfect sense.

That's how we interpret the mystery of a whole personality, with nothing to go on but just the data points we know. An essential part of that ongoing process involves the flexibility of adjusting our impressions when new information is presented.

When it comes to interpreting the messages encrypted in artwork by an artist known to tease the viewer by embedding cryptic clues, the composition itself remains a mystery. It's still a work of art, and as such it stands on its own merit: *res ipsa loquitur.* You might like how it looks or you might dislike it, and either way, you might be utterly indifferent to the intentions of the artist to imbue the image with significance.

But even if the artist is trying his best to send a message, each viewer will make of it what they will. That's the given fate of any work of art. It's like that old children's game Telephone, where each one whispers a message in the next one's ear; by the end of the chain of whispers, the message bears no resemblance to how it started out.

For many reasons, my own observations and interpretations are no different than those of anyone else. I don't have a degree in art therapy. But in consideration of the years I spent delving into the thoughts and dreams of Danny Rolling, I will tell you how I interpret "Rooftop," a story comprised of the oil painting and the exegesis by the artist, along with his remarks about the circumstances at the time of composition.

In viewing what he called his masterpiece, I see Danny Rolling in something like the past-perfect tense. I spent five years corresponded with him daily, studying his art and his criminal history; and "Rooftop" was done in the interim since then.

The three letters he sent Anthony Meoli about the painting are reproduced here in full, as his formal calligraphy is meant for display. He illuminates his pages as elaborately as a fifteenth-century European monk. The Danny I knew so well would affect an elevated tone when he wanted to present an impressive effigy of the man he wanted "Danny Rolling" to be. This carefully crafted persona was another way of insulating himself from the primitive horror of his crimes.

First, in his introductory remarks, we notice the arrogant, disrespectful way he manipulated his long-time correspondent, who the record shows had been faithfully sending him art supplies when nobody else would; telling Anthony he doesn't deserve the great honor of this masterpiece. Then after all that, he relented and let him have it after all.

It reminds me of what producer Jackie Giroux told me about working with serial killer Aileen Wuornos on a documentary: "A kiss and a slap, a kiss and a slap. That was Aileen all the way, a kiss and a slap." That's instability, at the very least, a form of which shows up in borderline personality disorder, as well as dissociation and psychosis. It could also be nothing more sinister than moodiness and irritability, secondary to extended solitary confinement on Death Row.

He speaks of "intricate dichotomies... poised forever in dynamic syllogism," and warns, no one knows what it means. With the grandiosity of narcissism, he assures Anthony that "Rooftop" is amazing, and calls it an understatement to say there's nothing like it anywhere.

Now, I've received many letters from Danny Rolling, waxing lyrical about his work in progress. It's not unusual for any artist, in any medium, to feel his latest is his greatest. So you have to put such an effusion into perspective. I have studied the widest spectrum of his art work, from the very first time he sent me a sketch scrawled in the margin of a letter, which he didn't even sign because he did not know he was an artist until I told him so. And I could name half a dozen compositions I would rate more ambitious, significant and compelling, than "Rooftop"; for example, "Fait Accompli," which appears on the cover of this book. So even though the artist himself declares "Rooftop" to be his masterpiece, I would file a dissenting opinion granting that at best, it may be one of his masterpieces. With 126 paintings in his past, painted and then sent away with no copies to remember them by, it's most likely much of his best work had faded from his memory.

"Rooftop" is a complex self-portrait of a killer's existential journey, a phantasmagoria of dramatic imagery that unreels as reality fades away in the distance of time, and the haunting dreams assert their urgent presence. One can only surmise how vividly such sagas are experienced by one held in sensory deprivation for over a decade.

The man describes the essence of his being in words uncannily close to those I chose to describe him as I interviewed Anthony Meoli before reading Danny's written portrait of himself. He describes seeing himself as forever the outsider, consigned to the darkness, alone in the rain, his face pressed up against the window of life.

I commented earlier on the significance of the little extras added to what was requested in the *House-Tree-Person* test. And this principle applies equally well to handwriting. The theory behind the practice of graphology is that you are incapable of making any gesture without revealing something about yourself.

When I first started working with him, I noticed he signed his name "Danny" with a little splash at the tail of the *Y* or he'd put the splash at the end of the *G in* Rolling. When I asked him what that meant, he said his signature was not complete without it. Maybe it did have a deep psychological meaning, but it was not one he could articulate.

Even though he deliberately hid clues in his artwork and dared you to find them, he did, however, have chastening words for those who would pore over his imagery to mine it for significance. This, from *The Making of a Serial Killer:*

> If people out there misconstrue my symbolism to
> mean something other than intended, I can't help that.
> If it's not the star, it will be something else, like the

toes on my fallen angel looking like **666**. Blahhhh...
pure poppycock. Sometimes a star is just a star, and
toes are just plain toes.

Without ascribing too much significance to his calligraphic
stylings, I do notice that by 2003, he had increased his use of
idiosyncratic embellishments, and some he even used in his
more quotidian script. He fashioned many of his capital
letters in a Gothic Blackletter style and used a stylized
version of his own hand. He perched a dot up over the letter
Y, and sometimes he drew a hard line right on top of the
lower-case *G*. The capital *K* had grown a gratuitous new
stroke, making it look to me more like an *F*. When he wrote a
TH diphthong, he slanted the *T* so as to cross over the *H*.

These embellishments did not help convey his message any
more clearly. Instead, they drew attention away from the
meaning of the words, and more towards the appearance of
the script, leading the reader to speculate about the writer's
persona, instead of being drawn into his story line. His
ornate script individuated him, with the intention to charm
and disarm his audience and show off how special he was,
how worthy of attention. But more importantly, the elevated
style of the calligraphic text gave him another way to
distance himself from his own bloody deeds.

Perhaps it also helped discharge some of the tension from
his still-extant homicidal obsessions. Back when I was still
working with him, he wrote to me from Death Row about
plotting the murder of another inmate; he did in fact make an
attempt on him, and was punished for it. So much for the
deterrent effect of the death penalty.

So in 2003, ten years after Danny first reached out me, we
see how the *mens rea,* or guilty mind at the heart of the most
heinous murder, was still animating his imagination, as
limned in the tale he called "Rooftop."

He presents himself as a hapless loner and outsider, who is
under the spell of a beautiful woman, an evil vampire queen
who summons her minions, including a sorcerer, a ghoul, a
chauffeur and a ram.

1-8-2004

Anthony

Soul sings...
soul cries, and
spirit of creating bleeds onto an
expressionistic plane. Where inner
eye sees visions only seen by that
universe called "The Artist".
No one knows what it means. Or
how beats the heart yearning to
convey what's there in that secret
place behind the face. Because I
am bound by my word. "Roof Top",
my 178 th painting is your's. Otherwise I would not give it away.
Not to you. Not because I feel you
unworthy, nor for all as anything as
shallow as gain. Because it means
more to me than you'll ever comprehend, and well... Even tho
we've been corrisponding and have
even spoke face to face you remain distant and a stronger to me.

D.R.

By Danny Rolling © Anthony Meoli

1-8-2004

Something as special & dear to me as "Rooftop". Isn't easy to let go. Not even if it were to someone I feel close to. I do not feel close to you, Anthony. Yes you've been forthright and Trueblue thus far. Appreciate that. Are we friends — YES. Anything more — NO. Not yet. Prehaps over time I'll feel closer. There are degrees of friendship, no? Can't help but wonder how you portray me to others. Especially your on going project. Am sure my contribution is bound to further that aspiration. Glad to be of service. Time, I give of my time ... you give of your's. It is different for me. Months to years Time is Time and it's expensive. As time goes by — I grow older [I'll be 50 this coming may] this world seems more remote and distant to danny. ah... suppose it was always so with me. I the

D.R.

By Danny Rolling © Anthony Meoli

1-8-2004

sad face pressed against a wet windowpane rain drenched in a storm. The lone figure [always, "even in a crowd"... alone] wondering down endless dark streets searching for the elusive will-ó-the-wisp of belonging. Few could ever understand, Fewer still ever will. "Roof Top" is an enigma that draws the eye to wonderment. Several intricate dichotomies work within it's borders. The angelic. The demonic. The beautiful. The hideous, The lost. The wicked. All forever poised in dynamic syllogism. as if to tell a story, a rather amazing canvas. am proud to offer it to you. although I doubt you'll ever know how much of me went into creating it. To say there's nothing like it anywhere is an understatement.
      About the canvas returned.
Sigh... forget it. Consider it a loss. I do.
                                    D.R.

By Danny Rolling © Anthony Meoli

1-25-2004

ANTHONY...

Good to hear "Rooftop" arrived in excellent condition. as always a pleasure. Will I be interested in writing a piece discribing what it means to me? Yes indeed I would and so I begin the task here-in.

"Rooftop"

by ➤➤➤➤➤ Danny Rolling ∴ 2004 ☺

It came slinking through his thoughts, raindrops splatting on objects of concern... When a logical out could not be derived. Each drop of hope snaked into gutters of dispair. Where he thinks himself [on one hand] fortunate,

D.R.

By Danny Rolling © Anthony Meoli

1-75-2004

but to what end? "The sun will be up soon", he speaks to himself [no one else is there]. Just an exhausted, emotionally spent man in black, a shadow 'mongst shadows. To some a will-o-the wisp. To others the boogyman. Intense hazel eyes stare 'tently down at dark ground. The only sound his pounding heart, and an occasional whine of rubber rolling o'er concrete overhead. Mechanical exodus of those misfortunate few who haven't left the seething carcass of a dead & dying city. He found the perfect hiding place, an enclave at the top of a concrete hardened pillar support holding an expand above in-place over a yawning gulch. How did it come to this? Him a creature of the night running wild from God knows what, and then they come... twist-creeking 'round his fevered mind like hurtful branches of an evil tree.

D.R.

By Danny Rolling © Anthony Meoli

73

1-25-2004

Twas demonic – spell cast from
an evil – yet beautiful witch. She
charmed an entire city to embrace
darkness cloaking her true self. ah
but once found out. Too late. For
all hell doth trail the banshee's wail,
and suddenly one finds one's self in
Lucifer's house, and you don't step
on the queen's tail. For the lord of
the house will surely cleave you in-
two.

Oddly it started on a night not
unlike anyother night. How often things
begin that way. a foreigner, a hearse,
a coffin, and the strangest pau you...
ever laid eyes on. metallic black the
hearse crept crunching o'er gravel
down a lazy, shrub hidden driveway,
parking behind an abandon english
style cottage at the edge of Merry
ville. The chauffeur, his age ravaged
face a skull scowl fitted head to toe
in tailored black, emerged from the

D.R.

By Danny Rolling © Anthony Meoli

1-75-2004

driver's side compartment, stood ghoulish and surveyed the area for prying eyes. There were none. Then apeish opened the passenger side door bowing white struggles of fine hair protruding from 'neath an old battered pilot's cap.

The vampire slinked 'cross crimson leather standing glorious before a full blue moon.

"Ahh... night's breath sweet", Mauvais Sujet coos exhailing dead soul. Black licorice feral hair framed obelisk brown eyes ... brown as grave-yard dirt thrown 'pon caskets of her [many] victims. A cute upturned nose beguiled innocence. Full pouty mouth whispered wicked sensuality, a wide gold neckless donning a massive green emerald graces an elegant neck. Strong shoulders [for a woman] drape a long black cape inner lined blood red velvet. With a flip of hand she

D.R.

By Danny Rolling © Anthony Meoli

1-25-2004

tosses oneside o'er and behind her back partially exposing a plump, perk, milk white breast peeking out from an open, tight fitting turquoise bodice. a thin waist supports the torso. Shapely hips. Long, athletic legs fit snug into black velvet lace-up pants. Princess feet press daintly into knee-high strap-up boots. On her left hand a perfect ruby glows in an ancient setting. Regally she lifts the hand to a hideous, but loyal servant... her voodoo zombie protector, Goath. Who clunk shuts the hearse, and together enter through the back door their new home.

— TO BE CONTINUED —

And so we begin a journey, no? For the painting has a story to tell, and I shall tell it. Hope the first glimpse sparks an interest. On that

D. R.

By Danny Rolling © Anthony Meoli

1-25-2004

the spinning wields it's magic splendidly. For now I bid you God's Speed.

Till next time ∴
Danny ∴

D.R.

- main Character -

diagram -

Danny Rolling 12-3-2003 ☺ Sketch & diagram for "Roof Top"

By Danny Rolling © Anthony Meoli

Anthony

1-28-2004

What does "Rooftop" mean to me? Baring bone with a scalpel of truth. Being as each passing day pushes me further along the appeals process. I know not how much longer danny has before the executioner takes away my life. Dwelling in the valley of the shadow of death it is understandable my paintings take on an urgent sense of it could be the last one. I put so much of myself into my craft. ah... it will probably be after I'm dead & gone before people will say," You know he had something, a certain unusual style that caught your eye". Then there's all the negative elements I struggle with to even place myself in position to paint. Don't have a studio. am confined to a 9'x7' concrete box. Don't have a proper easel. Have a makeshift cardboard backing that must be propped-up on a lockerbox with a rolled-up bedroll & pillow. But before that I have to dig out my material; paints & brushes. Don't have a proper palette. Have a small cardboard square with a clear plastic panel toped over it. Don't have all the brushes needed to be effective. Somehow I make do with what I have. my brushes are over 8 yrs. old. once

D. R.

By Danny Rolling © Anthony Meoli

1-28-2004

everything is just so [considerable moving around is required], & sit on an iron footlocker to sketch & or paint my vision. once completed & go through considerable red tape to mail it out! now would you like to ask that question again. Hmm... thought not.

Anthony, you'll have to overlook my cynicism. Guess it comes with the terro-territory. actually my tone more than likely stems from flustration. nothing personal towards you, & do grow to care about you.

Well now how's about a furtherance of "Rooftop". O'kie-dokie! Here we go...

"Rooftop" continued...

Though old and in need of repairs the house offered retreat, a safe haven against dawn & oblivion. Plus it had a coveted feature — A DEEP CELLAR. The kitchen covered in years of collected dust long since gave up it's crumbs to curl-tailed rats. a single fine china plate sat at a hardwood table where ghosts of distant past sat to dine on lambchops & redwine. only cobwebs remain. Passing 'neath a high doorframe they enter a spacious living-

D.R.

By Danny Rolling © Anthony Meoli

80

1-28-2004

room. Dark, dank covered with grimy films of dust obvious no one lived there for ages. Looking through pones of broken glass the vamp cast a longing glance east. While her servant with-draws back to the hearse to retrieve a long maple coffin.

"All roads lead to Disboli... The world a juicy, red, plum", thus spoken Mauvais sujet, the creature, the monster, the temptress come to undress humanity reducing it to bloodless corpse-shells littering a bleak shore. Could anyone imagine what walked among us that fate-ful night? Noy... The city slept dreamy childlike on pillows of ease.

Myself? Who am I? How do I fit into this theme? Might complicated, but let's cut pass the chase, open a vein of simplicity and make a long story short. Was just a regular guy trying to get by. You know 8 to 5 day gig chasing the dream. Well... onenight in november all that changed. It was to be a stroll through the park. I liked the sol-itude of a late night excursion. Could collect my thoughts. Never occurred to me id happen upon a horror that would change me forever, but there it was——

D.R.

By Danny Rolling © Anthony Meoli

1-28-2004

That Scream!!! It came from the otherside of the duckpond. Several mallards and a snow white swan wing fluttered into the middle of the pond squaking as though a cat startled their sleep. Instinctively my head wanted to investigate, but my feet refused. Dilemma quickly resolved. Forced one foot infront of the other 'til at a careful lope stumbled unto business should of stayed clear of.

"O-o-o little boy... Did you lose your way? Or have you come to rescue a damsel in distresss..." hissed the vamp white-ivory fangs dripping hot red blood of a fresh kill. Bleeding twin wounds in a soft neck testified to nightstalker's hideous intent. Gently laying the pretty head down 'pon dew kissed ground. It stood eyes burning deep red through shadows of rising oaks rooted near a stone walkpath. Throwing both arms up it announced non-chalant blood spewing from it's animal mouth; "Mavvais sujet, a wondering bet. What does that mean? Rogue: black sheep, and within this breast shadows weep". Pulling down oneside of a velvet bodice long red nails bite into subtle flesh drawing crimson lines of

D.R.

By Danny Rolling © Anthony Meoli

By Danny Rolling © Anthony Meoli

1-28-2004

stolen blood that ran down collecting
'round an erect nipple where it dripped
unto the path' neath our feet.
   Mezmerized as if in a trance I
failed to notice the other hand remove
a necklace o'er curling raven locks
and arrowing a large emerald gem my
way it emanating a greenish glow.
Captured by magic I was a buck caught
in headlights of a hell train with no
will to move out of harm's way.
   "Come doll... taste sugar's breast,"
she beckoned. Unable to resist my mouth
found the nipple and did drink. From
that moment on I became her slave. She
took me to places never embraced in
the wildest nightmare. Nor could I
fathom the wicked sin that stilled her
dead heart. Night after endless night
me by her side we stalked lonestreets
for prey. Entire families. Whole com-
munities fell under her bloodthirsty spell,
and as tho that wasn't enough, she con-
jured up a devilish wizard, who sum-
moned an ancient ram. It's singly
horns crowned a mystical head and
knifing sharp hooves 'cross graves woke
the dead. Streets ran with tormented
blood. As walking dead did the wizard's
bidding.

D.R.

By Danny Rolling © Anthony Meoli

By Danny Rolling © Anthony Meoli

1-28-2004

Lost and dumbfounded I couldn't find my way. Time had no meaning, but somewhere in a vogue recess of my wretched soul — I HURT. Would I could reclaim myself and be the man I'd once aspired to be. Then the moment to break free arrived. a pin-prick of light at the end of a long, dark tunnel. after a terrible night of satanic decadence a thunderstorm roared in. The dead claw-crawled back into their graves before sunrise. The vamp & wizard retired in the cellar of the house & was prisoner. only Goath & myself were [as usual] left to face dawn. Sneaking 'woy, found a barren hill overlooking the city below. Sitting Indian style rain pelting my face [as if to wash 'way my sin] I contemplated what I should do. a lightning bolt cracked open a crevice and an angel of magnificent beauty rose from consecrated earth. Waving hand stilled th' roging storm. a break appeared in the clouds allowing streaks of dawn to lance 'way the dark and bleed morning onto a chaotic world. Piercing eyes she did not speak. Rather drawing nigh drew from 'neath a silken robe a flaming heart. Spreading heavenly fleece white wings she flew up into a brightened sky, hovered and

D.R.

By Danny Rolling © Anthony Meoli

86

1-28-2004

descending stood before me immaculate flaming heart in hand. Nodding I knew what she meant to do. Pressing it against my heaving chest it burned into me restoring my soul and sense of self. Renewed! Reborn! Searching a dead city for remnants of trapped souls I purposed to fight the evil. Wandering hither & yon found sanctuary where'er I could. So much sorrow tomorrow brings when heartstrings refuse to sing. Then they came searching... the dead led by Mauvais sujet & her devil spawn the wizard. Oft' I could hear their callings spearing shadows'er prodding for me. Retaliating I torched the house they slept during daylight hours pilling Goath in a bath of fire, but because the vamp & wizard slept in the cellar survived and took residence in a plush penthouse atop a major hotel.

The defining moment, the coup-degrâce. A fierce battle commenced. Blade & gunpowder 'gainst dead flesh. Screams & howls of the damned filled the night. Mauvais & wizard commanded their demon forces from atop their penthouse perch.

— TO BE CONTINUED —

D.R.

By Danny Rolling © Anthony Meoli

By Danny Rolling © Anthony Meoli

"Rooftop" continued:

1-29-2004

The future? a grain of sand fallen from ffather Time's ageless hand. another heartbeat closer to what? If tomorrow becomes today & today [all to soon] yesterday. then is time moving forward or backward? Perhaps all we see, hear, touch, taste & feel is in reverse reflected from a mirror of what once was is & now never was. all merely a fragment of predestined possiblities poured from a dreamer's mind.

All appeared lost. Legions of undead marched gruesome carrying in their slack jaws apocalytic dragons tailwaging morage. Facing them head-on armed to the teeth: long sword scabbarded over one shoulder, 12 gauge pump shotgun slung over the other shoulder, AR 15 auto rifle in hand, bandolier of frag grenades criss-crossing my chest, and dual ivory handle 44 magnum revolvers hugged my hips. I would have used nightvision tech, but undeads give off zero heat signatures. Instead a befriended wolfhound sniffed them out, and one by one, or in bunches the indignation of those felled by un-

D.R.

By Danny Rolling © Anthony Meoli

1-29-2004

presented evil lashed out through us dispatching cold skins back to the hell from which they came. on the hunt canine side-kick & I fought our way blood & bone to reach the threshold of Mavvis-Wizard's tower of horror. The structure took on an eerie alien appearance. Thick vines burst from wounded concrete finger-ing loce-like up and 'round the dark building. overhead a silver crescent moon winked a satalite eye shimmering in windows not yet broken — a ghastly haunt. The frontdoors loy splintered, flung open by some powerful force! Within this black orifice groans moaned unspeakable blasphemies. Sound thereof sent the wolfhound into fits and spider crawled shivers up my spine causing neck hairs to stand on end. Then they came ... a torrent of putrid flesh crippled & gangrene.

"Rail-on legions ... destroy. Drink his blood. Feast 'pon his bones. Eee-ahh!!!", came the cry highabove. & was on! Tooth & toenail, hand-n-hand, foot-arm & fist my weapons exploded! Round after hot round of molten lead slammed into rotting corpse 'til heap 'pon heaps did pile barring the entrance, That's when & felt it. at first a whispering breath

D.R.

By Danny Rolling © Anthony Meoli

By Danny Rolling © Anthony Meoli

1-29-2004

moth fluttering down the collar of my shirt goosebumping flesh. Then without warning the vines unfurled wraped-way 'round me hoisting me picking & scratching into the air. No matter how hard I fought resistance was ineffective and exhausting. Skeleton finger branches tore at me stripping 'way my weapons as an angry child tosses aside unwanted tinker toys ... That done rudely ripped 'way my clothes. Naked as day born, was spent and completely helpless. Once again a prisoner to that which I fought so hard to overcome. Up-up! The vines raced 'til my effigy was held suspended a stone throw from Rooftop and my fate.

"Well-well lookie what th' cat drug in. Pity ... Didn't I show you a good time, hun? Where did I go wrong" shaking head vamp mocked.
"Bloody bitch", replied I, gasping for breath.
"Uh-uh ... be nice", wizard opened a gnarly hand casting a spell of transluscent ball of energy that engulfed me. It felt as though sinew pulled against bone and I would be ripped limb from limb.

D.R.

By Danny Rolling © Anthony Meoli

1-29-2004

Ahh.. at the point of no return anguish gave way to a peace I'd never known. The heavens opened up and my soul took flight winged' way up - up a golden ladder that took me through countless dimensions. The awe. The wonder of what my eyes saw filled my soul with a great sense of belonging, a higher purpose where light reigns eternal o'er darkness that once possessed me with blindness.

(Far below temptress "The Whore Of Babylon" lay on her couch of sin. The world spun on Ole Scratch finger, and for the first time I SAW CLEARLY — THE BEAST that slept with her, and understood.

        – THE END –

                              D.R.

By Danny Rolling © Anthony Meoli

Danny Rolling with Don Sider

In 1997, *People Magazine* sent veteran journalist Don Sider
to Florida State Prison's Death Row to interview Danny
Rolling. The nearly-inaudible interview was recorded on a
mini-cassette, and when the magazine killed the story, he
very kindly gave the tape to Sondra London, who has kept it
under wraps until now, 25 years after it was recorded. Here,
then, are the highlights.

Exercise

Rolling There's not much to do on Death Row. Because we
wanted to go out twice a week, we average about
five hours a week exercise. Before I took this fall
and was incarcerated, I was a highly athletic
individual. I was very much into that. It got to the
point where I think it probably scared some of my
neighbors, when I was living in Shreveport,
Louisiana. I used to tote an 85-pound log on my
shoulders around a mile-long block. People were
ushering their kids off the sidewalk. Because I was
in such robust health. I had so much energy and so
much health, I just didn't know what to do with it
all.

Sider What do you do to keep yourself physically fit? Do
you have a routine? A regimen?

Rolling I run about a mile, when I exercise out, and I play
volleyball, and I do stretches in my cell, and I do
isometrics. That's about the best I can hope for.

Remembered

Sider   After you are gone—

Rolling Yeah?

Sider   How do you want the world to remember Danny
         Rolling?

Rolling As a man that set out on the right path but he got
         confused, he got deterred. The problem is he didn't
         just get off the path, he got beat down morally.

Ennad

Sider   Who is Ennad?

Rolling You brought up a whole ball of wax from A to Z. I
         knew we were going to cover some difficult
         questions, and I knew it was going to be hard for
         me to answer them. But Ennad has always been like
         an individual I could depend on, like in a real tough
         situation. Like you take for instance when I was in
         Tampa, Florida, when that robbery took place in
         Tampa, Florida. That was a pretty chaotic situation,
         They shot the windshield out of that car, it had
         nineteen holes in it. Bullets were coming through
         the dash. Glass was flying everywhere. Ennad is an
         outlaw. He might rape you, but he wouldn't want
         your blood. Unless you were causing him a
         problem. He always been a big help to me in
         situations.

Sider   Does Ennad ever reappear in your thoughts now?
         Ever come back to you?

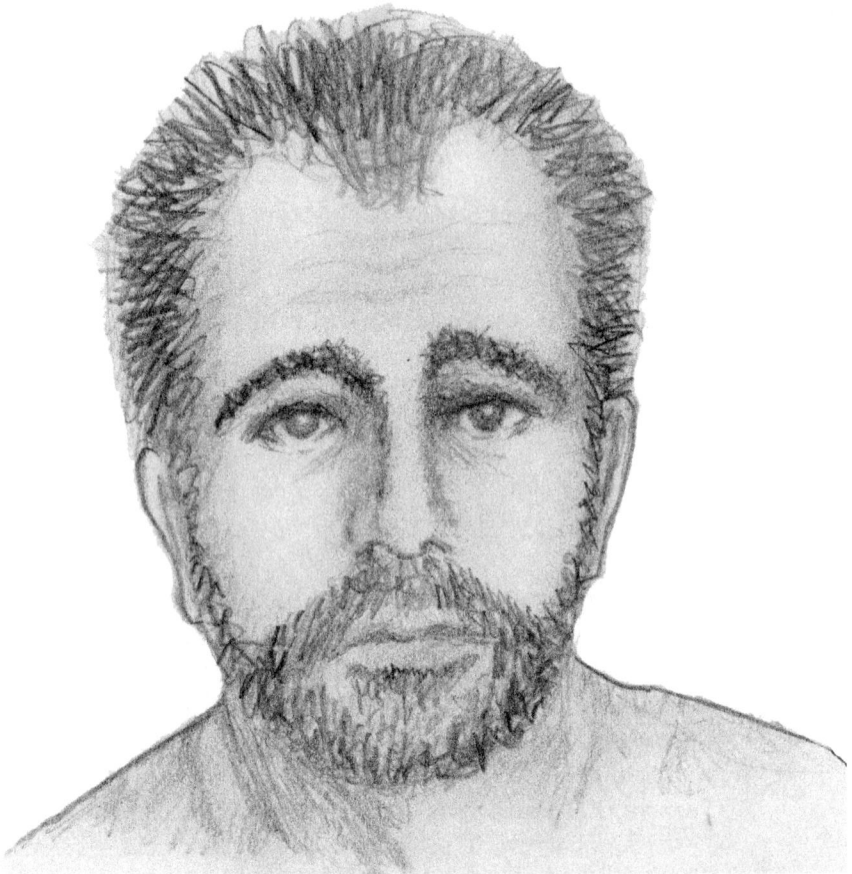

Sketch by Sondra London

Rolling   From time to time, yes. Sort of thing happens in the streets you'd never believe. A lot can happen like an armed robber or a burglar or a car thief or whatever, but I didn't know I was capable of violence. I didn't really have an inclination that I had a tendency towards violence. It is confusing to me. All right? It is. Because I want to be a complete, total, total individual, but it's still inside the baggage that I tote. I've got some pretty heavy baggage.

Married

Rolling   Once I was married. I had a beautiful wife. I had a
            beautiful little daughter. I would go to church. I
            drove the Sunday School bus, to pick up children to
            bring them to Sunday School. I sang in the choir. I
            visited the old folks home and carried my guitar.
            And I had a great love in my heart for humanity, for
            all my fellow creatures of this world, and the Good
            Lord put that love in my heart, for everybody. But
            you see, my friend, it was spiritual warfare between
            Heaven and Hell, between Lucifer and his demons,
            and My Lord and all the Angels in Heaven. One
            night when I came home from church, and we put
            the baby in her nursery to bed, and then my wife
            and I, we laid down. My wife, she went readily to
            sleep, but I couldn't, for some reason, I couldn't fall
            asleep. I was tossing and turning. I looked out the
            window, and in our bedroom, the curtains, we had
            these real long, they were drab olive green-colored
            curtains that were old, and my mother gave them to
            us. They were very heavy and they went from the
            ceiling to the floor. And there was a crack in the
            curtains, and the window was opened. I'm looking
            out across the front lawn and there's a streetlight
            out there. And the light spilled across our bed. And
            keep in mind that at this time I was the sort of
            individual who was an asset to the community. I
            wasn't about breaking the law. I wouldn't curse or
            drink or smoke or anything, you hear me? I was
            about trying to help people. And I'm looking out the
            window, I'm looking across the street, and
            everything was still calm and quiet, it was like a
            midsummer night's dream. And all of a sudden out
            of nowhere, this big strong wind come through the
            window. It was so strong it made a howling noise
            sorta like *ZZZZZRRRRRRRR*, like that? And I
            know it was real cold, it was freezing, and I'm
            looking out the window, and I remember looking at
            something outside the window, it was like it was on

the roof, like it was crawling down outside of my window. And it was like a dark cloud and it pooled underneath the window, and it pooled up and hovered in the ceiling. It was a dark cloud, and it was taking on all these different kinds of hideous shapes. I remember looking at this thing. And my wife, she was lying over there next to me but she's asleep. And I couldn't move. Like I'm paralyzed or something. It was like this thing, if you put your hand into it, it would go somewhere and you would never get it back. So I'm laying here. I'm trying to wake up my wife and warn her. And there's things moving around in the room, like pieces of paper and stuff. And I said, no I didn't say it then, I said it later. I'm moaning, I'm trying to say it, and my moaning woke her up, and she said Danny, she said what's wrong? And all I could do was moan, but somehow or another, I managed to get out "Jesus." It was just like, it was like a breath, it was a whisper. But it gave me courage to say "Jesus" a second time, and then a third time, and the third time I screamed it. I said *"JESUS!"* And when I did that? That thing went out the window, *pee-yong*, like that, lickety-split. The curtains went down and everything was real peaceful. And I turned to my wife and I said, Omatha, don't worry about it. I said, we've got Jesus. I went to sleep and I slept very well that night. The next morning I explained to her. She didn't believe me. Well, it's debatable whether I'm insane or whatever, but I should have took it as a premonition. It wasn't very long after that, my life fell to pieces and I ended up in prison.

Signs

Rolling   There are signs and guideposts, people are going to notice, that are telltale signs, of people who are going to end up going down Murder Road.

Sider   Can you look back now and say there was a certain
          point where if I could have turned myself around,
          or if Fate could have turned me around –

Rolling   You know, I've thought about that, Don, and I think
          probably the only thing that could have prevented
          me going down that very road, would have been be
          to have gotten some psychological help, like my
          people begged me to do. They knew something was
          wrong, they just didn't know how deep the problem
          was.

Sider   Who urged you, your mama?

Rolling   Yeah, well, and my girlfriend at the time, Bunnie
          Mills.

Sider   Why didn't you do that?

Rolling   I tried to. But the people I went to go see, just
          didn't impress me that they really cared or were
          interested, so I didn't follow through.

Sider   And then the time you were in the psychiatric
          hospital, you were writing it was kind of a joke.

Rolling   A terrible place, man. You talking about Bryce.

Sider   Yeah.

Rolling   Terrible place, boy, I ain't lyin' to you or puttin'
          y'all on the spot. There was this one kid in there for
          burning his whole family alive, right? And after
          that, he didn't speak, they couldn't get him to talk,
          right? This guy was way off, man. I think it's in the
          book. One night, man, I walked into the bathroom
          and he was perched up on the—

Sider   Mm-hm.

Rolling   And he had his hand up his rectum, and he pulled his guts out. Blood spurting everywhere. I couldn't believe my eyes.

Sider   Yeah, I found that tough to read in the book.

Rolling   Yeah, well he'd done it before. Wasn't the first time he did it. They laughed it off, like it was no big deal. They took him to the hospital, sewed him up, and the next day he was just out there on the floor.

Sider   And no help at all for you there?

Rolling   No.

Photos

Rolling   I'm not surprised at anything I did. And I don't like to remember the scenes, I wouldn't even look at the crime scene photos when they brought them to me, do you hear me? I remember the time that they showed me the first one and I said whoa. No. I do not want to look at them. So I didn't even look at them. But there were moments during those horrible bloody moments, that my mind, it was, I don't know how to explain it. I believe at the time I didn't want this to be credited to me. You know what I mean? And so therefore, that's the reason why the vaginas were washed. To get rid of evidence. I'm thinking over now something that happened over seven years ago. And that's the only conclusion I can come to.

Parchman

Rolling   Yes, I know the reasons for what happened. And there have been many times I have questioned myself on that. When I was at Parchman, I was in a cell that got flooded out once or twice, sometimes three times a week with raw sewage. This happened over a period of about eight months. I begged them to let me out of that cell. I'm a clean person. I can't stand filth like that. I had to eat in raw sewage, you hear me? They denied this, but I bet if you would get ahold of Donald Cabana that was the previous warden of that prison, I tell you what. He'll confirm that.

Possessed

Rolling   I'm detached from my body during that time. It's like another intellect, another mind. Absolutely. Ah, I firmly believe I was possessed. You hear me? I firmly believe that. And the reason why I say that is because when I was in Parchman my mind snapped. And I couldn't deal with all that filth and everything there, and being in solitary confinement, I was in solitary confinement for like about a year. It was all because of an escape. I ran off from the county jail. That's the reason why, they had a reason to put me in solitary confinement, but they didn't have a reason to make me live in pure raw sewage. I remember one cold night. And you know, this is another strange similarity. The way the prosecutor tried to turn the fact that I went to see that movie, uh—

Sider   The Exorcist 2, I believe?

Rolling   Naw, I think it was 3 or 4, or the last one. And he tried to say that the similarities, and well, to all the things that happened to me in the course of my life, was all concocted because of that movie.

Sider   Mm-hm.

Rolling   Which is not so. When I was in that cell in Parchman, it snowed in Mississippi, which is a rarity, but it did that year. And I remember I was looking out, and it was in the evening time, it was a gray sky. And a sparrow flew down and landed in the snow. I didn't land on my window sill. It rained a lot and snowed. And it froze to death, is what happened. Then it wasn't long after that, I remember that spirit Gemini come to my window, and he whispered to me, he said *Danny, aren't you tired? Aren't you tired of getting the bitter end of the stick? Aren't you tired of suffering? Don't you want somebody else to suffer for a change? If you'll just let me in, I'll give you your revenge.* And I said okay. And I opened the door. And I let that thing in me. I let that spirit in me. But at the time I never thought it would go as far as it did. I never thought it would escalate as far as it did. But right on down the line, it happened. He said, *I'll give you a soul for every year they've kept you in prison.* By that hour, I'd been in prison for eight years.

Reasons

Rolling   I don't think a sane individual could do some of the things I've done. I want to be a good person, but I'm sure that's highly debatable. There were reasons, there were several reasons for what happened, sir. I don't remember if there are any sins that are covered up, or that I might have tried to withhold from my Maker. I firmly believe that one day we will all stand before our Creator. And I don't want there to be anything hidden when it comes my time. I want to apologize to the victims. Certainly they have the right to feel against me, any way that they wish. I mean, they have that right. The tears I have shed over these, they won't believe they are real. I can't blame them for not believing that they are real. I have learned a lot of factors in my life that personally proved that. And I'm not shirking responsibility for what I did. I'm a confessed serial killer. I laid my cards on the table for everyone to view. I basically laid my soul bare before the world. It's not an easy thing to do, you know? But I did it.

Sketch by Sondra London

103

Dangerous

Sider   Could you kill again?

Rolling   I've thought long and hard about that. And I made a
            vow with my Maker that I would never shed another
            human being's blood. Unless it is for self-
            preservation or self-defense. But I can't really
            honestly answer that question, cause I don't really
            know all the workings of my mind. It betrays me
            sometimes, you know? And so I'm on Death Row.
            And because I am a dangerous individual, that's
            where I am. And I have been condemned to die by
            my peers. So I must face that.

Demons

Rolling   I would like to say this. In the world that we live in,
            there is a battle going on. We see it every day in the
            headlines. We see the violence, we see the terror
            that is going on in this world, not only on a
            physical level, but it almost seems like there, and
            there is, a spiritual war going on. There are human
            beings that are born who have an adaptive eye that
            can see into the supernatural. And not everyone has
            that ability. I believe it to be both a curse and a
            blessing. Take for instance people who are psychic,
            who are able to have visions of crimes, and are able
            to interact with the different law agencies to solve
            the mysteries. What happened to me, it's a different,
            even to discuss it, as you can probably tell kind of
            riles my thoughts, because it messes with me as an
            individual, because I try to displace that from me as
            far as I can. But I'm talking about demons here.

Devil

Rolling   This is the Devil's House. This is where every kind
of being you can think of dwells. So it's a constant
warfare for anyone who has lived in Darkness, to
embrace the Light. The Light is what we are all
seeking to have. If there are redeeming qualities in
those souls. If not, then you lean towards the
Darkness again.

Death

Rolling   I am against the death penalty. Not because it is the
ultimate punishment for the ultimate crime, but
because it does not work on any level of conscience
for healing. Society hasn't learned anything from
history. Our worldly activities continue to focus on
symptoms of an ailing civilization, while
disregarding the apparent cause. You won't find a
cure for crime in your microscope. Greed won't be
conquered by armed soldiers. No. The serum to save
mankind won't be discovered in some laboratory by
a well-meaning chemist. The cure is spiritual. Only
God in his infinite wisdom can redeem the human
race. A common denominator circulated amongst
intellectuals is that all reasoning is circular, which
means you can think I'm deluded and I can think
the same of you. And where does that take us? Back
to zero. For all our ability to equate the distance
between the earth and the moon, we can't seem to
see two feet in front of our face. If that were not so,
all people who deny can truly solve the age-old
problem of equality and prosperity. And that is
what I feel about the death penalty. Death. It's not
even a means to an end.

Dad

Rolling   You know, my dad was a policeman. And he was
highly respected as a policeman. But when my dad

came home, he was a different person. Altogether, if my dad would just, if poor Dad would just admit that he had a mental problem, and that he did things to my mother and my brother and me, when we were so young, that it hurts when I think about it. Because deep down in my heart I still love my dad, and I'm not honoring him by talking about this. And I want to honor him. But there were things that happened in my childhood when I was very young that formed and fashioned the way my mind works. He was an extremely brutal father. And I hate certain parts of my father, but he would open up those parts that, when he'd open up that door to his true, vulnerable self, every now and then, you couldn't help but love him. But then as soon as he opened the door, and let you spend a little time with him, he'd slam the door in your face, and then, there would be that cold, granite figure of my father that I hated.

Christa

Rolling In Christa Hoyt's memory, Lord God I hope when I see her on the other side, and I know she has forgiven me. I'm sure that the families of that precious woman can never find it in their heart to forgive me. And I totally respect that. I'm sure Christa Hoyt's in Heaven. I know she's an angel now. No doubt about it. And I'm sure Christa Hoyt wouldn't want anyone to be cast into the pale of eternal Hell.

Fish

Rolling I wrote another little piece here. It's called, "It Will Be Here." And it goes: "On a Greyhound Bus passing through Gainesville, that selfsame voice Gemini who called *Danny, come out to the night, come out and play-yay,* whispered in my ear: *It will be here.* I didn't know how or when, but I sensed I would be back, and that something terrible would happen there. Ride the wind, reap the whirlwind. And if you grab the Devil by his writhing tail, he'll sling you to & fro like a tempest sea whose troubled waters churn up the bottom, casting strange fish to the surface, horrible ugly finned creatures that bite you if you are in the water with them."

Legends

Rolling   I do an awful lot of illustrations. In fact, most of the illustrations you are looking at there have to do with *Legends of the Black Marsh.*

Sider   Really.

Rolling   Most of them are from one called, um, it's about a voodoo rock called Mojo. I think it's a pretty cool little short story, and I'm illustrating it. Sondra has it.

Sondra

Sider   I'm just trying to get some sense of the relationship.

Rolling   I highly respect Sondra London in every aspect of the word, and yes, there is a spark. There is a big chunk of my heart that will always be hers.And the media, the profiteers and all of them, they tried to play it off, as if it was just some sort of, I don't know, some sort of a promotion or something. And knowing the integrity that Sondra holds in her character—

Sider   Yes.

Rolling   —and the letters she has written to me. Sondra is not, Sondra is not an individual to perpetrate any kind of hoax. Sondra is genuinely believable—

Sider   I know.

Rolling   And you can count on her word as being good. I
                thank the Good Lord for Sondra. I really do. I think
                so much of her. The officials here have denied us
                the right to get married. They denied her our
                visitation privileges. So over a period of time I just
                felt like it was unfair to her to continue to be
                engaged, because let's face it, now. After so many
                years, I would rather be able to have maybe a
                simple kiss or even hold hands. It's unfair to her.

DON SIDER began a journalism career spanning five
decades at the *St. Petersburg Times*, then moved to *Time
Magazine*, where he helped set up Pioneer Press weekly
newspapers in key markets. In 1975, Sider was promoted by
Time to deputy bureau chief of their Washington bureau.
After twelve years covering politics, the Pentagon, and
Vietnam, he founded *Money Magazine* and *People Magazine*,
then went into semi-retirement, relocating to Florida while
working part-time as a correspondent for *People*.

In September of 2003, the dauntless reporter was busted
committing first-degree journalism. *The Smoking Gun*
reported:

> A *People* magazine correspondent was arrested Sunday
> in Georgia and charged with criminal trespass after
> sheriff's deputies found his car stuck in the mud on a
> private road near actor Ben Affleck's property. The
> reporter, Don Sider, was booked briefly into the
> Liberty County jail and hit with a misdemeanor count.
> Sider told a sheriff's deputy that he was a reporter for
> *People Magazine,* and acknowledged seeing the No
> Trespassing signs and locked gates at Affleck's 83-acre
> private estate called Hampton Island, near Beaverdale.
> Sider entered the site via a private gate that had been
> left open by workers putting gravel on the driveway,

where his car got stuck. Sider declined to talk about the incident: "As the lawyers say, I cannot comment on an ongoing investigation."

Don Sider's Georgia Mug Shot 9/14/03

Less than a month this heinous offense, Sider, 70, died of heart failure. A high-flying sky-diver, his will called for his ashes to be poured from a plane at 12,500 feet, and his estate paid for a plane full of jumpers, along with four cases of beer to be consumed in celebration.

"There is to be absolutely no ceremony, other than the above, to mark my passing," the distinguished journalist's will read. "No service, memorial, weeping or gnashing of teeth. The best thing the people I love can do is just to carry on and enjoy their lives too. I wish them all the fun they can stand."

Danny Rolling on WFTV

On February 15, 1993, Danny Rolling granted a televised interview to Kathy Belich with WFTV, Channel 9 in Orlando, Florida. He did this himself, without the participation or approval of either Sondra London or Rolling's attorneys.

Rolling read from a handwritten statement he had prepared, describing his relationship with London, calling her at one point his "agent and media go-between." He also stated that nobody was using him and that he had not been coerced.

Danny Rolling on WFTV 2/15/93

WFTV was hard-pressed to find a scrap of footage that was not devoted to enthusiastic praise of Sondra London. All of that, of course, was destined for the cutting-room floor.

All Channel 9 was able to air was a clip of Danny solemnly intoning: "The wheels of justice turn slow, but they do turn." They called it *enigmatic.* (The uncut footage may be viewed on Sondra London's YouTube channel.)

Rolling's public defender Rick Parker was standing at the prison gate, with every right to access, but was refused permission to be present at the interview.

The uncut statement was later played for the jury at the sentencing hearing for the murders. Rolling's naïve statement that he had not been coerced was used in support of the State's argument that giving Danny hope for visitation with London was *not* coercion, though coercion of a confession is defined as using fear *or hope.*

Rolling's ill-advised use of the word "agent" for London's role later became central to the State's civil suit under the Son of Sam statute preventing the proceeds of accounts of crime from going to a felon or his *agent.* Sondra London, of course, is a *writer* who also serves as a TV producer and media go-between. Though she was the co-author of Rolling's life story, she has never been anyone's *agent.*

Rolling did write a letter to London informing her of his intentions before doing the interview, but that letter was held back in the prison mail room until several days after the interview had occurred.

The interference with the correspondence predictably caused friction between Rolling and London. Once Rolling realized he had jeopardized London's commitment to *A Current Affair* to produce an exclusive interview, he sent her the following letter, writing out his unaired Statement in full.

Rolling: I don't understand you, Sondra. One minute you want me to give a statement about my wanting you to represent me, and I did. The next minute you say I've betrayed you. That whole interview with Miss Cathy Belich of Channel 9 was to set the record straight. Here's the statement I read, word for word:

> At this time I feel it necessary to comment on the blatant statements Mr. James H. Williams has made concerning Sondra London, Bobby Lewis, prison authorities and

myself. I am compelled to bring this matter into the light because Williams has caused undue pain & problems for those mentioned and on his own tried to muddy the waters and hinder the investigation in progress.

1. Ms. London and myself have been corresponding for almost a year now. Regardless of what Williams has said, Ms. London is of the highest caliber, sincere and honest, a woman of extraordinary talents. If I were here, I would sue Williams for slander and defamation of character. She did not deserve the things he said or what the *Gainesville Sun* printed about her. It's just not so. I do not know Williams reason to do such a vicious thing. It was totally unmerited or called-for. I think Williams has left himself subject to be charged with criminal mischief and/or obstruction of justice.

2. Sondra London is a colorful & bright woman, intelligent & talented, and it's a shame the way the media has bashed her as of late. She hasn't done anything to deserve that. Sondra is a worthy soul who only tries to bring the very best out of all she does.

3. Sondra London did not seek me out. I inquired her services because I had seen some of her work, namely a screenplay under the title of *Redbone* about the dramatic story of Bobby Lewis escape from Death Row, which would impress anyone. And so I wanted her to do my story. Sondra London is not... I repeat not... using me, period. No one is using me. I don't care what her previous lawyer Chet Dettlinger said about her. Can you imagine that? Her own lawyer sold her up the river. If I was a client of his, I'd find somebody else to represent me for fear that one day Chet Dettlinger would have something publicly to say about me.

4. Over the past 180 days, Sondra and myself have tried by protocol and through proper channels to get her approved to visit me, and she was allowed one visit behind the glass.

5. Any and all parties involved in the investigation underway concerning the Gainesville murders have been and will be dealt with in an honorable fashion.

The wheels of justice may turn slow, but they do turn. You don't ask of Justice. It asks of you.

6. The prison officials here at FSP have not made any deals with me... period. Nor have they made any promises to Bobby Lewis or myself... period. I have not been coerced into making any statements... period.

7. Mrs. London represents me as an editor, agent, and media go-between. From this point on, I shall make no further statements to the press unless Sondra London arranges it. You want to talk to me, speak to Ms. London.

8. Any further statements you wish at this time, please consult my lawyers Mr. Richard Parker or Johnny Kearns, who are excellent lawyers for the defense, and very capable of answering any other questions. I have nothing else to say. Thank you and good day.

Rolling: That was the end of the interview. She tried to get me to answer some questions as I got up but all I said was God bless you, and left the room. So, you still feel I let you down? I tell you, Sondra. Sometimes you say things that strike me harder than a punch to the solar plexus. Do you think I'm having a good time at this end? Hell! At least you can get away from your misery. Mine is everywhere I turn. The woman I love has been taken away from me, my best friend has been moved permanently, I don't have anyone who visits me, I have to look at Breeze's ugly mug every day, and I get letters from you that blame me for it all! Damn! Everything I've done, I've done for you. But it looks like it's not enough. I've pulled my hair out trying to find a way to make things easier for you, but my efforts seem in vain. The only other thing I can do is agree to be on *A Current Affair* as you wish. You can keep all the money it generates. I don't want any of it. You keep it. It's my gift to you. You get on my case about not writing you. Sondra. I do get letters from you every day. But lately, they tear me up so, I have to wait a day to get over the hurt to answer.

Danny Rolling Sings in Court

September 27, 1993. At a resentencing hearing for a 1990 Winn-Dixie robbery in Ocala, Florida, Danny Rolling made another noteworthy appearance. When given the opportunity to address the Court, he used it to serenade Sondra London.

"Sondra, they may keep me from you, but they cannot stamp out the love and affection I have for you in my heart," he said, then sang an original song. After two verses, Judge Thomas Sawaya interrupted, "Mr. Rolling... Mr. Rolling... Mr. Rolling..." but Danny kept on singing as multiple videocameras kept on rolling tape.

Finally Danny stopped singing and sat down. With Order restored to the Court, Judge Sawaya instructed the impassioned defendant: "You get one song, that's all. You're not here to address your friend. You are here for sentencing."

The Fifth District Court of Appeals had overturned the original sentence of life plus thirty years, but Judge Sawaya's resentencing decree retained the life sentence, and only reduced the extra thirty years to fifteen.

WESH-TV reporter Steven Stock later informed London that the hearing had been closed to the public and moved three times in an effort to prevent her from getting close to Rolling.

Stock quoted two official sources as stating that they believed London intended to smuggle in a knife to Rolling, who would then take London hostage in an escape attempt. No evidence for this canard has ever surfaced; however, off the record, it was suggested that disgruntled rival serial killer GJ Schaefer had a hand in starting the rumor.

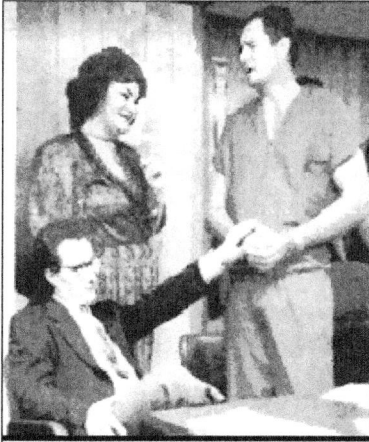

While Danny Rolling did sing to Sondra London in Court, it did not look like this. This photomontage placing Rolling close to London was created by ...

WHAT WERE MY WORDS?
by Danny Rolling © Sondra London

I recall the day I first saw you.
I reached out to say I love you.
But it was hard to say
Cause I couldn't touch you.

So tell me, baby (Chorus)
What were my words?
All my tears run together.
What were my words?
All my tears run together.
Baby, just like rain.

Someone said to me, you
Can't run from your shadow,
And all you wanna be
Deep or shallow
And all you wanna see
Along the path you follow,
So tell me, baby (Chorus)

In response to pressure from Judge Sawaya, Danny Rolling stopped singing after the second chorus, but the last verse, which remained unsung, was sent to London in a letter, and can now be revealed here:

No one seems to know
Or even care why,
Or how the story goes
They'd much rather lie.
So on goes the show
Do or die?
So tell me, baby (Chorus)

Sondra London on *True Murder*

On October 23, 2020, 1997, Sondra London appeared on the *True Murder* podcast, to discuss *The Making of a Serial Killer* with host Dan Zupansky.

Dan Zupansky

Zupansky   The man convicted of the vicious murders of five college students in Gainesville, Florida, discusses his motivations and actions in committing the crimes. Reflects on what made him into a killer and has struggled to come to terms with what he did, including new prologue, new illustrations and a new preview of the companion volume *Beyond the Making of a Serial Killer*. The book that we're featuring this evening is *The Making of a Serial Killer: Second Edition* with my special guest, journalist and author Sondra London. Welcome back to the program and thank you so much for this interview.

London   Oh Dan, it's always a pleasure. You're such a good interviewer.

Zupansky   Oh, thank you so much. It's always an absolute pleasure. You have some of the most – unique is not even an apt word. But you have definitely a must-read true crime book, especially here, with *The Making of a Serial Killer*. Incredible. Can you explain when this book originally came out, and then tell us now the reason for this new second edition.

London   In 1996 Feral House published it, so that is the edition that most people are familiar with. It is selling for a couple of hundred dollars on Amazon, because it's been out of print for many years. I had published the original on my own, as an independent publisher. And I had so many attempts to steal my work in progress, that I would copyright every fifty or hundred pages. And I called it *The Rolling Papers*. And so 1993 was when the first copyright was placed on it, while it was still work in progress.

Zupansky   Luckily, this Second Edition of *The Making of a
            Serial Killer* gets people to not only hear it from
            the originator, being you; and then we have
            these added bonuses, the Prologue, the new
            illustrations, and the preview of the companion
            volume, *Beyond The Making Of A Serial Killer*. A
            new cover. Let's get to this most incredible book.

            You say, Pulitzer Prize-winning historian
            Douglas Southall Freeman said that the
            biographer should provide no information
            beyond what his subject possessed at a
            particular moment, so as to take the reader into
            the past as it was when the life was lived, rather
            than to distort the historical record to conform
            to newly-formed standards and customs. And
            you say that such is your purpose with this
            book. Can you explain?

London   Yes, that is an immense challenge, because it
            was 25 years ago and things have changed.
            Expectations have changed, and even at the time
            it was published, it was way out on the edge of
            freedom of speech, in terms of publishing things
            that you might underplay by calling them
            politically incorrect. So it was already like that
            when it was published. So to bring it forward
            into today, now, that occasioned some
            discussions with the owner of Feral House, who
            held the copyright. And Feral House was a one-
            man operation, which was Adam Parfrey. And
            when he died, his sister inherited the business.
            Well, Jessica Parfrey wants Feral House to be a
            kinder, gentler publisher. And when I wanted to
            do a second edition, I sent her the letter, so if
            she chose not to print a second edition, then I'd
            get the copyright back. And so she started
            actually reading the book – because Jessica had
            not been involved in the business when Adam
            published the book. And then she came to the

part where Danny was raving about his enthusiasm for rape, and she said, you can't publish that, you know?

Zupansky   Right.

London   I just I have developed a philosophy about censorship and very much so when it comes to presentations involving violence. And I feel that whether you are cleaning it up or sexing it up, or making it palatable for a wide audience, it creates a dangerous motif, a current of belief that enhances the glamour of violence, because it's a quick and easy dramatic device to resolve any conflict. We are constantly fed with these scenarios through entertainment. And people are given what they want. They show what they like by what they buy, then they get it more of it.

Zupansky   Right.

London   And so I feel that some of that influence would persuade someone to cross the line over into something that would ruin their life forever. And they could never be who they were or who they could have become, because they are guided by these images and stories that don't tell the whole story. And so, from working with a guy like Danny Rolling, there was always the sense of what suffering that these explosions of violence brought on, and how he lost who he was. And he was very eloquent about showing me that side of becoming a killer. And I felt that all of this needs to be included, and as the readers, we need to grow in terms of being able to incorporate it all into one picture. And don't just skim for the sexy part and get off. Instead, follow the whole story line, where the sexy part brings on a great deal of suffering that is inescapable, that ruins your whole life. Because that is what gives the story meaning, that connects it to real life.

Zupansky   Now you write that the first week of July of 1992, you received the introductory letter from the high profile prisoner Danny Rolling, who had been charged with five murders that were committed in 1990 in Gainesville, Florida. And Danny Rolling was housed in Florida State Prison next to Bobby Lewis. Tell us who Bobby Lewis is, and your relationship with him, and what Bobby Lewis had shown Danny Rolling.

London   Bobby Lewis was a murderer from Jacksonville, and when he saw all the attention Schaefer was getting from Killer Fiction, he said he wanted me to do his stories because they were better than Schaefer's. And I told Bobby, you know, you don't get any money and you have to be honest. You have to show respect. And he's like, yeah, yeah, so he signs on. So from that point, I published, under my Media Queen imprimatur, his story of being on Death Row with Ted Bundy and his story of escaping from Death Row, which is why he was on Death Row with Ted Bundy, because they were both escape risks. So Bobby had presented himself to me as a good guy who was very popular and influential in the prison. He said he could get anything: money, drugs, guns and girls, you name it. And that was a completely con-man type of a description of who he was. Well, I found out what Bobby really was. He was a snitch. And that's where he got all his power, from working for the Man. Bobby had been involved in multiple situations, where the administration would give him privileges, and then they would get some information on an inmate in return. And that was who Bobby really was. So they placed Danny Rolling next to him on purpose, so Bobby could work him.

Zupansky Now before we go any further, for everyone that doesn't know this entire story, you mentioned Killer Fiction. And we haven't talked about how you'd come to this honestly. You didn't just come to true crime and decide to write to serial killers in prison. So we'll have to go backwards just a bit briefly to talk about your relationship with Gerard Schaefer, when you were seventeen years old, I believe, and what you saw in that relationship, and why you broke it off. And then a few years later what you learned about Schaefer and his criminal career.

London Well, I don't want to give Schaefer too much of our time today, but I will try to touch on what I think of as the relevant points. Schaefer was in prison, sixteen years into a life sentence on a double homicide. He had been convicted of two murders in 1973, and he was connected to thirty-four other dead or missing women. And when that case hit the news, they didn't have the term serial killer, that was developed later by Robert Ressler, who in fact based his definition of the organized type of serial killer in part upon the Schaefer case.

So now, what did that have to do with me? Because when I was a junior in high school, I met John Schaefer and he was one year older than me. And he became my steady boyfriend for a year. As I turned from a junior to a senior, I dated him exclusively. So we were both, you know, 16, 17, 18. And then we broke up. And then nine years later, came the headlines in the Palm Beach Post. They had just pages and pages of this story about this deputy sheriff who was perpetrating behind the badge. And the thing that excited everyone so much was the writings that he had done, because they were about murder. In the nine years since I knew him as a kid, John Schaefer had gotten two degrees, one in criminal justice and one in creative writing. And he studied writing fiction under the Southern Gothic novelist Harry Crews, who wrote a recommendation for him about his short stories. And that fiction was the big deal in his murder conviction. So meanwhile, I went along with my life, and then years later, it was 1989, the technical writing business wasn't going so well, and besides, it was boring; so I said, well, I want to do something different, something I can put my name on.

So while I was mulling that over, they executed Ted Bundy and there was quite a lot of interest in him and in serial killers. That let me to read The Stranger Beside Me by Ann Rule and my reaction was, shoot, I can already write better than that, and I knew a serial killer a lot more than she did, so I could write about that. And so then on February 7, 1989, I wrote to Schaefer in prison. I asked him, do you want to write a book with me about your life and crimes? So that is how it all got started. Because I wanted to figure out what in the heck is going on here? How could you know someone that well, and yet you can't tell they have a whole 'nother life going on at the same time? And I wanted to figure out what kind of a mind it takes to be a serial killer. I asked him a question: John, I said, do you still write those stories? Oh, God. I was opening Pandora's box at that point because after that, he began to assault me virtually by sending me these grossly offensive sexually violent stories. Well, little did he know that this was my way of getting him to admit what he had done and to commit himself as a killer. So that's what I did.

I was coached by Roy Hazelwood, at the Behavior Science Unit. He was an instructor at the FBI Academy, and he was very helpful, because Schaefer was very difficult. Well, a half-dozen of the stories Schaefer sent me for Killer Fiction, I called them the Starke Stories. Starke is where Florida State Prison is, with the electric chair. And these stories were about atrocities going on in the prison. And that's what got me in trouble with the authorities, because the stories were atrocious. They got Schaefer in trouble too. They didn't mind when he sent me the original handwritten letters with the stories written out, page after page. But when I sent them back to Schaefer with titles like "Death House Screams" over his byline – nicely edited, typeset, illustrated and copyrighted by Media Queen – they confiscated the print-outs as contraband, and sent Schaefer to the hole for thirty days for receiving "pornographic filth" in the mail.

So that explains why I was already known to the authorities in Florida State Prison as a *persona non grata* when Danny Rolling came along. The difference in the two projects was, Schaefer's case was old. He was arrested in 1973 and he was not in the news by the time we started working together in 1989. But Danny Rolling was a huge news story, and I was already putting news stories on national TV for *A Current Affair*. So that's what was different about the Rolling case. There was this whirlwind of intense attention. And that story came to me through the good offices of Bobby Lewis. Bobby Lewis was drawn to me because he saw what I did with the Schaefer story. And then he saw what I did with his own stuff. So he showed Danny Rolling this screenplay I had written about his escape from death row, and Danny was impressed with that, and made up his mind he wanted me to help him tell his story. So that's how Bobby introduced me to Danny. And Danny was presented to me by Bobby as quote-unquote, highly suggestible. And I was told, he will do anything you tell him. And so throughout the rest of all this, there was Bobby trying to manipulate Danny to Bobby's own benefit. And it was kind of throwing a stick in the spokes of the wheel, so to speak. But Bobby continued to play a role there. The problem with Bobby was, he lied too much. And he expected to be the star of the Rolling trial. But they could just barely use him, because they knew what a liar he was, so they could only risk putting him on the stand for about three minutes to just swear to some facts and then get him off quick, right?

Zupansky   So Bobby Lewis now is trying to manipulate the situation, and he shows your writing to Danny Rolling, and Danny says, who wrote this? Bobby said, Sondra London, so Danny said, well, who is Sandra London? And Bobby says, oh, she's just my editor. But Danny Rolling realizes very soon after reading this screenplay, that you are the person he wants to write his story. So now with all your experience, and with your coaching with Roy Hazelwood from the FBI Behavioral Science Unit, you were prepared – you had an extraordinary preparedness for this interaction. We know it's in Danny Rolling's own words, and that will be shocking to many people. But what was your goal? And you did write that Hazelwood gave you some really important advice about what not to do with Rolling.

London   Well, my goals were multiple. I still had a mystery to be solved of the mind of a serial killer. Now I graduated from a college that put us through independent study. We didn't have classes and we didn't have grades. We learned how to structure our own studies, so I knew I had to go from the particular to the general. I knew I had to read all of the published literature. And then I started going back the other way from the general to the particular. By the time I had copies of Killer Fiction, I sent it to some name-brand serial killers to get their reviews, so I could use a blurb to promote the book. And from that, I became acquainted with a litany of modern serial killers of different types that helped me broaden my general knowledge. So I know what to compare it to and, then but I have a philosophy that I have developed, Dan.

Everyone who interviews anyone is always pressing for a generalization. In my case, I'm always continually asked, what is it about serial killers. And so you try to be nice and give them what they want, because they want that sound byte. They want you to boil it down, cut to the chase. But I'm afraid that, too, does a disservice to comprehending the phenomenon of serial murder because it involves a very subtle and complex pathology. And when you start generalizing, your preconceptions will blind you to what is right in your face. And if you please, just open your eyes and look at the next five human bodies that pass your vision. You will note that each one is completely distinctive in different way. And if you worked up their biochemistry, you'd know that each one is different and there's a kind of a meme that is often repeated serial killers are all alike. And, I try to resist the pressures that are brought to bear to make people say things like that. I don't know who gets so many people to say that serial killers are alike in any way, but it's not true.

Thinking of a human being in front of you as a statistical average will blind you to their unique traits, and that can get you in trouble, because you will miss the unique human being that you're dealing with here. It would be foolish to say, he's another serial killer, so he's just like Gerard Schaefer, I need to deal with him the same way. Well, he's not the same, so then what good are your learned preconceptions?

It's better if you take everything you've learned from other cases, from books and news, and studies that have been done, from dialogue with experts and authors, trials you've attended, cases you've worked on, and put all that on the back burner. Don't ignore what you have learned. But don't let it get in the way of the fresh data that you are privileged to be the exclusive holder of. So that's why my mission was to get as much data as I could and to publish it. Go where the data leads. Elicit the data, organize the data. Fact check it, of course, since we're dealing with reality here, and then publish what I find.

And my goal was not to create a best-selling novel or something that would give you a warm fuzzy, that the bad guys are really obvious in the good guys will catch them quickly, identify them and punish them. And every little thing's gonna be all right. I wish I could get ahold of a story like that, because the ones that I have been presented with are nothing straightforward like that. I would violate the integrity of my unique data by squeezing it into a procrustean bed, trying to comply with the need for a sound byte. So I think the most productive a way to examine my work is to dwell on the one case under the microscope, and draw out the unique features of that case, rather than try to look for the lowest common denominator to everyone we know of who has been classified as a serial killer.

Zupansky   This book includes everything about Danny Rolling's life and his disturbing upbringing with his father, James, and his mother, Claudia. It also includes the graphic details. It may seem even exaggerated, but it is the gleeful recitation of his rapes and murders mixed in with other things like his incredible artistry. I mean, his illustrations, his poems.

Light's on
11-27-95 ☺

London   His versifying. Yes, that's what Danny's like. You take a letter from Danny, and you know, most people just write one line after another down the page. Well, in his letter Danny will just burst into pictures, you know, right in the middle of the line, so that graphic imagery is true to life. If I'm going to deliver a complete portrait of Danny Rolling, to present his complex character in all its contradictory parts, I have to include his artwork, because it helps you get a feel for what Danny was really like, the way he literally illustrates his own thinking with his pictures.

Zupansky   Very much like your other investigations for book projects, one of your goals is to get the absolute truth about the murders, but also you delve into it by asking Danny Rolling the motivation behind all of this.

London   Absolutely. That's what it's about. The guilty mind, mens rea. Well, it went beyond the motivation for murder with Danny Rolling, because with him, there was a strong death wish that was on the record since childhood, and he made multiple attempts, suicidal gestures. And he hated himself. He had tried to kill himself again just three weeks before he contacted me. When Danny presented himself to me, he had what I called zero self esteem. And you know how I mentioned a minute ago how he would burst into pictures, well, I had to tell him, Danny, these pictures are really good. I believe you are actually an artist, I said, and from now on, everything you do, whether you write it or whether you draw it, I need you to sign it and date it. And to this day, anyone who ever corresponded with Danny Rolling can confirm that he faithfully initialed and dated every page, he dated and signed every artwork.

Well, that's one sign of improvement in his mental status, that allowed him to see himself as worthy of living, worthy of receiving recognition and encouragement as an artist. Whereas before, he was completely buried in shame and guilt and unworthiness. He had that guilty mind, that mens rea. He couldn't confess to murder before he went to trial, but he could deal with the darkness of his life leading up to becoming a serial killer, if the process was gratifying. So a big part of my contribution to making this book come out was coaxing him to keep on living, and giving him a motivation for using his talents to probe his own mind. I gave Danny a college-level course in creative writing. When he started, he was writing at about an eighth-grade level. But he caught on fast. I gave him instruction, training and explaining, examples and plenty of practice. Each time he would send me a piece, I'd edit it and send it back, and I'd explain the principles behind the edits. And Danny would pick it right up. He was open to any suggestion. The improvement in his writing was rapid and dramatic. He was parched for learning and recognition. He had been a talented, imaginative, sensitive child. He was abused before he was born, and he was abused again as an infant. And these incidents were witnessed. So you can multiply in your own mind, all the things that went on that were not witnessed. So that is how he came to me.

Zupansky   This psychological investigation here. You also make it so that he's attracted to you. You say he's in courtship mode from the very beginning, that he wants to meet you, and wants to get you to visit.

London   Yes.

Zupansky   But he also wants to please you. And some of the terms of that, to satisfy you in this endeavor, is that he needs to include every bit of his background, of course, which is important, but also the shameful parts.

London   The ugly parts, the painful parts.

Zupansky   Exactly.

London   He can't be preening around like a peacock because that will not impress me. I need to see his pain. I need to see the turning points in his life. I need to see how he got hurt. It's very, very hard for a big hardened criminal to talk about how he has been hurt.

You know about Ottis Toole, right? Very brutal upbringing. And I was privileged to debrief him with Joel Norris in a prison interview. And I had asked him to do some drawings for me, and he'd sent me a dozen or so drawings of faces and figures of people. And he always drew enormous ears on his little stick figures. We asked him why the ears were so big. We asked if there had been a lot of yelling, was that why? No, he muttered under his breath, they were handles. You see, that was how he was being sexually abused. Well, that's all he could say. And he had to turn his face down and nearly whisper it very low. But through working with that, it was very gradually able to bring him to talk about what had been done to him. Oh, he was blithely happy to chat all day about what he had done, bloody murder and who he had hurt and the crimes he had committed. But when it came to how he had been wounded, he could not speak and he had to be worked with at that point, to be able to bring that out. So anything that would go to the really painful part, that's what you're not gonna get.

Now, here's the thing, Dan. People think, you wanna know why did he kill? So you're gonna walk up to him, stick a mike in his face and say, hey, buddy, why'd you kill 'em? And then you think they're going to carefully sit down and explain to you in a way you can understand why all this happened? That is not possible. Oh sure, you might get a reaction, but it will not be the answer to the question you asked. In order to really answer a deep, painful question like this, it requires a great deal of personal investment in terms of your time, your energy, to get involved.

Or let's say, for example, you are doing a psychological assessment. You know, you just do a drive-by, you say, he clicks off these symptoms in the DSM, so therefore, his diagnosis is X.

But, you know, I dealt with Danny personally day after day for years. I read all in investigative reports. I went to the press conferences, the hearings and the trial. I heard all their testimony live, and studied the transcripts later. And I think the most productive thing to talk about with Danny is borderline personality disorder, because he really had a lot of borderline traits, regardless of his dissociative disorder. I think you'd call it co-morbidity, with different conditions in the same person.

But what I'd like to talk about is how he did not respect people's boundaries and how he violated them. And as soon as a person was around him, he would try to befriend them. The investigators who were working for the police to try to find him guilty, Danny would welcome them and try to be their friend. He had no discernment when it came to boundaries of people and that was why his early pathology involved violating boundaries and they started with the voyeurism where he called himself The Eyes, and he would just look. But even nonviolent looking was still violating boundaries. And then that same impulse escalated, as it will, to breaking and entering. That's violating boundaries. And so it goes on to rape. And then it goes on to murder; and all those are forms of violating boundaries.

When you listen to the girls he tried to romance in Sarasota before the murders, they all commented that his social behavior was prematurely intimate, and he would try to exert a proprietary control over a girl he had just met.

We see him violating their boundaries even in a benign social setting. So if you will go back to your question about his being in courtship mode with me, you see, he was violating boundaries. Okay, so whenever it's Danny Rolling, he's gonna do that. He's gonna try to make a connection.

And then there's another aspect of the borderline personality which is called splitting. And it doesn't mean that Danny himself splits into Danny and Ennad and Gemini. No. It means his perception of you will split. You are an either angel, a princess, a goddess, or else you are a demon from hell. That's splitting.

Zupansky   Interesting.

London   So you would see that as a strong tendency with Danny toward emotional extremes. Well, look at his take on Bobby Lewis. At first, he's the greatest, he's my partner, I trust him in everything, he's a real stand-up convict. And then after Danny realized how Bobby had betrayed him, then of course, Bobby was a beast, a toad, the enemy.

Zupansky   Absolutely. You write about his past, his background. I know from reading hundreds of books that everybody attributes their crimes to their background, especially when it's a death penalty case. People come out of the woodwork to say he bumped his head, and he was acting weird from then on. And there was always some reason to attribute it to their background. But in this case, this is a particularly disturbing childhood with his father, who's police officer. Tell us a little bit about his background.

Sketch by Sondra London

London   Okay, I'll do that in a minute. But first, if you will, let me talk about how that kind of statement gets into the case. It is the work product of defense attorneys doing their due diligence. They have to put on some kind of defense. Now with Danny Rolling, in most states you have aggravators and mitigators, and these are aspects of a case that will make the penalty more or less severe. Okay, so that's what comes in on the penalty phase of a capital case. The hearing is to present aggravators and mitigators for jurors to weigh. Well, Danny Rolling pleaded guilty to all charges, and went into his sentencing hearing with nineteen aggravators. They were statutory violations that required no evidence or argument, aggravators that were not up for debate, like having a weapon while committing a felony. Okay, he had nineteen aggravators. On the other side he had one paltry mitigator, which was his mental state. He did not plead mentally ill, or not guilty by reason of insanity. His plea of diminished capacity was only introduced in mitigation of his sentencing. Okay, so it's not like they were saying he was insane. But the long-suffering public defenders, their thankless job is to go find people to stand up and present something on behalf of the defendant. So that's why it's there.

Zupansky   Certainly, I understand that, but what I'm saying is that this background, this upbringing is particularly disturbing, even compared to the other people who wound up on death row and in prison as a serial killer, this is stands out, this childhood.

London   Danny was the first son of a Shreveport, Louisiana, deputy sheriff who wore his Sam Browne belt around the house. He was the stereotyped Southern cop in every way. And he was a war hero. He had been in Korea and had experienced what could only have been severe trauma during war, which we need not to go into here. But some of the only moments he ever spent with his sons were when he was telling the stories of the war atrocities that he lived through, the most horrifying scenes. And he would tell them over and over to the boys. And that was how they got to be around him. Then, on the other hand, when he got mad at his wife he'd threaten her, remember, he'd say, my granddaddy cut my grandma to death at the dinner table. So you've got to do what I say. And he would use that as a threat. It was true. Danny's father had witnessed his grandfather cutting the neck and killing his grandmother at the dinner table.

Zupansky   You have the corroboration from people to get
            everything he did say you write, that you got
            that corroboration, that verification, that that
            actually happened. And then you get Danny
            Rolling's take on it in his own unique way,
            encouraged by you to be a writer and to be
            insightful and to express himself. Throughout
            this book Danny Rolling is talking about
            wanting love from his father, sending him
            letters telling him I love you, I love you. And we
            haven't even got to the confrontation between
            the two that ends up with one of them wounded.
            Let's talk about just what happens that prompts
            him to go into the military and from there, what
            happens afterwards in his life.

London   Well, I think that he was always cruel to the
            boys, even when they were small, before
            puberty. He would torture them. He would put
            them in handcuffs and then leave the property,
            leaving the boys in handcuffs. He would beat
            them both, but especially Danny. Danny's aunt
            Agnes saw him beating Danny so severely, that
            she called the police. They referred her to Mr.
            D'Artois, who was the police chief and she said,
            he is gonna beat that boy to death. And Mr.
            D'Artois said, well, Officer Rolling has always
            been a very good officer, and we don't want to
            interfere in domestic situations or do anything
            that would reflect on him.

            So, my interpretation of why Danny became a
            serial killer instead of merely a patricide is that
            society let this go on; that there was no help for
            him; and that because the father was in the local
            law enforcement establishment, whenever they
            saw Danny, they would go, you're Sheriff
            Rolling's son, right? So in that context, I think
            he grew to conceptualize the enemy as society,

especially those who belong in society and are loved and welcomed and sustained and strengthened and nurtured, because he always felt that he was on the outside looking in on those qualities in life.

Zupansky   When he finally made it into prison, what was his experience like? And didn't he later vow revenge for the treatment he received every year he spent in prison?

London   The way Danny tells it, he was in and out of every dusty joint in the South. And that's true. He was in multiple state penitentiaries and county jails, and he was in state mental institutions – Bryce in Alabama, and then later Chattahoochee in Florida. He writes about his experiences in each of these. One thing that we will run into in the book, especially with these prison encounters – some of the people involved happened to be black, and so Danny would use the kind of language that everyone used to address their opponents in these unpleasant contretemps. So we come back to my editorial philosophy that says we're here to learn how these people think, so we mustn't jump in and cut off their tongues when they finally do start to talk.

Zupansky   Right. We need to hear what they are saying.

London   That explains why the book has such graphic language, with the real fighting words used to start real fights. These were some rude, crude convicts, right? Trying to aggravate each other forty or fifty years ago in the deep South. Danny was kind enough to give us his story, tell us what he saw, what he heard, and what he did, just how it really happened. So my editorial approach is, while we have such vivid descriptions of scenes of real violence, it would just cheat the reader to be squeamish about the harsh language you'd hear if you were there. That was my editorial position when the book first came out, and once again in this 2020 edition, I made the same decision, to leave the historically accurate language just as related to me by the source.

That goes to the agreement I've made with anyone I've worked with: If you lie to me, we're done. So you've got to tell me the truth. And if you don't disrespect me, and you don't talk to any other writers, I will guarantee you that your story will come out just like that, as you want it told, in your own words. I know from being the target of mainstream news hit jobs myself, that when you give one of these reporters an interview, and then you read what they write, it could really put you off the idea of giving any more interviews.

It's shocking how selective they can be with what you gave them, and how biased the writing is, with much of it just plain wrong. So I offered an alternative way to get a story out, and that was my side of the bargain I made with Danny. I don't want to come out with a story that has been altered to conform the demands of a mass market, always wanting another best-selling book that provides dramatic entertainment by tracing the same predictable arc as the last one. And these pressures are insidious.

Zupansky   Oh, I know, they can be.

London   And I've talked to these young first offenders who popped off and killed someone all of a sudden, and they don't know. They're not thinking, they are just acting out a script they

have seen over and over on TV since the
Roadrunner days. They don't know the
difference between fantasy and reality, because
in the cartoon version, when you get flattened,
you just jump right back up. And the shooter,
he's the winner of a contest that's over as soon
as he pops that cap.

Zupansky   Yeah, that's the fantasy.

London   But now so many of these kids have crossed a
line and they can never, ever go back. And all
the dreams they had for their life are wasted. All
their friends are gone, all their gang members,
with the brother-brother talk, you know, all of
them, they don't know you. So if I'm going to
tell the story of a crime, I've got to put that part
in there—the aftereffects, the crash after the
rush.

And anyone who's ever been in prison knows
that it's a very racist environment. So when you
have a prison fight, and someone calls you White
Boy, you know you are going to call him
something worse to even the score. And all of
that belongs in the book, because this is not a
book for those who are easily offended, though
perhaps the language issue is more sensitive
these days in the parts about prison life.

Zupansky   I can see your dilemma.

London   I'm getting a little philosophical about how I
handled this violent and offensive material, but
let's just say I wanted the result to serve the
public interest. I wanted to stretch the readers'
perception of the mind of a serial killer beyond
the impressions we get from entertainment
media. Because so often people will say, oh, I've
got really good instincts, so I can tell if a guy's

off the wall, and I just go the other way. Well, that's great for the 99.9% of the freelance nut cases floating around who might commit a murder or two, if you will. Sure, most of these sketchy characters you meet who are disturbed troublemakers prone to violence, and they do project a palpable menacing vibe. But that is not the impression you get with a real serial killer. As different as they may be one from another, still there's one thing they do share in common. Somehow or another, they have been able to get away with presenting a complete picture to other people of who they are, so that when you have your encounter, you come away thinking that's all there is to it.

Zupansky   Sure. That's just natural.

London   You connect whatever dots you know, and then you fill in the blank spots with a composite picture of other people you've known, until that image you create is all you see. This tendency is so powerful, to project a normalized image over the blank spots in the screen, that it blinds you by blocking the real nature of what is there to behold. You will think you know this person. You may work with him, go to school with him, even date him, but you remain oblivious to the danger he presents, because you fail to discern the significance of his complexities and contradictions. And that natural tendency towards blithe oblivion that we all entertain provides this subtle criminal the cover he needs to keep racking up enough kills to reach the serial rank.

Zupansky   I see.

London   And you just accept it. That's the kind of person they are. Only if you're dealing with these people for years, do you begin to see striking illustrations of completely opposing ideas, manner of speaking, manner of handling things. They were developed in order to help you cope. So if you were in a situation you could not cope with, you could learned to snap over into a different part of your mind where you could cope with it. It only becomes a disability when that ability you learned is out of control. And it starts snapping over here, snapping over there without you driving it, and you find yourself at a loss. You're trying to explain to someone that you don't know how that happened, and that wasn't you, and you're sorry it happened, and you got to go now, right?

You see in the book how Danny does this several times with rape victims. He takes them and does all the preliminaries, and he's ready to kill them. And then something unexpected happens that triggers his better instincts. He looks around, he comes to himself, he says, I don't even know what I'm doing here. Lady, I'm so sorry I hurt you. Go ahead, you're free to go. He did that several times. So that is a disability because he can't control it.

Zupansky   He talks about the personalities that are a struggle. He describes it as a struggle in his own mind. And as time goes on, more of the domineering personality. Maybe you can explain this these two personalities, especially, and then Danny Rolling, I guess.

London   Well, let me try to explain There is a lot of skepticism about the diagnosis of the dissociative identity disorder. There are people whose careers are dependent upon discrediting this, because it is the mechanism that is used in mind control. MK Ultra Labs, in order to create a new alternate personality that can be, as I said before, "easily led," to do things that are even against their own interests. That's the definition of the MK Ultra goals, and they used this dissociative identity disorder to further those goals. So a lot of these characters that get picked up, iand they are called serial killers, you might call them Road Kill on the MK Highway, because they've been processed. So that's why you have people so vociferous about saying there's no such thing. Okay? So we'll set them aside because a person like Danny Rolling is not using this as a defense in court. He's not trying to get away with murder. He's not pushing himself on you and saying, "Look at this. Look at this." He's reacting to probing where he is asked questions over and over and over. "What is it like for you?" And so he answers them. He doesn't answer them to give an excuse for being a murderer. He answers them because he's under this process where psychiatrists, one after another, come in and ask these questions.

Zupansky   Right.

London   And so he answers them as best he can, saying this is what it's like for me. And so that's what he did with me to write this book. I said, I want to know what it's like for you. And yet I have also experienced his switching in our interpersonal relations. Also, besides him talking and writing about it analytically, you also notice it in his everyday life. And it's quite striking. And it's good thing this is rare, because you really don't have to completely reshape your mind in order to wrap it around this. But people keep saying they want to understand the mind of a serial killer. They say that, but I don't know if they really do, because

you have to do some work on your own mind.
Because your mind has algorithms that say, if
this is true, then the opposite cannot be true.
And chances are, that will work for you for your
entire life. Because circumstances are almost
always ordinary. The extraordinary is so rare it
is unlikely you will have to actually deal with it.
So if he is a sexual sadist, a violent offender,
then he cannot be a prayerful church attendee,
who drives a school bus and goes and tends to
the sick and shut-in, plays them songs, and just
does random acts of kindness here and there.
Girls who dated him told the writer that he was
always a gentleman. And indeed he was
honorable with me throughout some very
stressful circumstances. Okay, so it's your mind
that has to develop the ability to see that that
he's not fake. He wasn't pretending to honor our
agreement not to talk to anyone else about the
murders. He gave his word and he kept it. Okay,
so it's not a mask to cover his secret depraved
desire to torture me, me because it's not there. If
he had a secret desire, it was to honor his
commitment, and to respect all the suffering
that I've had to go through from being
associated with his case. He said anything he
could do to help, that would be it. And once he
figured out all he had to do to help was just to
keep his mouth shut from talking to these other
authors, and he did it. So I realize the audience
is not going to be impressed by that, because it
has to do with the business of getting a story,
rather than sex and violence. But that indeed
was what was going on. I was working with *A
Current Affair* with Steve Dunleavy, who I
brought this story to at the beginning as a part
of a batch of stories I was pitching. Steve was
always so blunt. And he said, forget all those
other stories. Concentrate like crazy on Rolling.
So I was being encouraged from the top. And

every day Danny got all these letters, attempts
to get his attention and alienate him from me.
He sent me the letters from the journalists and
the autograph seekers, the provocative pictures
from the girls.

Zupansky   Yeah.

London   And there was the legal challenge against our
               project, the Son of Sam lawsuit. That was just
               insane. And at the same time, the other thing
               was that Danny wanted to confess and be
               executed. I mean, do you understand that?

               I don't know if that comes through there in the
               book or not, because people continue to react as
               if he was trying to get away with murder. Danny
               wanted to confess and be executed because of his
               crimes. So in order for me to be his friend and
               his partner, I had to represent that, whether I
               agreed with his intention or not. It's not my life.
               And I was there to delve into what drove him to
               kill. It's not for me to tell him, Aw, come on,
               Danny, don't do that. If that's the way he feels,

that is the situation there before me to document. That's how he came to me, that's who he was. He wanted to die. And he wanted me to cooperate with the State so he would go along peacefully, to his death. He defied his defense attorneys, while he was talking to Channel 9, and while he was talking to the State with Bobby Lewis as his interlocutor there.

And you can safely ignore what Jamie Fox, the great professor, put in his book about the defense attorneys assisting with that interrogation. The truth is, his attorney was standing outside the prison gate, refused entry by the Department of Corrections, refused to come in to represent his Death Row client who was in talks with the State about his guilt. These are the kind of circumstances that surrounded this case. Highly irregular. Then, you could see everything was irregular. We began to call them Rolling Rules because he started to become such a great artist that they outlawed having paint. They changed the rules so prisoners couldn't have paint anymore. They shut down art for the whole prison. New rules, new rules, no art supplies for anyone.

Zupansky   The thing is, there is a certain understandability in terms of law enforcement and the judiciary, because Danny Rolling isn't infamous just because of the things that we've already talked about, but especially because of the incredible atrocities that were the crime scenes. And then his description of that outraged. But Danny Rolling is unique insofar as the crime scene, and the particulars of posing. And so we have this shock value, which is quite unique. So he describes the process in *The Making of a Serial Killer*. And in it there are these incredible crimes, like August 23rd, 1990, in Gainesville.

Christina Powell, seventeen years old, and Sonja Larson, eighteen, they lived together.

London   I'll tell you the worst thing about that one. He started with Sonja upstairs, and he pounced on her while she was sound asleep. He had his duct tape in one hand and his knife and the other. And he threw his body on top of her, slapped the tape on her mouth and stabbed her right in her heart. And as she lay dying, he whispered in her ear, "I'll come back for you after you're dead." And to me, that is just beyond the pale. I mean, you got your thrill, you did your kill, did you have to go that far just to profane her spirit? You know? Yes, that was what was happening. And he admitted it. And then the rest of that story is that he went downstairs, then came back up to Sonja Larson because remember, he said he was going to come back.

Zupansky   Yeah.

London   And when he came back, behold, his comment was, "She was too bloody to rape." Wow.

Zupansky   Through this whole graphic description, this third-person description that Danny Rolling wrote, that only he witnessed, of these murders. Who is this? People have criticized and said that there's one of the personalities, Gemini. And he got that from an Exorcist movie. So we're gonna ask you about these personalities. What does he attribute this loss of control of Danny Rolling to? What personality? Tell us about these personalities, Sondra, including Gemini.

London   Okay. Let me go back to things that his mother testified about. She had witnessed these changes in him, and she put that in her taped deposition, that she had seen this herself. And she said his body changes. His voice changes. His posture changes. And his mother also made a very piercing observation, for being an unsophisticated layperson. And she said, Danny just seems like a little 15-year-old boy. Seems like he never got past fifteen. And when I think of Danny myself, to me it seemed like he never got past thirteen, because he was not sexually mature. And he had a child's psychology. But because he was going to jail, getting locked up in juvey for voyeurism, all of a sudden he had to be a convict. And so in this creative ability of the mind, he said, I can't do that. I don't know how to do that. I'm inadequate for that. And yet it has to be done. And so with this spontaneous quality that the human mind has, probably just latent in most people, he is able to come up with a new personality that can do these things that can walk the walk of the convict, and can take on the burgeoning sexuality and own it. Because little Danny cannot own those things at all.

So the deviant sexuality, first of all, would be what would be the split in his personality. And it would be a process that some psychiatrists call life-saving, or a way to stay sane. In the intolerable situation, in order to protect the core personality, another personality has to be created that can absorb the kind of punishment that is too painful for the core personality. That creates a pressure that is relieved when the personality splits off a part that is able to survive the ordeal, while somewhere inside, the weak little person just collapses. So that would be the incarcerations and the crimes, all the mannish behavior, and that tolerance of stress, or that ability to absorb pain and continue to function, that whole cluster of traits, would be accumulated up into his Ennad side, and with that, he could go along like that pretty well. And then this Gemini thing, according to Danny, it had a specific time and place of onset, and that was in Parchman Prison.

That whole penitentiary was in deplorable condition. It was infamous for treating prisoners to cruel and unusual punishment, and down through the years, Parchman was found at fault in lawsuits and investigations. In fact in 2020, yet again a class-action suit over inhumane conditions was filed on behalf of Parchman prisoners in federal court. But Danny's story was so poignant. Down the end of a sloping hall where all the sewage accumulated three inches in his cell and being treated very callously, like everyone is at Parchman. But he couldn't give any relief from the horrible housing situations he was kept in. And according to his narrative, there came a time when Gemini appeared outside himself and upon that occasion, Danny agreed to accept this into his own self.

Well, it all sounds kind of fanciful. But I can't change the way Danny expresses himself. You can interpret it some other way if you want. But he says that Gemini guaranteed him revenge for all he'd suffered, in terms of one life for every year that he'd been in prison, which made eight years at that time. And Danny agreed to it. So I'm conveying to you his description of his own inner experience.

But now I'd like to introduce the concept of ego-dystonic. That is where you know you're doing wrong and you're not happy about it, okay?

Zupansky   Right.

London   Ego-syntonic is where you just joyfully love to do wrong. With ego-dystonic, know that you're

committing these behaviors that don't conform
with your idea of who you are. The lawlessness,
the deviance, was ego-dystonic to the core
personality of Danny. Yet Danny could own
Ennad. He was everything Danny was not, and
he was an important part of how Danny
survived. It was how Danny found a way to grow
up, though he would still remain a kid. It was
how he could carry himself in prison. He knew
how to perpetrate, how to be violent and tough.
It's almost like Little Danny had a big brother
who would back him up.

Zupansky   You write about this situation where a doctor at
the trial talks about the incisions made on the
victim who was posed like The Thinker, Danny
calls it "a grotesque replica carved from human
flesh and bone, its sculptor the Devil's Advocate,
Gemini." That's what Danny writes. But the
doctor called it very meticulous scalpel work,
and this Dr. Copeland commented that this
person was "either expert or very lucky." But
then in the book, Danny said it was not luck, it
was knowledge acquired. But Danny Rolling
didn't have that kind of background.

London   Oh, but he did. It's mentioned in the book, that
he had been employed at the LSU Medical
Center. He attended an autopsy there, and he
learned to handle a scalpel. Then he was able to
observe when students at the VA Hospital in
Shreveport dissected cadavers. And as an avid
deer-hunter, he had field-dressed many deer. He
told me these details in response to one of my
challenges over testimonies. He said that Ka-bar
was razor-sharp, and he knew how to apply the
force in exactly the right place, so it "took the
head off easily... cleanly... quickly."

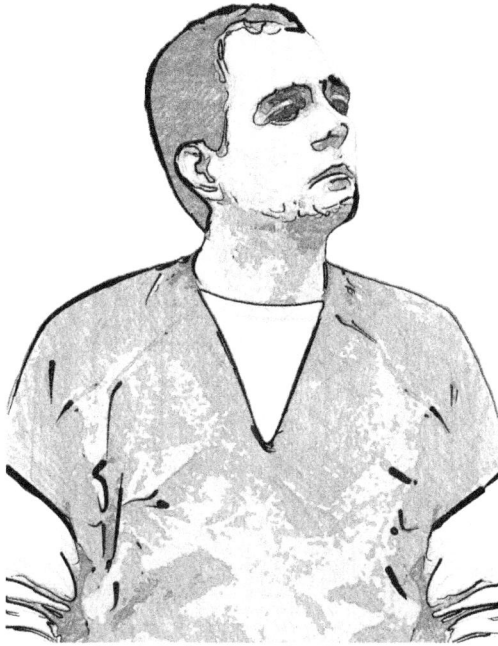

Sketch by Sondra London

Zupansky   I see. Well, let me ask this then. Is this Danny
            Rolling's idea of rationalization? You talk about
            the different personalities, Ennad and Gemini.
            And, like I say, Gemini that people are familiar
            with from Exorcist Three. But is this some way?
            How much do you believe in these personalities
            being responsible for all of his criminal
            behavior?

London   Yeah. You know, that's like asking me about
            demons or something that's not my training or
            my belief system. It's abnormal psychology. And
            that's the best he could do to describe his
            experience. And I've had to deal with different
            parts of Danny. Remember that part where they
            said he wrote them a letter saying, "I love you, I
            love you, I love you"?

Zupansky   Exactly.

London   He did that to me. And he covered a whole page
          like that. And then you turn over the page, and
          it says, "But do you love me? Do you really love
          me?"

Zupansky And that's what he asked his father. He always
          wanted that that statement from his father, but
          incredibly, he could not do it at the best of
          times. I think once in the book, he did say it,
          reluctantly.

London   His father hated him and he said so, and he
          wanted him dead. And let me talk about that
          shooting.

Zupansky Sure.

London   It was James Harold who discharged his service
          revolver on his first-born son.

Zupansky That's right.

London   He shot at Danny three times, and his shots
          went wild all three times. And then when Danny
          came back and approached him, and he shot at
          Danny three more times. He emptied his service
          revolver at Danny, without laying a bullet on
          him. It was then and only then that Danny fired
          back. He fired three shots. The first went wild,
          the second was mid-center mass, hit him in his
          abdomen, and the third went right between his
          eyes. And Danny quotes the medical
          professionals: It was a wonder, because the
          bullet between his eyes entered the skin, then
          went all the way around the skull and exited out
          the rear. Now, I know that sounds crazy, but
          that's what happened. And the bullet to the
          abdomen didn't hit a single organ. It went
          straight through and through. So those are the

facts about that shooting. Psychologically, it was an attempted patricide. But legally, it was pure self defense.

Zupansky   You write about the pathology of the husband, James Harold. His wife has got terminal liver cancer, and she's watching the trial coverage of her son. He's likely to receive the death penalty. And James Harold comes home and sees her watching their son on TV. He flips out, he beats her, he throws her out of the house, and he gets a divorce. Incredible.

London   Yeah. James Harold was a really disturbed man. And please consider that he was a veteran of many perilous situations, the things that he had done and the things that he had witnessed in the Korean War. And when he came home, I mean, we don't have a diagnosis on the record, but surely he was post-traumatic. And there was a time mentioned in the book, when he was asleep and dreaming, you know, flashing back. And he tried to strangle his wife. Well, listen to this. That identical scenario took place with Gerard John Schaefer. His father had been shot down behind enemy lines by the Nazis, and he had suffered unknown traumatic experiences during the World War Two. He brought those experiences home. And they impacted the dynamics of his relationship with his son. And I would like to just posit for a moment that perhaps the victims of those sons could ultimately be accounted for, as victims of war.

Because as the Scripture teaches us, when we suffer a trauma, the impact of that is going to go on for seven generations. If you know anything about epigenetics, this theory shows how the trauma that impacted our parents will be written into our very genetic code. And so I would like to point out, in the two cases of serial murder that I studied in the most depth, they could both be traced back to wartime atrocities suffered by their fathers. So there was a certain toxic generational dynamic, with the sons working out the unresolved post-traumatic stress issues of the fathers.

Zupansky   All right, on that note, I want to thank you, Sondra London. Our time is coming to an end, unfortunately. We didn't get around to talking about the companion volume, *Beyond the Making of a Serial Killer*.

London   (Laughs) We didn't talk about hardly anything, did we?

Zupansky   Well, the time flies, there's so much to talk about. This is such an incredible case, and your involvement is just unprecedented.

London   I hope we were able to answer some of the lingering questions that people have about this case and this book.

Zupansky   Well, I'm sure they still have many more questions, but I think some of those questions can be answered by taking a look at *The Making of a Serial Killer, The Second Edition*. It's fabulous. Thank you so much, Sondra London. It has been an absolute pleasure.

London   It was my pleasure.

Sondra London on *Malice*

Sondra London appeared on Ariel Cooksey's podcast, *Malice*, on November 18, 2020.

Ariel Cooksey

Cooksey	Hi everyone, and welcome to a very special episode of *Malice*. I am so honored to be joined today by acclaimed author Sondra London. She is one of the most fascinating authors I've had the pleasure of getting to know, and I wanted to be able to share her insights with you, as she talks about her newest book, which is *The Making Of A Serial Killer, The Second Edition,* by Danny Rolling as told to Sondra London. Sondra, thank you so much for joining me!
London	It's my pleasure. I assure you.
Cooksey	I'm just absolutely thrilled. And I know that my audience will get so much out of this. So I wanted to start off, just for anyone who is not aware of you (which would be shocking to me, but it happens sometimes), would you talk a little bit about how you got interested in true crime and how you ended up being a true crime author?
London	Okay. Most people, I think, that pay attention to true crime, horror, and other dark subjects are there because they're interested in it. It's not why I'm there. It's because of the horrible, sad, scary, morbid, depressing things that happened to me, and then how I reacted. It wasn't something I sought out, and what happened was simply this: I was a kid, 16 years old, just a regular teenager from a good home, when I met a very attractive boy, or young man – he was one year older than me. He had all the social graces. His last girlfriend was a debutante. He went to the Catholic school, attended Mass every day of his life. He was tall, he was good looking. He was an outdoorsy kind of guy. He liked to go fishing and hunting, he knew how to navigate the waters, of the ocean and inland. And he was a golfer. He liked to go skeet shooting. He was

funny. He was smart. And I called him John. He was named after his father, Gerard John Schaefer, Senior, so he was a Junior. They called his daddy Jerry, and called him John. I always think of him as John Schaefer, as I recall when I first knew him. So he was my steady boyfriend for a year, long story short. I'm not gonna go into the whole story of Schaefer, I'm just touching the main points.

Cooksey   Mm-hmm, of course.

London   So at any rate, we did break up, let's put it that way. And I went my merry way for the next nine years. And then my sister and my mother confronted me with headlines and the enormous story in *The Palm Beach Post* about this bloody killer cop who was killing women and writing it all up in feverish prose. And they said "So that's what happened to your boyfriend!" It was something that was shoved at me aggressively in an accusatory way, like it was my fault. Okay, that's how I found out about it. Schaefer had gone to college, he had gotten degrees in criminal justice and creative writing. He had become a deputy Sheriff in Stuart, Florida, and as he was in uniform and in his squad car, he was perpetrating. He got caught because he picked up these two hitchhikers, trussed them up in ropes and suspended them by the neck in such a way that if they fell off of the little tree root that they were perched on, they would strangle. So he bound and gagged them, and he left. And as he wrote to me later, "I would come back and find them and be surprised." And then on that writing that he sent me, he went back and squeezed in a little note: "Funny, isn't it?" So now you're in the land of the cuckoo, you know? I mean, it's not normal.

Cooksey   Right.

London   He didn't just tie them up and kill them. He tied
            them up in a tricky way, and left them. And
            then, when he came back intending to get a kick
            out of surprising himself, they weren't there.
            The girls had gotten away. So he called his boss,
            Sheriff Crowder, on the phone and said, "I've
            done something bad." So the Sheriff said, "Come
            on in." He came in, they held him there, they
            found the girls, they were fine. They were
            tourists and they went home. And so he was
            charged with that offense. And he got out on
            bail. He was out on bail for six months. And
            during that time, at an unknown time and place,
            two teenage girls were murdered. They were 17
            and 18 years old. Well, he was charged and
            convicted of those murders. I'm just trying to
            speed through this.

Cooksey   Sure, sure.

London   There's a *lot* of weirdness around Schaefer's
            case, but I'm not going down that rabbit hole
            today.

Cooksey   Sure. Absolutely.

London   Okay. So in the course of investigating the
            double homicide, they found all these writings
            that John had done that were still back at his
            mother's house. So he'd done them years before,
            he was married and living somewhere else. But
            they found these, and they used them as
            evidence against him in court. And they
            misconstrued these writings as a diary, but you
            can tell from reading them that they were not,
            these were fantasies. And it was quite clear to
            me that they were just a utilitarian form of auto-
            pornography, where he would write it to the

point where he got off, and then he'd abruptly lose interest in writing, and the narrative would just end in the middle of a sentence.

Cooksey   Oh, my God.

London   So it wasn't really like he was working on his chops as a novelist.

Cooksey   Right.

London   He was fantasizing and writing stuff that was of a sexually violent nature. So those things were used against him to convict him. So he went to jail. And it was another sixteen years before I contacted him, which brings us to the question: why did I become a true-crime writer in the first place? Let's place ourselves in 1988, and a lot of people are aware that there was a little economic problem in 1988.

Cooksey   Mm-hmm.

London   I was not aware of that. I thought it was all me! And everything I tried to do wasn't working, even though it always had. I was a freelance technical writer, and every time I'd make a pitch I'd get the contract. All of a sudden, 1988: I kept making pitches and not getting the contract. Evidently there was an influx of low-ballers, and the low quality work satisfied my erstwhile clients. I sit down with client and I say, "Look at this crap!" "Yeah, it's crap," he says. "But it cost one quarter of what I was paying you!" So there you have it in a nutshell. The economic squeeze hit my trade.

So then they executed Ted Bundy in the beginning of '89, and it was the biggest hoopla you ever saw! And everything was Ted Bundy.

And then all you heard was serial killers, you know? I'm just sitting there, I'm still scratching my head about what I'm going to do about my career. And I said, well shoot, I knew a serial killer.

Cooksey   Right.

London   I could write about that. I said, I've been a technical writer, I wrote all these brilliant works that tell you how your systems work, and what buttons you need to push, what your preventive maintenance procedures need to be, how to troubleshoot malfunctions. Wow, beautiful genius work, right? Eloquent!

Cooksey   (Laughs) Right.

London   But who would ever know I wrote it? Well, I was about forty. And so it was like one of those "Is-this-all-there-is?" kind of things. You had the great economic collapse of '88, and I was just thinking, "Well, if I do this really well, I'll get to do this for the rest of my life, and I'm not so sure I wanna do that." I already had a whole career as a reggae queen in the seventies, where I heard those famous words one too many times: "It doesn't pay, honey, but it's great *exposure*."

Cooksey   (Laughs) Oh yes.

London   And I'm like: "I'm never going to hear that word again,' but sure enough, as a writer, I wind up hearing the same thing: "Doesn't pay, honey, but it's *great* exposure!" – that's the pivotal line, I guess that should be my epitaph, you know? (Both laugh) Anyway, I was thinking that if I wrote books that I would do the work once, and then the book would go out and do all the work for me, while I'd sit on the beach sipping margaritas and watching the everlasting royalties just roll in.

Cooksey   (Laughs) Right, right.

London   Yeah, I could do that! And I read that book, *The Stranger Beside Me* by Ann Rule. Everyone's read it, I read it and I said, "I could write better than that." Okay? Number two: I knew a serial killer a lot more than she ever did!

Cooksey   Sure.

London   Okay? So I said "If this is all you need to do to write a book, I already get out that covered, so I might as well just do it." At that point, those were my thoughts. There was nothing in there about murder, horror, crime, serial killers – it was just a change of focus of what I wanted to do with my ability to write. And you look at the *TV Guide*, and just run your finger down any column, any time, and what are the words you see? Murder, killer, kill, right? Murdering murderers, right?

Cooksey   Right! I mean, it really is considered kind of the golden age of true crime, that started in those late eighties, right?

London   I think that's over. And when I was interviewing Roy Hazelwood, who was a very well known guy, highest of the high experts along with Ralph Stone who was his Georgia boy, they select nine profilers from throughout the country, one per each region, and they bring them in and train them and then they act as a direct liaison to FBI. So Ralph Stone was the Southeast profiler. I was interviewing with them, and I was saying, "Why is everybody talking about all this serial killer stuff?" And Hazelwood said, "It's a fad, it's almost over." He said, "Don't worry," and he said, "The next fad's going to be terrorists."

Cooksey   He wasn't wrong.

London   Well, yeah, but it's true: serial killers really are kind of passé now, you've got your grand spectacles being put on in your public spaces, your mass killings...

Cooksey   Sure.

London   ...your school shootings, your terrorist events and your racially-charged events.

Cooksey   Mm-hmm.

London   I think that the Golden Age of being interested in serial killers is probably over. So that's okay, and in fact, I'm about twenty years late filing my story, but that's okay, too, because at least I'm getting it done.

Cooksey   It's so fascinating, though, and it really kind of lends itself to something greater than just serial killers, but the mindset of murderers and violent offenders. And I think that that's really important right now. Both as something we as lay people like to watch but also from the perspective of rehabilitation, of preventative measures.

So at this point I want to dive into your new book, which is the second edition of one that came out earlier, and tell us how you became acquainted with Danny Rolling and what that was like.

London   Alright, I'll give you a very quick segue to get from Schaefer to Rolling. Schaefer and I did write a book: *Killer Fiction*. And it became very well known on what I call the Convict Bullshit Hotline. (Ariel laughs.) And every convict in Florida was sending me letters saying, "Please do my story." And an alarming number of those were about malfeasance in the prison, by prison officials. Crimes being committed upon prisoners. All over Florida, the mail rooms were seeing these letters going through to me about things that had happened in their prisons. So I became *persona non grata* throughout the whole Florida prison system.

Cooksey   I can imagine.

London   So to pick up where I left off before, when I started working with Schaefer I contacted him to find out if he'd like to do a book with me. I said, "Do you remember me?" And he said, "How could I ever forget you? My love for you burned with a cold blue flame that will never go out!" I'm like "Awww..." (Laughs)

Cooksey   Wow (Laughs)

London   Well, anyway, we did the book. And I said, "Those stories that you wrote, that they seized," I said, "Do you still write those stories?" He said, "Oh boy, do I!" And so the writing of the rest of that book was more a matter of him assaulting me with these scenarios that he would write and send me, and I would edit them and add them to the book.

Cooksey   Mm-hmm.

London   I was advised by Roy Hazelwood, and it was just like in that movie that came out later from then, *Silence of the Lambs:* "Don't show any reaction, because that's what he's looking for. He will get off on it if you react. So your job, no matter what he says, is to keep a deadpan demeanor and don't jump when he's trying to shock you." Well, that was new to me, I'm an expressive person. Had to be as a singer, a lead vocalist interpreting songs.

Cooksey   Right.

London   Being deadpan was new. So I had to work through that. Okay, so somehow I maintained that demeanor and Schaefer kept upping the ante, sending more and more shocking and disgusting things. When he sent me one about nasty things going on during executions that was when the prison said, "All right, that's it, this little fun and games, you're done here." So next development was one of the prisoners who wrote to me saying "Do my story," and that was Bobby Lewis.

Cooksey   Right.

London   Bobby Lewis said, "I'm a better writer than Schaefer and I have better stories. I was alone on Death Row with Ted Bundy and I escaped from Death Row!" And I had a protocol I would put these boys through: "Here's the deal: you tell me the truth and I'll see that it comes out in your own words and it won't be altered or censored. Your deal is: You tell me the truth, you never show any disrespect for me. And you don't get any money from me ever, okay? So that's the deal. And if you should choose to abide by those rules, sign here."

Cooksey   Mm-hmm.

London   So Bobby came along with that program, and we worked up those stories. Bobby presented himself as being some kind of master kingpin prisoner. He was a convict king, right? He boasted he could get anything: money, drugs, women, weapons. Okay, fine: Bigshot Bobby. So then, when they caught Danny Rolling for robbing a grocery store and put him in Florida State Prison, they put him with Bobby Lewis.

Cooksey   I see.

London   Now, that was not an accident, my friend! Because Bobby Lewis was a long time snitch, collaborator with the administration. That's how-come he could get all those favors, because he was betraying his fellow convicts. For as long as he'd been in there, he' been the administration's boy. So when they put Danny in with Bobby, the idea was for Bobby to work Danny to produce confessions for the State.

Cooksey   Right. Pretty ingenious.

London   So all that, I did not understand for years. *Many* years. I didn't realize the setup that made it all fall into place. All I knew was Bobby wrote me and said: "You know that guy who's in the news? Well, he's with me, and I'm going to send him to you." So Bobby took the screenplay I wrote about his escape from Death Row and showed it to Danny. And Danny thought it was great, and that's how he decided that he wanted me to be the one to write his own life story.

Cooksey   Mm-hmm.

London   So let's just put it this way: It was a conspiracy! That's the word!! (Both laugh.) It really was! People had to know what each other were doing, and they had to do it together, so that's the definition of a conspiracy, okay? And just like a real conspiracy that you read about, no one in any part of it knew what was really going on. Each person thought they knew what was going on, okay? And then the other people involved had a completely different interpretation of what was going on.

Cooksey   Hmm.

London   So the main thing about Danny Rolling as he was presented to me was Bobby's assessment that Danny was easily influenced. Bobby had him under his influence. And when Danny came to me, I became his everything. I became his anchor, his lifeline, his connecting point to reality itself.

Cooksey   Right.

London   And if you want to go into all the different kinds of varieties of mental illness that you would see in Danny Rolling – right now, let me just talk about borderline. A borderline personality has a deep need to cling desperately to a connection.

Cooksey   Sure, mm-hmm.

London   A borderline will also flip on you, and enshrine you as an angel and queen, and then without notice strike you down as a demon from Hell. That's a borderline trait called splitting. Another thing that got Danny Rolling in trouble – but it was also so much a part of him that it would also manifest in benign ways – and that was the violation of boundaries.

Okay, he's essentially a rapist who is violating boundaries. It started out with voyeurism, that's violating boundaries; graduated to breaking and entering, that's violating boundaries, okay? Of course murder is violating boundaries. Then he goes to jail and escapes, that's violating boundaries. If you have that trait, it's going to permeate everything. And so you look at when investigators would come in to interview him with an intent to kill him, a prosecution psychiatrist would come in with intent to find him evil and bad, so everyone would be comfortable with him being killed by the State. And what would Danny do? He would try to make friends with them.

So when it came to Danny's relationship with me, it would be impossible that he would not violate boundaries. Although he knew what I was there for, and it was always foremost in my mind that I was there to get a story. And I made it quite clear to him, as I had to make it clear to other inmates throughout the years. I'd say, "You know what? I'm not interested in your story if you're innocent, because in the news business, it's just not a story. The only a story people want to hear is one of guilt."

Cooksey   Right.

London   And so that was made quite clear to Danny at the beginning, don't even waste my time with anything about being innocent. At the same time I had a long haul to go; if he were to give me any information about his murders, I would be made a witness at his trial against him, and I could not attend his trial because of The Rule.

Cooksey   Right.

London   I would be sequestered, couldn't attend the trial. And he was well aware of the facts. Now, he may have been crazy, but he wasn't nuts, okay? But the part that was very difficult, was that Danny

165

was half in love with death. It was on record since he was fifteen years old. So it didn't proceed from committing murder. He already had a death wish.

Cooksey   Right.

London   And he said it in so many words: "I wanted to kill myself, but I couldn't do it, so I wanted law enforcement to do it for me." So, suicide-by-cop.

Cooksey   Right.

London   They shot him down in a hail of bullets and none of them hit him.

Cooksey   Oh, my God.

London   (Laughs) Okay? Not one!

Cooksey   Oh, my God.

London   So, he failed at suicide by cop. He couldn't even get the cops to kill him. He fetched up in prison. He tried to commit suicide two weeks before he wrote to me. He tried to hang himself. If I was to be his friend, if I was to report his true story, it would have to be the story of a man who wants to kill himself. Now, I am not a minister, a therapist, a psychiatrist or a nurse. I am not here to help him or change him. If that's what he is, then that's what will be the story. And that was easier said than done. Believe me.

Cooksey   I can't even imagine, Sondra.

London   No, I absorbed an immense amount of stress, all along the way, being in that position. That was Danny's original idea, that he wanted to tell his story. He wanted to return his soul to a state of absolution. He wanted to come in from the cold. He wanted a friend to hold his hand. So we worked on this story. We could not talk about the murders because it was pretrial, and we did not want me to become a witness at trial, so we just proceeded to talk about anything and everything else, no particular order. So then he began to draw pictures in the middle of his writing. Okay? It would be like a musical where they're talking like normal, and then they burst into song.

Cooksey   Right.

London   Danny's letters to me would just burst into graphics. And I hadn't seen that before to the extent that Danny would go. He embellished his writing, he'd do it in ornate calligraphy and turn words into pictures. The first time he started doing that, I said "Danny, wait-wait-wait-wait! Wait just a minute. You are an artist. Every time you draw a picture, you need to sign it and date it because it's important. I want you to stop squeezing these pictures into the margins of your letters and put the picture on a page all by itself. Sign it and date it. Because Danny did not realize that he was an artist until I treated him like one.

Cooksey   How fascinating.

London   He did not have enough self-esteem to respect what came out of him in any way. And so it was really gratifying to see how exponentially he flowered under my attention. He began to sign and date everything he did obsessively, and anyone who ever seen any correspondence from him will confirm that every page is signed and dated.

Hello Princess ...   5-30-93

I miss my baby badly, Yeah I do ... I'm thinking of
you, my Love ... Faithful & True, As WALLy KeNNedy so
poetically put it .. "So woody AlleN sAys, the heart
wANts whAt it wANts, ANd you sAy, ... woody"?
That was one Super Duper INterview with W. KeNNedy
... LizAbeth StAr ... and you!

SoNdrA honey ... I rededicate my Love to you, as
though it were FRESH from my heArt-N-soul. & Love
you darling ...   I will always Love my MediA Queen,
SoNdrA LoNdoN   ... Forever and a day!

So ... WAlly   said, "The pAth to true Love
Never ruNs   smooth", Very profound ... you and
& have be-   come the Romeo & Juliet of Crime.
you, the   beautiful, talented, intelligent,
author & Editor

                      "I THE HuNchbAck
                      of NorteR DAme,"

What a pair we make?
Well ... to tell you the truth Princess ...
I dont give a rAt's ASS   what people
think? & Love you .....
I will always Love you ......
                                                    D. R.

Cooksey	Wow.
London	Because I had him under my spell. I bossed him, okay? I handled him. I threatened him. How can you threaten a guy like that? (Laughs.) I just threatened him that he would never hear from me again. And that was the kind of attention he thrived under.
Cooksey	Right. Mm-hmm.

London	Now he did lie to me twice, about writing to other females.
Cooksey	Okay.
London	He was constantly getting these letters from people begging him to write to them. I said look, these people don't care about you, they just want your autograph so they can sell it!
Cooksey	Right.
London	I was already doing stories for *A Current Affair* when Danny presented himself to me. I had done three exclusive stories for *A Current Affair*, which was at that time, the number one news show on TV. So when I presented my story pitches to Steve Dunleavy, I showed him three stories. One of them was Danny Rolling and then there were two others, and Steve said, "Forget about those other two. Just concentrate like crazy on Rolling." Boy, did I take that to heart. (Laughs.) So I just blame Steve Dunleavy for the whole thing!
Cooksey	Sure!
London	So when I was developing the story, I had Danny under contract, and Steve was constantly warning me: "Remember: If you don't have an *exclusive*, you don't have a story."
Cooksey	Right.
London	And Danny was being besieged with requests from big name-brand journalists all the way down to the local college paper. And I did have a little trouble with him, with that.
Cooksey	Sure, sure.

London   But when I did catch him corresponding with this student journalist, his lawyers were called to the prison to come see about him, and they told me they'd never seen him so distraught. I mean, look at everything he was up against. Not facing a death penalty trial. Not guilt, not the killers next door. Danny handled all that. But "Will Sondra ever speak to me again?" That is what sent him into a state that his lawyers had never seen. So that just gives you an idea of the relationship I had with Danny.

Cooksey   Right, sure, that connection with you was so important. That's all he had.

London   We only met once, and he said then, "You're the only one who ever understood me at all." So of course I would not want to leave Danny, but it was strategic. I could not put any more energy into a project when my partner was going to violate his promises to keep his story exclusive to me.

Cooksey   Certainly.

London   So yeah, I was manipulating him. I was there for a story. I was there to get confessions to murder. And there was no two ways about that. That was the introduction: "Here, Sondra wants to get your murder confessions."

Cooksey   Right.

London   So nobody was tricking anybody or anything like that. We both knew what we were doing, and we were both working on that story.

Cooksey   Right.

London   So that started in July '92. And then it was 1993, there was heavy-handed manipulation of us by the prison. We wanted visitation so that we could talk, and convey the story. So they were jacking us around to put it mildly, it was a full time occupation. And they would come up with some obstacle, and we'd overcome that, and they'd come up with something else and we'd have to overcome that.

     So, by February '93, it went like this: First of all, you had to choose whether you were Media or Friend. So we said, "Okay, Friend." And finally, after giving no response for months, they responded: "Your visitation is denied because your friendship is not leading to marriage."

Cooksey   Oh, my God.

London   Get it? Now what's your move?

Cooksey   (Laughs) Get engaged?

London   No, no, what's your move? Do you want this story or not, lady?

Cooksey   I guess. (Laughs)

London   Okay then, check and mate.

Cooksey   I see.

Sondra: So this is the circumstance under which the great romance was taking place, okay? If we don't say that we are leading to marriage, our visitation will be denied. They put that in so many words. Then we're like, "Okay, we're going to get married! We're engaged! So let's have that visitation!" But it was always "No, no, no, no." And I have a letter from John Schaefer. He was so crazy and so angry, and he was saying "I really admire you," he says, "You've got balls," and he says, "Look, what you need to do is marry him, because then they can't deny you visitation." To be fair, Schaefer was describing the way things were done in the Florida prison system. But when it came to Danny Rolling, they changed the rules again! We called them the Rolling Rules: "You can get married, but you still can't visit. In fact, you can't even get married in person. And even once you are married, you're still not gonna visit."(Laughs)

Cooksey   My God!

London   So Danny and I were both fit to be tied. And, of course, all of our letters were being read by a whole committee of lawyers, right? The better to analyze and strategize how to work this, how to channel this potential energy in their direction. So that went on and on and on. Eventually, I think Bobby broke it to Danny that he, Bobby, could arrange a conversation with the Florida Department of Law Enforcement that would result in him being able to visit with me.

Cooksey   Bigshot Bobby.

London   (Laughs) Ha! That is what turned into his so-called "confessions," which if anyone has seen the videotape of that occasion, they will understand why I say it's quite unlike anything that's ever been done in the history of criminal justice, period.

Cooksey   It is.

London   And you've got a so-called expert named Jamie Fox, who is very highly respected, he's a professor, for God's sake! He's written many books, and Jamie Fox never went to Gainesville, or sat in court, but Jamie Fox advises us in his book that Danny Rolling's lawyers were there and participated in this debacle. No. They. Were. Not!

Cooksey   Nope.

London   They were not there. Where were they? They were standing outside the prison gate, banging on it and being told, "No admittance"! Danny Rolling's lawyers were *not* admitted. And they were trying their best to get in, okay?

Cooksey   Wow.

London   So these are the real facts behind what happened there. And you will see something about that in a version published by someone other than myself, who has their own reasons for distorting what happened. So anyone that wants to come to me and say I'm lying, I'm like: *Molon Labe,* bitches, come and take it!

Cooksey   Mm-hmm.

London   And they were delaying our mail. So I was writing back and forth frantically to Danny saying, "What in the hell is going on? Bobby's writing me one thing, you're writing me something else. I'm getting your letters a week late, they're holding your letters, what is going on? I've written you every day this week with no answer," and we were both just really bouncing off the walls. And finally I get the letter from him where he says, "It's you, me and the FDLE, babes." And this meant going against his attorney's advice and cooperating with the State to ensure his execution.

Cooksey	Wow.
London	That's what that means: "You, me, and the FDLE." I'm like "Oh! Oh, okay!" So then my good-buddy Ed Dix, the Special Agent who was masterminding all this plotting, called me on the phone, and he said "Hey, hey, how you doing? You want to see Danny?" I said "Well, duh. Of course I want to see Danny! What do you think?"
Cooksey	(Laughs) Right.
London	And Dix said, "I can get you in. Come to the prison today." And I said, "How are you going to get me in?" I said, "It's not visiting day." I think it was a Tuesday. He said, "Don't worry about that." And I said, "Well, how am I going to get in?" He said, "We're going to get you a Special Pass." That was his word. "Just come to the front gate and tell them that you have a Special Pass," and that's what I did.

I jumped in the car, drove to the prison, went in and just said the words "I have a Special Pass." Now let me make something clear: There was no pass! A pass is a piece of paper, isn't it? A document, a ticket, a card? That's a pass. There was no pass. It was just words Ed Dix said over the phone: "Come to the prison, and you'll get in on a Special Pass." So I got in and I had my one and only visit with Danny Rolling, behind glass with two guards present, taking notes, and of course it was videotaped. And oh, you're not allowed to bring in any tape recorder, you're not allowed to have pencil, paper, anything. You just have to try to remember it later. |
| Cooksey | Sure. |

Sketch by Sondra London

London   And there came a point in our in our visit where
           Danny said, "I want you to release the story
           now." And I foolishly said "Okay!" So that's what
           happened. I did not say, "What story?" I did not
           say, "Eh, maybe not such a good idea, Danny?"

Cooksey   Right.

London   So when they ask me: "Did you make any
           mistakes?" Yeah, that was an actual mistake.
           When he said "I want you to release the story," I
           just said "Okay!"

Cooksey   Right, right. Hindsight and all that.

London   After I left, I begin to say to myself, "Wait a
           minute. What story?" (Laughs) Okay, so I sat
           down and wrote up a press release, and I'm very
           sorry to say that press release has been lost in
           my records. So if any of the people who received
           it would like to send me a copy for my records,

that'd be great, but right now I can't put my hands on it. Anyway, there was a phrase in the first draft I wrote in which I said: "In a visit *arranged by the FDLE,* Danny Rolling agreed to give his account of the Gainesville murders in exchange for the pleasure of my company."

So because we were on Danny's plan of "You, me and the FDLE," naturally I called up the chain of command to Ed Dix and said :"Okay, Ed, I just wanted to run this press release by you." (Both laugh) And so I read him that. He said "Okay, it sounds great, except for that part about arranged by the FDLE?" He said, "Better take that part out." And I said "Okay, sure!" (Laughs) Without appreciating the seriousness of the situation I was in, still naïve enough to believe we were all singing from the same hymn book, and that my Constitutional right to practice my trade would be affirmed in court in due time. I can hardly say this with a straight face because I was such a fool. But I'm trying to recapture who I was then; in all my naïveté, I would just make it up as I go and learn my lessons too late. So when it comes to getting involved in a screwball situation like that, I'm saying: "Don't try to do this at home, kids!"

Cooksey   Mm-hmm, sure!

London   Okay? Don't do it. Don't think about even trying to do what I did! I've had too many people contact me or send messages or say things to the effect that they're gonna do what I've done, and some guy who wanted to go on a podcast told me I'm the leader of a movement! I'm like: Oh, no, I'm just a writer! There can't be any movement to be like me or do like me. Because I would never lead or direct anyone. No one should ever try to follow me, or do what I did. I did not do my work, intending to have the effect that it did. I just wanted to find something a little more interesting to write about than how to run your new computer program.

Cooksey   Yeah. Definitely, yeah.

London   So I found myself in that situation, collaborating with the State. Danny went into this session in which the investigators would ask a question, and he would whisper his answer to Bobby Lewis, and Bobby would state his answer for the record. Now, why did he do that? And, we've heard a qualified expert speculate that Danny was afraid to take credit for what he'd done, he couldn't face it, and that it was a form of lying. But what he didn't understand was: Danny was under my control, and he was threatened by me. By this time, he had seen the immense amount of suffering that had been vented upon me because of him. And he was utterly aghast at what it had done to me to publicly support him.

Cooksey   Mm-hmm.

London   I said: "Now you listen to me. This is my story. You see what I've had to give up: my home, my family, my friends, my job and everything, just so I could do this story. This is my story, and you don't give it to anyone, and that includes the police, because then it goes on the public record! And then all those running dogs of the establishment press, all those authors... they are just wanting to do a book, and they will get my story for their book! Don't you dare!" And it wasn't that he was afraid, it was that it was horrible— the media had put through a FOIA request, to go into the mail cover that was on Danny and put all of our letters out on the public record. And they won, too! And thousands of pages of our correspondence was put on the public record.

Cooksey   Oh, my God!

Prosecutors seek Rolling letters

An Associated Press Report

GAINESVILLE — Prosecutors will ask a judge to make the fiancee of prison inmate Danny Harold Rolling, accused of killing five college students, produce letters and information about her relationship with him.

A spokesman for the state attorney's office Thursday declined to comment on how that information would relate to Rolling's prosecution.

However, court records show the property subpoenaed includes letters from another Florida State Prison inmate, Bobby Lewis, a state witness who says Rolling told him about the murders. Lewis introduced Rolling to his fiancee, Sondra London, through the mail.

Rolling, 39, who is serving multiple life sentences for a string of robberies, is charged with killing five community college and University of Florida students in Gainesville.

London, a free-lance writer and television producer, is being asked to appear Monday before Circuit Judge Stan Morris.

"She refused to provide certain information that our prosecutors believe is important and crucial te the prosecution," said Will Irby, spokesman for the state attorney's office.

Irby said the information is not being sought in connection with efforts to keep Rolling from profiting from the publication or filming of his story, although he acknowl-

edged, "Everything is connected to everything else."

Earlier this year, prosecutors had a temporary lien placed on any money London or Rolling make as a result of recounting his crimes.

At a pretrial interview, London refused to answer a myriad of questions or turn over letters, creative writings and artwork belonging to Rolling.

Most of the state's questions apply to her financial situation, court documents show.

Danny Rolling began writing London while in prison.

London   Yeah! Yeah, and this had already happened, we'd already had these people go in and try to steal the story, in different ways. It's not that the media were conspiring with the State, it's that the pressures exerted on me and Danny were coming from all directions at once. Multiple forces were determined to prevent me debriefing him and writing a book about his crimes. And of course it hurt, emotionally. We both just wanted to be able to visit and talk in person. And the irony of the situation is that by causing us that emotional suffering, they actually contributed to the making of the book, because this way, everything had to be in writing. So there will never be any question about whether I am telling the truth about what Danny wanted me to publish. I still have all of our letters, and nothing was communicated between us outside of our correspondence. So Danny did what he had to do, under the false impression given by the State that he would be able to visit with me if he cooperated. He admitted his guilt. That's why I refer to that session as *admissions of guilt*, not confessions.

Cooksey   Mm-hmm, sure.

London   The confession is *The Making of a Serial Killer*, which is an in-depth, detailed account of everything that he did and every thought that went through his head, the motivations that drove him, the voices he heard, the things he witnessed and did – a no-holds-barred, uncensored account that is shocking and gruesome. But we're talking about murder here, the real thing. This is not a *Murder She Wrote* with Angela Lansbury and your decorous corpse laid out in a shapely swoon on a chaise longue. (Both laugh.) No, this is the edge that really cuts.

I encouraged Danny to go back in his mind to the point where he was that murderer. I said, don't sit here as the man you are now looking back on it, but allow your mind to take you back into who you were then, and be that guy. Feel like him, see like him, talk like him.

Cooksey   It's unbelievable how you got to this point with Danny. We've talked a lot about how you built that rapport with him, but I'd love for you to delve a little further into what that experience was actually like when he divulged things to you, and what you learned about the way his mind worked.

London   Danny is... well, he *was*, I'm sorry. I might say "is" or "was," I don't know. To an extent, I think of him in the present tense today because I'm still working on another book, to follow the one I just finished. I've been working on that one for a couple of years there, and now I'm working on

another Danny Rolling book, so bear with me for
the time being, because Danny is still kind of in
the present tense with me. I'm not being spooky,
I'm just saying I think about Danny the same as
I did when he was living. I never hung out with
him, or hugged or kissed him, or had him walk
in the door of my house. It was always an
intellectual activity, me sitting alone,
concentrating on comprehending this mystery
and trying to inspire him to reveal more.

But anyway, I said one of the most essential
things about Danny was his neediness and his
violation of boundaries. Another thing that's just
absolutely essential is that he's unstable, okay?
Wherever he is now, it always changes. So that
permeated everything about dealing with
Rolling his mutability. A part of that involved
dissociation, but even without shifting his
identity, he was a lot more moody and emotional
than me.

Cooksey   You did an interview with Dan Zupansky for the
True Murder podcast, and I would encourage
everyone to go listen to that because there is
some really wonderful information there. But I
remember you talking about how you perceived
Danny not as just the adult that he was at that
point, right? That's really fascinating, and your
interpretations too, of the artwork you were
seeing.

London   Okay, let's go. I developed what I call a multiple
interface; it's a mental ability that you have to
grow into. It doesn't come naturally, okay? And
one way of understanding it is just keeping an
open mind so you can stay aware of the present.
Because your mind always tries to draw a
conclusion. It always tries to discriminate
between the false and the true; to throw out the

false and feature the true. It's just the way our minds work 99% of the time. So in developing this multiple interface, I think of it as an ability that constantly needs exercise. It's like you have to keep pushing away the cobwebs that press you to form conclusions.

Cooksey   Mm-hmm.

London   Because you need to continue to intake the raw data. And if you can't do that, you won't develop an appropriate response. You don't filter it by falling back on generalizations. When something is a contradiction, you resist the impulse to immediately say: "It's a lie, there's a mask, there's an attempt to deceive," which are all knee-jerk reactions to the common distribution of traits throughout humanity. You're only gonna find maybe 1% of humanity that really gives you a multiple performance. So let's say 99% of the people use the thinking process that works 99% of the time. That's normal, for you to say "Well, he said this, then he said that, so he's obviously just lying." Because most likely you would go your whole life and never have to deal with a true multiple personality.

Cooksey   Mm-hmm.

London   So I had to develop that trait working with Schaefer, because he gave me things that were diametrically opposed. And I had to confront him about it. Why was he doing that? I'd say "You're lying! Either you're lying to them or you're lying to me, one or the other. And I'm not gonna take you lying to me." With Schaefer, again, this double identity was a trait that permeated everything about his case. He had two stories: he was a framed ex-cop who was a really good fiction writer, and he was *also* the greatest killer of women in U.S. history.

Cooksey   Of all things!

London   Now you're supposed to be writing about him and presenting these stories to newspaper editors and TV producers. You write this piece about how oh, he is just a framed ex-cop who is a really good writer. So Schaefer makes copies of that. And he scrawls a note on it to the editor: "There were 18 unsolved homicides in your jurisdiction while I was at large. For further information about them, contact Media Queen, Sondra London." So, here he is sending me out one door reporting one story, while he attaches the opposite story to my piece, and tells them to call me to explain it.

I learned to deal with the different behaviors in different ways. I believe this is a trait that adult children of alcoholics develop. They have that in their teaching about how adult children of alcoholics will develop hyper-vigilance, because they need a clue as to whether the guy coming in the door is going to be Good Dad or Bad Dad. So, they develop the ability to instantly assess the different behavior in that person and respond appropriately, as a survival mechanism. I'm sure that multiple interface I developed is very similar to the ability someone in a situation like that has to develop. I didn't grow up with anything like that, but I had to learn to deal with Schaefer.

I was having to do intake of vast amounts of information that contradicted each other and to keep it all simmering on the back stove, not throw any of it away. On this day, this witness said this. So, maybe I have to wait twenty years in real time before something confirms it. I had to keep all that dubious, confusing information alive. So, that's kind of what my mind was like by the time I got to Danny. I was keeping a lot of information in the back of my mind and watching for patterns.

As fractious as Danny was, dealing with him was not the most difficult part of my situation. Don't forget, Schaefer still hadn't been murdered yet. He was in the mix, believe me, causing plenty of trouble. I was being stalked and harassed. I was driven from my home and was having to flee from one sketchy place to the next.

And there were prosecutors and investigators and reporters and editors and producers and prisoners and victims' families.

They were worked by the Florida State victims' advocates office to the extent that they purely forgot about Danny Rolling. They rechanneled all of their angst at me. That was with the encouragement of the State. The gentleman who was the brother of Manny Taboada, was the Vice President of Marketing for a top Miami radio station. He quit his job and told the press that he was going to go to work full-time practicing up to debate Sondra London.

When the case did come to trial — but of course, it wasn't a trial. It was an evidentiary hearing on the penalty phase of his five murders. Taboada stood up in court and made a grand gesture pointing at me and screaming at me in a frankly menacing manner. Then the brother of Sonja Larson came up to me in court. He said, "If you make one cent off this story, I'll kill you myself." Things were very difficult for me to deal with.

And remember, I had Steve Dunleavy hovering over me the whole time in the background. To us simple Americans, we're just not really geared up to be quite as vicious and devious and domineering as a bull-goose Australian journo. I swear, they're a different species, like the killer bees and the murder hornets. Steve was legendary, he was the prototype.

There came a point where Danny Rolling got so frustrated with all that was going on against me that he called a press conference. Now that was exactly the opposite of my vehement orders: "You don't talk to no-fuckin-body but me!" It was much later that I learned Danny thought he was doing this to come to the rescue, and defend the honor of his Lady Faire.

Again, the prison would not allow his attorneys to enter the prison. They just let the reporter and her crew in, and they had about eight grim faces in suits lined up to witness this. Danny had written a script of his statement, and he read it before the cameras. The script just goes on and on, all about Sondra London. "She is of the finest character. I just can't believe the way the press has tried to destroy Sondra London. She is not trying to use me. She has tried to help me tell my story." The entire time he spoke, that was all it was. Well, they couldn't run *that*, now, could they? So, they ran about three seconds, where Danny said something vague like time is ticking away. That's all that they ran. They were blaring their brag: We got the *exclusive* interview with Danny Rolling!

I was just a viewer. I didn't know any of this. I see him standing there talking to a reporter, and I'm just like: "Gee, thanks, partner! You know? There goes my whole career with *A Current Affair.* Steve Dunleavy is going to literally send out a hit man on me. I'm sitting here, promising Steve an exclusive and you're off the chain, calling a press conference I know nothing about!" And it was true, too. Steve was disgusted with me, and I despaired of my future.

Because they were jacking with our mail, it took at least two weeks for Danny's letter to reach me, and he sent me the script he had read on-camera, which I had not heard until I got ahold of the original tape from another TV station some time later.

He said, "You get so mad at me. I'm just trying to help you. I'm just trying to do all I can." He said he was just sick when he saw what they put on TV, he was shocked that no one even mentioned my name, when that was all he talked about. That was when Danny wised up, when he realized that he got *took.* But meanwhile I had to spend two weeks in this state of absolute betrayal. I was sending him letters that were being delayed. I'm like, "Damn it. All this time I put into this, and all the things I had to give up to be here for you, and this is how you thank me?" And the way we were being jerked around caused so many hurt feelings, because that was not what was in his mind at all. He was trying to do a good thing, to the best of his understanding. If we could communicate in real time, it would have been cleared up immediately. But it caused a major upheaval. And even now, today, I have to live with comments on the internet, where people say that I wrote that statement, that I made Danny do that appearance. And that is just so wrong.

When we very first started working on this project, within the first three months, three times he wrote: "Okay, that's it. I'm done. I can't do this. Goodbye." Then I'd be like, What? There was no problem. Just BOOM. What the hell? And so, when he finally did apologize and tell me, "Okay, I'm not going to do that anymore," I never believed it. I was constantly like, any minute now you're just going to jump up and fly. I was always on the edge of my seat. I was like, what next? So, that gives you an idea of what it was like dealing with Danny.

Because I did not make it easy on him. I was very hard on him. I questioned him repeatedly on the same things. I had no way of knowing if it's going to be the same answer. It might be a different answer. Sometimes it was the same, sometimes it would be different. I sent him all the police reports that I got ahold off. I said, "Is it true? Is it not true? Do you have anything to say about it? Respond, respond, respond." I compiled his responses to everything that was printed about him, in my Rolling Case Chronology.

I did that with that entire Mary Ryzuk book. He was so upset trying to go through that book, because it was just so full of nonsense. Paragraph one, line one, word one is *Daniel*. She says, *Daniel* Harold Rolling was born on... I'm like, "Oh, really? Is that right? How many official documents did you have to disregard to put Daniel for his name?" Because nowhere in any official history does the name Daniel appear. It never was his name. He was born Danny. He was married Danny. He was charged Danny. He was convicted Danny. He was executed Danny. Yet this crazy broad comes up with Daniel.

Cooksey   Just the lack of integrity and due diligence.

London   There's more along that line, but it's never
                 flattering to down-rate your competition. I'm
                 just saying that going through this experience,
                 there was a lot more to it than Danny. That was
                 my point in going on about these various
                 difficulties. I don't mean to complain. Just to tell
                 the truth. Look, Danny was a perfect gem, as far
                 as convicts go. He was cooperative. He was
                 guilty. He was sorry. He wanted to talk to me
                 about it. Danny had undiscovered talent that
                 flourished when I gave him a bachelor's degree
                 level course in creative writing. He couldn't
                 write at all when he first came to me. But he did
                 learn. Whatever I told him to do, he did it. He
                 never tried to trick me, bully me, betray me.
                 Your average convicts just live for someone who
                 will pay attention to them, someone they can
                 maneuver into doing something wrong. That did
                 not happen with Danny. Danny earned my
                 respect. At first, I had no respect for him
                 because he seemed like just a sad sack, and a
                 yokel, and a crazy person. He really had to earn
                 my respect. The way he earned it was by
                 respecting our agreement to keep this story
                 confidential.

                 Then he had another case in Louisiana. He sent
                 me a handwritten detailed confession to that
                 case, but I did not publish it, because of what
                 had been done to me for publishing the
                 Gainesville murder confessions. This was not
                 what you'd call a rewarding activity. Why should
                 I do it again? Danny wrote to me and said, "It's
                 yours. You do what you want with it. I totally
                 release it to you." Well, he made me a promise
                 that he was not giving that confession to anyone
                 else, and he never did. On his dying day, he did
                 give an admission of guilt to his pastor, Mike

Hudspeth, who released it to the press. He never said, "Sandra has the written confession." Because he understood by then, that would put me in a bad position. I respect him so much for that.

Cooksey   Right. That was one of the things I would really like to talk about more with you. There is a knee-jerk reaction among people that once you do a horrific thing, that becomes your entire identity.

London   Right, you are considered to be immoral in every sense. If you kill someone you are guilty of everything, and that includes profaning the Sabbath. Of course, that's a very naïve supposition. I'm sorry that a lot of people still say that they don't believe Danny Rolling's account that he gave me on principle, without even reading it. Because he chose to reveal his story to someone who is sympathetic to him as a person. But I will say this about our project: In 25 years, no one has ever shown a single word of *The Making of a Serial Killer* to be untrue. I stand on the truth of my work, and I take that as my rebuttal to the challenge that is often hurled my way: that you can't be a journalist if you get personally involved in a story. They teach that in J-school, that you're not a journalist because when you are involved, your bias distorts the story, so whatever you report, it can never be true.

You might be surprised to hear me say there is some wisdom to that, because in general, journalism is practiced by salaried employees. If you worked full time, you got a good salary, you had a reliable employer who ordered you to write a whole bunch of stories every week, you couldn't afford to care that much about any one story. Because you'd have to finish it up, send it off, and move on to the next one. So I'd agree that you mustn't even try to practice that narrow definition of journalism while getting emotionally involved in a story.

But if you don't happen to work for a big, reliable corporation that pays a nice, juicy paycheck and sends you out on 20 assignments a week, then the rationale of that proscription doesn't pertain. A freelancer can do things an employee can not.

I would do this story because I would be able to help the State close all these homicides and get a heinous killer to come along nicely to his execution. Yet my contribution was downgraded because I openly admitted enjoying a personal relationship with Danny Rolling while we worked on his life story. Now, I'm not saying that was my strategy. No, it was not a wise move. On the day I visited Danny in person, I said, "I can't tell the world that I'm in love with you." He said, "No, of course not. I understand." I said, "That would be it for my career." He said, "No, no, no. That's fine. You shouldn't do that."

Yet the very next day, I took the plunge and released a story about our relationship. That was a mistake, because I was the executive-in-charge of the whole story. It should have been my decision when and how to release it. It just happened that way because Danny said to release the story, and I agreed. It wouldn't make any sense to tell people, "I'm working on the story of the murders. Boy, is it going to be big when I finish!" He said to run with the story, so I told the only story I had.

Then the State of Florida sued me under the Son of Sam Law, which was preposterous. The law forbids a felon from profiting from accounts of crime. That's the formula. Now, that law was struck down by the Supreme Court of the United States two years before I even started my project. The language that used to strike down that law is just sheer poetry. It's so powerful. It makes such pure unequivocal sense that you shall not penalize any speaker for their identity, nor for the content of their speech, period, no matter what the content is, and no matter who they are. It's that fundamental to freedom of speech.

So, I, upon advice of counsel and with full confidence, embarked upon a contract with Danny Rolling under which if we were to sell anything from his story, Danny would get nothing; his brother would get half, and I would get half. Well, that was the predicate for the lawsuit.

Now, there are several things wrong with this picture. First, I was sued before my codefendant was even convicted of the crimes at bar. It was pre-trial, so the status of his being a felon did not exist. Next, I was sued under prior restraint, because no one had written any such accounts of crime. Prior restraint is unlawful. Third, I was never served. No one ever served me with papers. I heard about the lawsuit from a reporter calling to get my reaction. Number four, I'm not a felon, and I am not married to a felon. And number five, every reporter, every commentator who goes on TV or goes into print with something to say about the crime of the day is profiting from accounts of crime.

Cooksey	There is no difference between what you were doing and what they were doing.
London	The only difference is they are on salary, while I get paid directly for coming up with a story none of them could get. I was targeted, personally, because I'm sure it hurt people's feelings to see a murderer have a friend stand by his side while the whole world shunned him. But that doesn't mean I have to forfeit my civil liberties. I can understand that emotions run high, but that's why we have laws, to keep from getting carried away by emotion. No one else before or since has been targeted under this law but me. That's a form of *ad feminem* discrimination, and a violation of my civil liberties. In practice, it is equivalent to the old Bill of Attainder, an antiquated legal procedure that was banned by our Founding Fathers, because it is specifically directed against one single person, penalizing them and ostracizing them for who they are, without any form of resolution or restitution provided to restore their previous standing. It's a life sentence in the court of public opinion.
Cooksey	That's wild.
London	The Assistant Attorney General of Florida called George Waas received a Lifetime Achievement Award for what he did to me. He boasted to the Associated Press: "I don't know of any other case where this law has been brought against a person who's not a convicted felon." But instead of admitting what a flawed concept that was, what a failure to bring a proper prosecution, he was bragging of how creative he was, because sure enough he won in court.

The concept that was invented especially for me, in order to tie me together with this murderer, was declaring our relationship to be *unique and special.* Now, to me, *unique and special* means there is no precedent for it under common or statutory law. But instead of being a weakness in their bogus prosecution, it was reframed and celebrated as legal creativity.

Sure enough, I, having a *unique and special* relationship with this felon, at one time had an agreement to give his brother half of the profit from sale of stories about his crimes. Although they attached that agreement to the lawsuit, when Danny Rolling saw what was being done to me, how maliciously I was being attacked, he filed a statement with the court saying: "I give all profits and all copyright ownership to Sondra London. I do not want any profits at all from anything that I give Sondra London."

The court just completely ignored that sworn statement. Never acknowledged it exists. They also completely ignored the fact that I never sent Danny Rolling one red cent. He was a prisoner. His account was on the public record. If I had sent him any money at all, much less "profits from accounts of crime," the records of those transactions would have been attached to the lawsuit as Exhibit A. There was no such thing. So the case convicts me of allowing a felon to profit from accounts of crime, without any evidence of such profits existing.

Cooksey   Absolutely. It's really interesting. As you are recounting this part of the story, facing these obstacles specifically because you were involved, it occurred to me that it suggests a great deal of power on your part. They were so fearful of what

you would illuminate for the world that they
went to great lengths to stop you.

Sun-Sentinel, Thursday, February 24, 1994

State files motion to take
profits from Rolling story

London   When you say that, what flashes through my
mind is all those letters crossing my desk, from
prisoners all over Florida about murders that
were being committed in prisons. And then, you
know, John Schaefer was murdered in prison.
Vincent Rivera was the fall guy, but that was
bogus, he didn't do it. And why would they
frame him? Because he was right next to
Frankie Valdez when he was beaten to death.
Vincent Rivera filed a grievance as a witness on
his behalf against the five guards who beat
Valdez half to death a couple of months before
they finally did beat him to death. When John
Schaefer was murdered, his body was found
covered with boot marks. Testimony was given
at Rivera's trial that those treads matched the
government-issued boots worn only by the
prison guards; and no prisoners were allowed to
wear those boots. Even after that compelling
testimony, they still found Vincent Rivera guilty,
and sentenced him to another life, on top of the
two he was already serving.

Cooksey   It's so much easier to convict a convict.

London   It was explained to me by my attorney that the
mainstream media within the state of Florida
were co-opted, that they would never run any
exposés of the prison system because of access.
If they were to expose prison corruption, they

193

would be denied access to interview prisoners, and that would interfere with their ability to profit from accounts of crime. So reportage of prison malfeasance is traditionally quashed by the editors and producers; reporters just follow orders from above, and that works out for everybody in the circle jerk. So you see, by my coming in on my own hook as a freelancer, that required a *unique and special* approach to stopping me. People just see the Rolling case, and think that's all it is. But before Danny contacted me, I'd already been red-flagged for years because prisoners all over Florida believed here was someone at last who would dare to publish the crimes being committed behind bars.

When they filed that lien against me, as I told them, I told the attorney general, I said: "If I were a corporation, all my shareholders would insist I stop this project because it's not profitable." I said, "But that's not why I'm doing it. I'm not doing it for the money. So, your taking the money is not going to stop me." What it actually did was make me dig my heels in more. I started this project, I said, and I am going to finish it. I don't care what they do to me.

Telling me I could not do this story sort of got a rise out of me from my rebel blood. I'm a proud rebel, and my people fought for their home. I feel that my rights were violated and that what was done to me in Florida was a part of a transition in rewriting the law and in denaturing the First Amendment, vitiating our civil liberties. The people were going along with it. They were able to successfully marginalize me in such a way as to sell the proposition: "It's okay for us to take her rights away, because she is so heinous that she is in love with a serial killer." That's the most heinous thing that they could say about me since I was still not married and I had no legal connection whatsoever to Danny Rolling. But in the public's mind, I was firmly attached to the things that he did in Gainesville before he ever knew me.

Cooksey   Certainly. If it bleeds, it leads, right? The more scandalous that they can make it, the more salacious, the better.

London   Exactly. I was a part of that process as well. I knew as well as any other journo that if it bleeds, it leads. That's why I want the guilty murderers to give me their stories, but the book *The Making of a Serial Killer*, it was very difficult but the result was solid. I will put it up against any other account of the Gainesville murders. Time will tell who wrote the real story.

If anyone else says something happened there, and I say the opposite, I would look very carefully at that source. I'd look into their associations. I particularly would like to know how Mary Ryzuk got a Book of the Month deal for that mess of a book she wrote about Danny. Now that's a real murder mystery! She has him committing a crime while he was on furlough from prison. Let me ask you this. You've done a lot of crime stories. When was the last time you heard of someone being on furlough from prison? I'll wait.

Cooksey   I can't think of one.

London   How about that?

Cooksey   Nope, not a single one, Sondra. I'm sorry.

London	Did Danny Rolling mention doing anything on furlough from prison in his authorized autobiography?
Cooksey	Not that I recall.
London	It happened in a peach orchard, she said. Daniel was in a peach orchard on furlough from prison.
Cooksey	Maybe Daniel Wallace.
London	She also insisted that Daniel lusted for this mother. There's not one scintilla of evidence of that anywhere either on the record or off the record. Not one scintilla. And while I'm at it, John Donnelly is not going to get out of this either. There was a gag order on this case. John Donnelly put his book out before the trial was over. He had all the stuff in it, that was still under gag order when he was handing out his book.
Cooksey	Just outrageous.
London	The book was written and published before the trial ended. Why was he given an unfair advantage?
Cooksey	I don't know. Even the people who would be promoting that would be...
London	These people were all helped, so that by comparison I would suffer. I had an FDLE agent who called me up and said, "You'd better get to work on your book. All these other people are coming out with theirs." Just gloating. I said, "That's all right. Let them come out, then they'll look all the more foolish when I come out with the real story."

Cooksey   Absolutely. You had the exclusive with the killer
                 himself.

London   So, I got the book out. That was in 1996,
                 published by Feral House Books, which was
                 owned by Adam Parfrey. Years later, he died,
                 and his sister Jessica took over Feral House. I
                 wrote to her and asked her to issue a second
                 edition; or if not, I said I wanted the copyright
                 back. She looked at the book, and she felt that
                 Danny was too enthusiastic about rape. That
                 was not proper. I was going to have to do
                 something about that. She wanted Feral House
                 to be a kinder, gentler publisher.

                 At any rate, I got the copyright back, but the
                 book had been out of print for years, over a
                 decade. It was published in 1996, and people
                 have been writing to me for years asking where
                 they could get a copy. So, I got the rights back. I
                 added on a prologue that brought it up to date,
                 in which I explained why I did leave the writing
                 the way it originally appeared. I addressed how
                 things have changed, and with this politically
                 correct movement claiming to be offended so
                 gravely that the book itself should not exist.
                 Well, first of all, I don't agree with any of that
                 philosophically. Number two, this whole point
                 from the beginning was that it be authentic, that
                 it be uncensored.

                 When you really, really, really want to know
                 what it's like to be a serial killer, this is where
                 you're going to go. Because here's the good, the
                 bad, and the ugly. There's the sweet. There's the
                 charming. There's the divine, the sublime.
                 There's the devoted. There's the tender. There's
                 the brutal. There's the absolutely batshit
                 craziness and LSD hallucinations, all of that. If I
                 don't put all of it, then I'm distorting reality.

Some writers do that so that their story will be more of a fun, recreational ride. That is why we distort these horrible stories, nice them up. Drop the parts that don't fit the profile.

But I say you're doing your audience a disservice because you came here to find the truth, not to make up a story that goes the way you want. If it doesn't go the way you've been trained to expect by entertainment, then the better for you, because that means you are onto something significant.

I love this part that Danny gave me to put in about security tips on how to protect yourself from somebody like him. That's a good example of the socially redeeming value that derives from *The Making of a Serial Killer*.

Cooksey   I think that that's so very important. One of the things that I really admire about your work that I encourage people to look into, is that you treat Danny as a complex human being. Because just like you mentioned earlier, they're not one thing. You're not going to find someone who is completely evil. You're not going to find somebody who is absolutely altruistic and good. Every human being is complicated. Some of us go to further extremes than others, as you have continuously found in your career. But I do appreciate the radical sense of empathy with which you approach this. You try very hard to put your biases aside and report as accurately as possible.

London   I think one of the hardest parts is probing into the injuries and pain of the childhood. I found that in every case. It's always difficult to uncover what hurt. In Danny's case, he did not even remember most of his childhood until he was at trial. He saw, for the first time, the videotapes that his family members and neighbors made for his defense, sworn testimony about what they saw. The trial was traumatic for him because it brought back these deeply suppressed memories.

Now, when you talk about what made Danny Rolling a serial killer, you have to go back to prenatal abuse that was witnessed, sworn and testified. Danny's father kicked his wife's pregnant abdomen, he shoved her downstairs, and she was heavily pregnant. That's just witnessed behavior. He felt free to behave that way in front of company. So you can only imagine what went on behind closed doors. When the baby was an infant, he didn't crawl straight. He crawled on one leg and kind of scooched with the other leg. That outraged his father. He kicked his first son all the way across the room where he smacked into the wall. Again, this was witnessed.

As Danny grew older, he was bitterly abused to the point that one time his Aunt Agnes called the police. James had tied up the boys to a metal pole and left them there to suffer in the midsummer sun. Agnes called the police and Chief D'Artois told her: "Well, I'm sorry, he's a good officer for me. He does his duty here, and there's nothing I can do. It's a family affair." In a word, I would date the making of *this* serial killer from that incident. Because after so much rage was put into him and it was going to come out one way or another, but it wasn't going to be against a certain person. It was going to be against the society that stood back and allowed him to be abused. Of all the things that went on in his mind, his self-hatred was strong. He wanted to destroy himself, but he also wanted to destroy everything else.

The story I just finished working on is a phantasmagorical story with the oil painting to go with. In the core of the story is that the evil woman seduces him and betrays him. I don't know what, but he responds by destroying everything in the world. That's the storyline, very immature. The woman, at the end, there she was, the Whore of Babylon. I said to myself, golly Moses, I have come full circle now, because that was Schaefer's obsession.

There is a whole section of brutal fantasies Schaefer wrote in *Killer Fiction* called "Whores: What to *Do* About Them." That was his whole thing. Now I look at Danny Rolling of all people, and see that's where he winds up at the end of his journey. He isn't owning the violence he commits as a character in that story. He's saying that he existed on a high pinnacle of Good-Boi. The Evil Woman seduced him, grabbed him, and dragged him to bad behavior. And oh boy, is she is going to pay!

Cooksey   When the people you've spent time with share these kinds of phantasmagorical concepts of why they've committed their crimes, how do you treat them when they are sharing those things?

London   Oh, my answer to that is very simple. I just see it as more data. Whether you happen to like it or not, you just take it in. It has to be included in any theory or model you form in your mind as you struggle to comprehend all of it. Don't get drawn into it. Don't let it get a rise out of you. Don't evaluate it as being good, or bad, or worthless. Just keep it. Preserve it. You never know when it's going to come into play, when you might find it will fit in with something else and unlock another unsolved mystery. As for how I treat anyone who is confiding in me, I pay close attention. I show respect. I respond to their moods in kind. If they're ready to laugh, we share a laugh. If it's a strain, if there is any tension, I'm being watchful and I'm dialing back my reactions. I'm not going to challenge or criticize or complain. I won't be the first one to crack a joke, unless I can tell they are ready.

Cooksey   A lot of the studying of the very beginnings of the Behavioral Science Unit with the FBI, which is now the Behavioral Analysis Unit, is when you have these stories of John Douglas and Robert Ressler, their interviews, and the things that they talked about, it is very much the same as what you're saying. It's that if you do pass judgment, or react, or whatever, in some ways, you're allowing them to manipulate you. And you're breaking their confidence in you.

London   That is the FBI training. Those guys are FBI cadre, they are certainly up at the top of the heap. There's one thing I forgot to mention, I remembered when you mentioned Robert Ressler's name. In his book *Whoever Fights Monsters,* he talks about developing his theories of the modern serial killer. He says, "Every time I do a presentation about this to law enforcement, someone inevitably raises their hand and says, "You got all those markers from the Schaefer case." Ressler says, "That's not really true, but it is accurate in that every aspect of the theory we developed about the organized serial killer is exemplified in the Schaefer case."

When Schaefer went to court in 1973, we didn't have that terminology of "serial killer." When I started writing to him in 1989, he still referred to himself as a mass murderer. Evidently, that was the language that was used in headlines about him, mass murderer. So I was the one who explained to him the difference between mass murder and serial murder.

Cooksey   It's fascinating that they could learn from you in that way. It's really interesting to me, the evolution of your ideas. You mentioned looking at the roots of their childhood. I know I personally find it difficult – coming from a very similar mindset that you do, it's hard not to see the child in the adult.

London   Well, we'd work at revealing the things from the childhood. The thing is that there's so much *shame* involved. There is something I wrote. I've been looking for where the heck that I published it because I wanted to quote it.

Well, I don't even know where I wrote about this before, but it comes from what Danny was talking about his father trying to teach him a lesson and by being the giant with the big stick. What lesson was he trying to teach and what lesson was he actually teaching? He was intending to teach the small, weak person that he was bigger and stronger, and that he needed to do his will. What he really was teaching him, he was giving him a closer look at how it feels to be dominated and to look at the giant with the big stick, get a good close up look at him. That's how you behave to get on the other side of that state you're in, you become the giant with the big stick. Because all he could ever be was that measly little crybaby who is no good for anything, who's weak, who's a loser, who will never be anything.

You have this beaten into you. Then you learn the lesson: There is an alternative. You become the giant with the big stick. That was something I learned from working with Danny and how he went from one to the other. His mother filed a sworn statement for his hearing. She couldn't attend because she was dying. In that statement, she said she didn't believe that Danny ever got any more than 15 years old emotionally.

Cooksey   I can understand that.

London   I would put it at a little earlier. I would say pre-puberty and that he was emotionally in arrested development right at that stage. He was not able to develop and to become the person that a man has to be. Because he knew he was never going to be that. He was always going to be the weak little weasely loser. That was all he could ever be. That was the child in Danny.

He got put in jail, and behavior was demanded of him that was not in his repertoire. I believe that is how he came to split into a part he called Ennad, which is a name he made up. It's just Danny backwards. Everything that Danny can never be. That's Ennad. So, then the man could enact the behavior of a sexually mature man. As Ennad, he could walk the yard like a convict. Ennad already handled the transgressive behaviors of the voyeurism, the violation of boundaries, while Danny would always be adherent to the moral principles he learned in church.

While Danny was too cowardly, weak, pitiful and depressed to go out and prowl around, break in and rape women, Ennad could do that because he wasn't limited the way Danny was. Ennad was a psychopath. He had no empathy, no respect for the law. All the strength this person had, Ennad knew how to use it. Danny did not. There came to be a difference there. It was natural for that to evolve. It was an adaptation. It was not possible for Danny to own his own mannish nature. But as Ennad, he could.

So, I accepted that that condition was functional. It helped him survive. But on the other hand, what starts out as an ability, a technique many people can use when they need it, becomes a disability when you can't control it. And Danny could not control it. Some people grow up, learn to adapt, and dissociation doesn't become a disability. It doesn't become a problem. It's just the ability like you've heard Beyoncé talk about her Sasha Fierce. And Herschel Walker writes candidly in his book *Breaking Free* about his own multiple personalities. That's when dissociation is an ability, not a disability. It's a disability when it's out of control.

You will see that very graphically in *The Making of a Serial Killer* after he shoots his father, in self-defense. I should put it this way. After his father discharged six bullets from his service revolver at his first son, Danny was forced to defend himself. With one shot, he hit his father between the eyes. Let's describe that incident accurately.

Danny left his father shot down, and ran to the home of some rich folks he'd met in a bar. That narrative, which he so brilliantly described, shows the way his mind changed. And his account did match the one they gave the FDLE.

He pulled a gun at them and said, "Give me all of your money." They had very little cash on hand,

and were trying not to upset him, when he said, "Oh, I don't know what I'm doing here. Take this gun. Take it. I'm sorry. I'll leave now." "Look how you messed up our white rug." "Oh, let me clean up where I messed up the rug." "Oh, look, I've got another gun." And he pulls another gun out. The guy tells him to hand it over, and he hands it over. Then he says he will leave, and they try to give him twenty dollars; he refuses the money, but accepts an apple. He's switching back and forth very fast. So you can see in just that one scene how he's not functioning. If he could just be Ennad, he could dash in there and pull off a robbery, get some money, and keep going. But because his condition was a disability, under stress the structure of who he was kept dramatically fracturing.

Cooksey   There's a conflict between his hating the violence that was inflicted upon him and others, and at the same time, he had that need to overcome his helplessness and to take some control over his power, right?

London   You can be the giant with the big stick, that was his choice. That was the choice that was presented to him from the very cradle.

Cooksey   It's difficult when we really delve into who these people are and what contributed to putting them where they ended up. I try to deal with it on my podcast, and that's something that, once again, I really appreciate so much about your writing and your approach to it.

London   Let me go ahead and take you to the next level with Danny Rolling's development problem, of his coping ability or disability, if you will. The next stage of it occurred in Parchman Prison. Parchman Prison lately has been in the news for torture and inhumane conditions that persist still, these twenty-five years later. Parchman was originally a plantation. So, its nature still has some of that history clinging to it.

At Parchman, Danny was housed on a corridor that sloped down at the end, and his cell was the very last one at the bottom of the slope. All the filth from the sewage would back up into his cell. Then they didn't have any heat in the winter, where it was frozen ice and snow. The sewage in his cell was forming ice. It was under those conditions that he had his epiphany of evil. As he puts it, "Gemini appeared." Gemini was a spirit of evil who promised Danny that if he would let him in, he would give him revenge for all that had been done to him. He put it as a pact. Gemini promised Danny would take one life for every year he suffered in prison. That number came to eight. Now, you cannot shake him from that story. You cannot get him to say anything else. Gemini appeared, then Danny invited the Evil One into himself. Gemini didn't force himself, Danny said. "I invited him in."

This shows his indoctrination by the Pentecostal Church. This is why he puts it in those terms. That was what he was taught to expect of the unseen realm. That's why he sees it that way.

When Danny's defense was being prepared, the attorneys contacted the former warden of Parchman, whose name was Donald Cabana. Donald Cabana had been the warden of Parchman Prison when Danny was incarcerated there. Cabana was no longer a warden; he had moved up in Mississippi Department of Corrections. A couple of years after Danny's trial, Donald Cabana went on to write one of the most important books ever written about the death penalty, called *Death at Midnight: The Confession of an Executioner.* I highly recommend this book. Cabana describes how he came to loathe state-sanctioned murder after years of serving as the State Executioner of Mississippi.

Danny's attorneys wanted Cabana to testify to the inhumane conditions at Parchman. He was agreeable, but then he had to renege, because the Department of Corrections told him that if he were to testify on Danny Rolling's behalf, then his career in corrections would be over.

So, in order to counter the impact of Danny Rolling's account of his conditions at Parchman Prison, Florida sent our good-buddy FDLE agent Ed Dix, to visit Parchman Prison in person and examine the records and look around. Golly, what a surprise! Agent Dix couldn't see a single thing out of order. He saw nothing in the records he examined. He found no evidence at all of any substandard conditions. That was the rebuttal that the state of Florida put on to weaken Danny Rolling's account of how his mental illness erupted into a virulent psychosis.

Cooksey   One of the things that strikes me in so many of these cases, and I definitely see it in Danny Rolling, is that these are logical precursors to a completely avoidable pathological situation.

London   Right, number one. And number two, these are social issues. Guess who's guilty? We, the people. That's something we don't want to hear. We, the people, want to draw a big, bright line between us and the offender. Over here on this side, we never do anything wrong. Then there's them, and they do everything wrong. The underlying concept that I'm getting at here, it's a little bit subversive. Because it undermines the foundation that we rely upon. Our prison systems throughout our entire country are indemnified. They have such clauses in their powers as *discretion*, and everything can be done at their *discretion*. They tell us everything is just fine. Prisoners should not have any rights. They should not have friends. Nice people should not have anything to do with them.

In fact, they shouldn't even pronounce their names properly. As we see resolutely demonstrated by the likes of Nancy Grace. I have no love for Nancy Grace. She covered my trial, when I was sued by the State of Florida for publishing Danny's confessions. I was the only person on the stand in the entire proceeding. Nancy Grace said on Court TV in a voice-over: "Sondra London is what we call a *hostile witness.*" When I watched the footage later I was yelling at the screen: "*No*. You stupid bitch. Sondra London is the *Defendant* in this action."

Cooksey   It's amazing.

London   She was a prosecutor! She's supposed to understand the difference between a defendant and a witness, but she wasn't there to treat me properly. That was not her assignment. She's not there to treat Danny Rolling properly either. She flaunts her contempt by calling him *Rawlins*. She loves to call him *Rawlins*. Even when called on it, she'll go right straight back to deliberately calling him out of his name.

People hate crime, they hate criminals, they just want them to go away forever. Look. You can't kill them all. Most of them are coming right

back out into our side of that bright line. So,
great, have it your way. You put them in cages
with career criminals and violent, insane people
who can't be held responsible for their actions;
you subject them to inhumane conditions. Prison
is a monster factory, a crime college. You put
novices in with professional criminals so they
can learn new tricks of the trade and make new
criminal alliances. You cannot kill them all. You
can't keep them all locked up. They are coming
back out. That is the fatal flaw with all these
underlying assumptions that law enforcement
and corrections will separate the bad from the
good, and exterminate the bad.

If you thought I was radical before, I am going
to get really radical now. There's no use talking
about Death Row. There's no use talking about
murderers and career criminals. Let's just look
at our first offenders. What if a first offender
enters this system and gets a complete workup?
What if their blood levels are taken? What if we
have our own in-house MRI equipment inside
the prison? Then they won't have the security
problems that cause judges to deny the defense
these procedures to document brain damage.
Find out what their defects and deficiencies are.
Give them tests to find out if they have any
literacy at all. Put these kids onto
supplementation with vitamins and minerals
that they're deficient in. Give them education
and literacy, and a therapy I call theater.
Because it involves learning how people act, how
to talk to people without killing them, how to
get along with your fellows. You might develop
an enthusiasm and interest that will carry over
and give you something to feed your spirit. Give
these kids at least four hours a day of hard
labor, hopefully outside. If that's all we could do

differently, that would be enough to make real changes.

You could put them on a contract. You go to these classes, you do this work. You get detoxed, you take these vitamins, you eat this good food, you go to bed early, and you get up early, and you work hard. If you don't cause any more trouble, then you're free to go. You've completed the course. If you're not going to respect our attempt to help you, then we'll have to move you into the next level of correction.

I would like for us to see these first offenders as failures of our system, and I'd like to see our system take responsibility for turning them around. Many of them cannot get this support at home. They need to get help from society. That's because we, the people need these young failures to become barbers, auto mechanics, artists, lawyers, therapists, and television personalities. That's what we need of them. They fell down and they came to our attention. If they are unable to become a fully functioning citizen, the human potential will just run in reverse. Danny Rolling's case throws this dynamic into stark relief, and the way we, the people handled him only exacerbated a bad situation.

If they've got a brain problem, there's no use trying to give them the kind of therapy you give a patient with a normal brain. If you can identify these deficits, they can be addressed. I'd just go broad slightly here. Autism cannot be cured, but an autistic can be trained. The therapy consists of behavioral training just to learn that when I say, "How are you," we want you to say, "Fine, thank you. How are you?" You don't go into a detailed discussion of how you are.

Even conditions that can't be remediated can be treated, so that this person will be functional when they leave here. The addictions have to be treated. If they come in addicted, their medical needs in detoxing have to be met, not just ignored. Until we accept responsibility as a society for those of us who fall into criminal behavior, we're going to continue building walking time bombs like Danny Rolling, bouncing from one blow to another, adding insult to injury, until they explode.

Cooksey   Everything that you're saying, it's not a new concept. It's just a radical concept, right? We can hearken back all the way to *Utopia*, the book by Thomas More. This was centuries ago. He said: "Is it not society's fault that we create criminals and then punish them?"

London   Well, we don't want to hear that, it doesn't let us be morally superior, so shut up.

Cooksey   Absolutely right.

London   We're a part of the problem, too. They'll say to me, "We will put you in an electric chair right next to him." But until there's some change, we're still going to be winding up costing quantum levels of money trying to deal with the damages done by people who can't find a way to be productive citizens. There is no system of assessment upon intake, because gathering those data would imply an obligation to address remediation of the deficits.

I do know that a human being has potential. Here's Danny Rolling. He is at the end of the road. He can't be saved. He can't be healed. But his creative spirit— which was hidden, repressed, undeveloped— but it could be brought into being with nothing more than healthy human attention. If that level of attention could be given to that child all along, he could have become a great artist. He could have been a singer, a songwriter with considerable talent.

I have the highest respect for Danny because he respected me, and he respected our agreement. He never treated me improperly. So, he deserved the attention I gave him. In return, we're all the beneficiaries of the work we did, to create the book.

You can take this book, *The Making of a Serial Killer.* You can read one page, and it's the cute little boy. You read the next page, and he's tearing the nipples off someone. It doesn't play to your sympathies the way a good Ann Rule book does, where your sympathies are squarely with the victim and against the offender. This book is not about the victims, because no disrespect, but there's no story to tell. There's nothing to be learned from talking about what these victims did and who they were. It literally did not matter. They were chosen at random. This is not Nicole Brown Simpson where you want to know what she did, because it matters. In this case, it was Danny Rolling striking against a system. His victims were emblematic of being cherished, emblematic of belonging. That was what he could never have. My image of Danny Rolling was as a little orphan with his nose pressed up against the window of life, yearning to be on the inside with all the other people.

Now I almost sound like I am all warm and fuzzy about Danny Rolling's criminal behavior. But he was still actively homicidal even on Death Row.

He wrote to me about plotting to kill an inmate; so much for the deterrent effect of the capital punishment. He didn't say anything about Gemini. He owned his intent to kill in proper persona. And then sure enough, he made an attempt, jumping the guy with a shiv, out on the yard. He was caught at it and punished for it. So, don't think that I was unaware that Danny never got over being a bona fide homicidal maniac.

Sketch by Sondra London

Cooksey   That's incredible, Sondra.

London   Don't let one side take away from the opposite side. Try to make your own mind bigger, so you can hold them both in your mind at the same time. That's what I was talking about, the multiple interface with a very complex personality. To *comprehend* means to wrap your mind all the way around the matter. You have to take a comprehensive look at all of the data. Your theory or your reaction has to take into consideration the contradictory information. It's not that this side is real, so that side has to be fake. That's just a really lazy, low-IQ way to understand a subtle, complex reality.

Cooksey   Sondra, where can we find *The Making of a Serial Killer: Second Edition*?

London   Well, it's on Amazon, you can always just go there. But I'd like everyone to visit my website **SondraLondon Dotcom.** You'll see *The Making of a Serial Killer: Second Edition* at the top of the menu. Click on that, and you'll come to great big link saying "BUY THE BOOK" that takes you directly to the Amazon page. While you are on the website, you can read reviews, excerpts, and my new prologue.

If you don't want to go to the website, fine. Just go to Amazon, and search for *The Making of a Serial Killer.* You will find the first edition, with the red cover. Used copies of it are still for sale for way too much money. Because the book is out of print, so now it's a rare book. So just skip that and scroll down, because *The Making of a Serial Killer: Second Edition* is the one you're looking for.

And soon to come, I will release *Beyond the Making of a Serial Killer.* In this book, we will have Danny Rolling's detailed confession to the triple murder in Louisiana, when he crossed over to being a murderer for the first time. We will tell you about the man who was considered for nineteen years the prime suspect in that case, and how that ruined his life. We will release some of Danny Rolling's short fiction. Two stories he wrote are set in the current era. Then there are a series of stories set in the medieval ages. He loved to write about princes and princesses, witches and gypsies, vampires and werewolves. We have an article called "Why Did We Kill?" going back and forth between Keith Jesperson and Danny Rolling. Keith Jesperson is a serial killer doing life in Oregon and he's what you call a real asshole.

Cooksey   Well, that sums it up.

London   A lot of people know about Jesperson. That secret is out. He'd trying to meddle with me and Danny, and writing Danny letters to turn him against me and stupid stuff. But at any rate, he poses the question of why we did kill. And Danny writes back on that subject. That's included there. You'll have my account about the lawsuit that was filed against us and all of the activities that surrounded it, the Attorney General getting an award, the victims' families threatening to kill me, and all the other things that went with that.

My final goal in that volume is to cover what I call *"L'Affaire Bourgoin,"* which is the completely unbelievable, incredible, outrageous story of Stéphane Bourgoin who billed himself as the world's greatest authority in serial killers, and who rode my coattails for 25 years in Europe. He'd taken my work and published it under his name, but that's not all he did. My story will tell about the other frauds he perpetrated as well. He was busted on this scam, and journalists all over Europe mobbed to the story. On May 6, 2020, *Paris Match* got him to admit to being a plagiarist, a fraud and a mythomane. Without my knowledge or permission, he had taken my copyrighted work and published a book with his name on it as the author in 2012.

Cooksey   I didn't know he had a book.

London   He's published forty books. He's been on all
          these TV shows, made all these documentaries.
          It's all lies, or if it is true, it is plagiarism from
          the likes of me. I will write up the details about
          that misadventure. It's ridiculous. Bourgoin said
          he visited Danny Rolling right before he was
          executed, and that Danny gave him all his
          artwork, which all has clearly drawn or painted
          on it the date, "1993." There are many pictures
          of me, pictures inscribed, "Dear Sondra." Like
          Danny would keep all that artwork there in his
          cell for twelve years. Like you could give
          someone artwork when they visit you on Death
          Row. Like he could even get in to visit anyone
          on Death Row, especially when they are on
          Death Watch. None of this happened. If
          Bourgoin had done any research, he would have
          come up with a better lie. But that's what he's
          been making bank on. So, anyway I will be
          writing up *"L'Affaire Bourgoin"* for *Beyond the
          Making of a Serial Killer* as well.

Cooksey   Fantastic. Sondra, thank you so much for
          coming on. This has been just illuminating and
          amazing. Like I told you, personally, I'm a big
          fan of your work. I've read everything you've
          written. I think everybody needs to check it out.
          It's really some of the most authentic true crime
          writing that's out there. So, I do encourage you
          all to go to **SondraLondon Dotcom.** Everything
          you are looking for will be there. Simple as can
          be. Sondra, it's such an honor, and I'm really
          excited that my audience will get to share in
          this. So, thank you once again for coming.

London   Thank you for having me. It has been my
          pleasure, I assure you.

Sondra London on *Court TV*

On Labor Day Weekend in 2000, June Grasso had Sondra London in the hot seat for a Court TV special called *Crimes of the Century* to commemorate the passage of ten years since the Gainesville Student Murders.

Sondra London on Court TV

Grasso   Now we're joined by Sondra London via satellite from Atlanta. Sondra is a freelance journalist who co-authored a book with Danny Rolling called *The Making of a Serial Killer.* There's been much litigation about that, which we're going to be talking to Sondra about.

217

Grasso   Sondra, we just saw you in a clip in the courtroom while Danny Rolling was singing to you. You met him while you were researching a book about the student murders. Can you tell us what he's like, and what attracted you to him that you wanted to or agreed to be his fiancée.

London   Well, June, we've worked together for quite a while and very closely on the project of his life and crimes, and it was in getting to know him during that process that we became closer gradually over the months. I've worked with a number of serial killers and other convicts, and Danny Rolling's quite different than most of them that I have encountered before and since. He was quite interested in being honest in terms of getting to what was wrong with him or what he had done wrong, and virtually all the others that I've encountered are more interested in running a game.

Grasso   Obviously he was in the courtroom fighting against the death penalty. How did he feel when it was imposed? What did he tell you about it?

London   He said in a letter that he felt like a cockroach. He was expecting the death penalty, and he really even wanted the death penalty. It was like suicide by law enforcement to him.

London   He had expected the death penalty all along and he was prepared for it. He said in a letter that he felt like a cockroach. He was expecting the death penalty, and he really even wanted the death penalty. It was like suicide by law enforcement to him.

Grasso   This is I know a personal question, but if I may ask you, why you were his fiancée. And obviously once he's given the death sentence,

that is not going to go anywhere. But why did
you break up your relationship with him?

London   The fact that we got engaged, you know, is in
the intensity of the situation that we were
under. We wanted to visit. He wanted to talk to
me. He had stated over and over to Ed Dix and
to the other investigators that he wasn't going
to talk to anyone except me. He wanted to talk
to me about his crimes. As he grew older he
became his worst nightmare. He had told
someone that what he hated and feared the most
was being stabbed to death at night in his sleep,
and that was exactly what he had committed.

Attorney Joe Tacopina
Tacopina   Sondra, if you could tell us, who made the
decision to plead guilty, rather than fight the
case at trial? Was that Rolling's decision, or was
it a joint decision between his attorneys and
himself?

London   That's a very interesting question. Danny
Rolling had gone against attorney's advice
throughout this entire thing. He had bonded to
me and he contacted me by a letter written on
February the tenth, and asked me to tell him
whether he should plead guilty or fight it. My
goodness. And I went to his lawyers and told
them look, you know, you need to get a grip on
him, go out there and visit him or do something.
But I told him I could not advise him. I told him
to pray, and to make sure he wasn't gonna
change his mind before he made a decision. And
I said, please don't ask me to make those
decisions for you, please talk to your attorneys.
But he was going against attorney's advice for
quite a while. I believe that was part of his
appeal, based on the fact that coercion, in Danny
Rolling's case, was using hope; that the State

had coerced him to trust them rather than his own attorneys, because they held out the hope that that he would be allowed to see me, and that was how they got the confessions.

Danny Rolling in Court with Lawyers
Barbara Blunt-Powell and Rick Parker

Grasso   Sondra, you said he was not surprised that he got the death penalty. Once you admit guilt to serial killings, there is , a slim chance to none that a jury is going to let you live.

London   That's right, but Danny's different than any prisoner I've ever known. He hardly even follows his case. To my knowledge, you know, he'll get the paperwork and not even look at it. Most prisoners are very much involved in their case. I had mentioned to one of his attorneys when he wrote me that letter about whether he should plead guilty, and he said there were a few things to consider. And he wanted to know how it would affect our book project. And I just was appalled. And said to his lawyer, my goodness, he cares more about this book than he cares about his own life. And his lawyer said, that's how it's always been with Danny.

Grasso   Sondra London, you were in that courtroom. In a lot of courtrooms you have a mood. there's a tension or something like that in the air. What was it like for, you sitting there?

London   For me? I was torn in so many different directions at once, and I feel the same way now. I mean, it's just a tragedy. It's not a matter of someone wins and someone loses. It's all so terribly tragic. Rick Parker, and Johnny Kearns, and the rest couldn't have been finer lawyers. They're working out of a public defender's office, chronically understaffed and underpaid. And they gave him the finest defense you could give. I have to say, even though I was sensitized to the suffering of the offender, this was just one mitigator. If you had put me on that jury, and instructed me what my orders were that I was to weigh aggravators against mitigators, I don't care how sympathetic I was to the suffering of this offender, there's no way that would come anywhere near approaching the weight of the aggravators that were presented to the jury. The whole thing is just a sad situation on every side.

Grasso   You're saying you would have had to vote for the death penalty?

London   Yes, looking at the position of the defense lawyer, it's an honor to be a part of a judicial system that takes even the most heinous offender and gives him every possible chance to present whatever case there may be. In this case, the offender had one paltry mitigator, and that was mental illness. And his attorneys did a great job of presenting that it. But there you go, that's

one mitigator, and he had how many
aggravators, twenty-three?

Grasso   Now, Sondra, you're wearing a sweater that says
                Crime Does Not Pay and that has I think a
                double meaning for you. Tell us about your book
                and what's happened with the book. You've been
                fighting for years to get the profits from the
                book you co-authored with Danny Rolling, *The
                Making of a Serial Killer.*

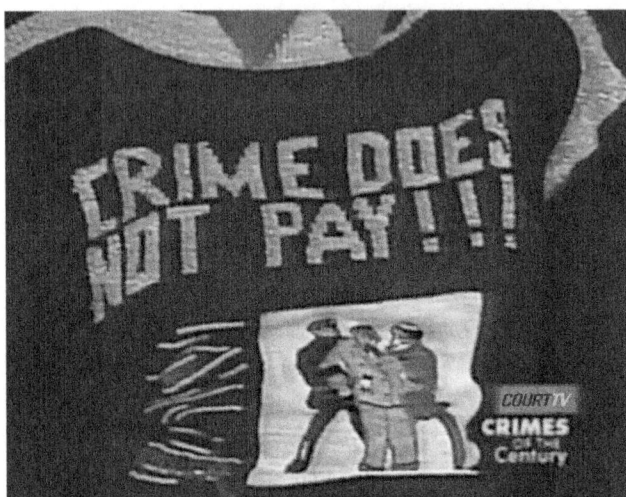

Sondra London's Sweater on Court TV

London   To tell you the truth, June, it was a struggle just
                writing it, of course. We started working on this
                in 1992. We were served with a lawsuit as soon
                as they got his admissions of guilt. They turned
                around and sued me and Danny Rolling, and
                that was in 1993. Well, that was prior restraint.
                We had not written the confessions, and they
                had no felony conviction, and there was no
                money, there was no contract, there was no
                book. Nevertheless they filed suit to prevent us
                from continuing to work together and to do this
                story. So from 1993 through 1994 when, you

know, we had the trial, or the sentencing hearing, after he pleaded guilty. So only then were we able to correspond about the murders. After that, when we finally finished up the whole project with the murder confessions and all, then we published it in the *Globe* and that was when they seized the money from the *Globe*. That was fifteen thousand dollars by the time it reached me. Danny Rolling had signed an agreement specifying that he would never get a cent.

Grasso   Sondra London, you were in that courtroom. We heard someone crying out. Who was that? We heard some crying in the background.

London   There were shouts. Judge Morris had warned not to make any outbursts, but they did have outbursts, and I know that Court TV did cover the part where Mario Taboada jumped to his feet and screamed at Danny, and then turned and threatened me. And then Jim Larson came up to me and threatened to kill me. That was the kind of thing that was going on in court there.

Grasso   Were you in fear as you were going in and out of the courthouse? Were the victims' families identifying you with the crime in some way?

London   It's worked out that way, but you know, I don't really consider this to be something that is their own original idea. I believe that this whole situation was more or less spun for advantage by the State's Attorney's office in order to redirect some of that animosity my way. Actually it would have been more advantageous to them politically if Danny Rolling had fought this, so that Rod Smith could be perceived as a victor. But because due to my assistance and cooperation with the State, Danny Rolling had pled guilty, it appears to me so that then all that animosity had been spun and directed toward me.

Grasso   Well, of course that's for how you feel after being through all these proceedings. I know you feel that you really deserve the money from this book that you wrote and that you're being cheated out of it, let's say, by the court ruling. Joe Tacopina, could you explain what the Son of Sam law is and why it's there?

Tacopina   Well in a nutshell, June, it really is on the books to prevent criminals, predators of victims in society, from profiting from their crimes, because obviously everyone likes to read it. The sex appeal in a real-life criminal story is overwhelming and people love to read it. But with Sondra, no one would accuse her being part of the Gainesville murders. No one would accuse Sondra knowing Danny Rolling during the Gainesville murders. And no one would accuse Sondra of having anything to do with the defense of the defendant during the trial, because he pled guilty. Sondra had a relationship that really was separate and apart, in my opinion, from the intent of the legislature in the Son of Sam laws. And she has got something in writing from Rolling, an affidavit for which he would not profit from the proceeds of the story. With that etched in stone, I don't see why the prosecution, other than either just pure overzealousness, or an attempt to sort of enact revenge on Sondra for what they perceive her role to be. I don't know why they would really go to take that away from Sondra.

Joe Tacopina on Court TV

Grasso Sondra, is there any hope left that you will get the money or is it at the end of the battle?

London Oh, it's not the end of the battle, but I'd like to comment that the ironies of this situation are multiple. First of all, without this Son of Sam law, any victim of any crime already has recourse under the law, to sue for wrongful death or damages, in which they are able to collect one hundred percent of the proceeds, regardless of where the money comes from. Now this law prevents such an action by imposing a preposterous construction, whereby the victims' families in fact only get half of what is claimed. And a full quarter of that money goes to the felon's child. That's right, because my money was seized under this Son of Sam law, Danny Rolling's own daughter gets one quarter of it. Because this State lien law is prior in dignity to any other. These are the details you never hear about this law. I just hope that I can emphasize once again, that it's not a win-lose situation, and that there's a tragedy in every direction, that the suffering that broke out in the violence there in Gainesville started many years before, and that there's a cycle involved there. Danny Rolling, of course, had a conflicted relationship with his mother, because she did enable the abuse to continue. I believe that an important part of why his violence was not just family violence, but why he struck out at society, was because society endorsed the conditions under which he was abused. And the key moment was when his Aunt Agnes tried to complain to the police about the violence that was going on in that house, they said no, Officer Rolling's a good officer, and we don't want to do anything to embarrass him. In that single moment, it became an issue of society's attitudes that bred the conditions that made Danny Rolling into a serial killer.

Grasso   And how does Danny Rolling spend his time on Death Row?

London   He writes fiction and he entertains himself with romantic affairs.

Grasso   How is that? Can you explain that a little? I mean, he writes to people or—

London   And then they come visit him, this-that-&-the-other.

Grasso   You've written a lot, you've had a lot to do with serial killers. What is the attraction? I know a lot of serial killers get a lot of mail from women. What do you think the attraction is there to write to someone, and to get involved with someone who's on Death Row and has admitted killing five people?

London   Well, I'm not in that position myself. I knew a serial killer when I was a teenager, and that's why I was interested in applying my education and my skills towards trying to understand what goes wrong in the mind, to allow the sort of thing to happen. And when the Gainesville murders happened, everyone was saying *why?* Why did this happen? Certainly the answer is locked within the mind of the offender. And it's the offender's choice what he's going to do about that. Some of them go to their graves without revealing anything. Certainly, Danny Rolling wanted to participate in the process of allowing what went wrong in his case to be studied, and that was what we did. We spent five years going over and over everything that he had done wrong. Most of these guys, again, their stories just self-justifying nonsense. Danny Rolling was not that case. He wanted to make amends in some way, to at least figure out what the story was, what happened there.

Grasso   Sondra London, thank you so much for joining us this evening and for your remarkable candor in discussing this case with us. Thanks again

London   Thank you for the opportunity.

Sondra London on Court TV

Sondra London on *NBC Dateline*

In 1997, Sondra London appeared on *NBC Dateline* in an episode called "Double Jeopardy." London was questioned by the anchor Jane Pauley. The focus of the program was Janet Frake, a woman whose rape was described by Danny Rolling in *The Making of a Serial Killer,* without her being identified in any way. Pauley strikes pious poses while publicizing the rape victim's face and name, and inciting so much animosity against London that over 250 death threats were turned over to the police in the wake of this show.

Pauley   You've probably noticed how often *Dateline* tells stories you would not believe if they'd been written for one of those TV movies. This is one of those. It begins as a crime that happens, sadly, every day. But after that this will be a story, one the likes of which you've never heard before.

Frake   I was watching videos at home alone, and was probably watching for an hour, hour and a half at least, and I went to the bathroom, and he was hiding in a – the spare bedroom, and he jumped out and attacked me.

Pauley   (Voiceover) Janet Frake, then 30, was a single woman who lived alone in this house in Sarasota, Florida. Though it was seven years ago, she remembers all too well.

228

Frake   And he threw me into my bedroom onto the floor, and he had the knife in one hand and he put the knife down and he tied my hands up. Then he – well, actually he – yeah, he ripped off my clothes and then he took me into the bathroom and he put me up on the counter, and that's when he raped me. He had the control and the power.

Frake   And he was – it was almost anger in him. A lot of anger and hate and it was – it was scary. It was – I thought I was going to die.

Pauley   (Voiceover) But she didn't. And it's probably because she did something totally unexpected.

Frake   I thought, 'I've got to do something to get him to stop doing this.' So I basically just said, 'Oh my gosh... Let's go have a beer.' And his – it's kind of like, God, that sounded good to him. And he never did rape me again after that.

Pauley   So he had to undo your hands?

Frake   Uh-huh. I went to the refrigerator, and I got a glass and I gave him glass and a beer.

Pauley   (Voiceover) He sat at her kitchen table drinking Keystone Gold beer. He wanted to take off his mask, get comfortable. She wouldn't let him.

Frake   He want to take it off, because it was so hot.

Pauley   But if he took it off...

Frake   Then I would have seen him, and I didn't want to see him.

Pauley   Because he might kill you?

Frake   Uh-huh.

Pauley   (Voiceover) But for the first time, she thought she
         might survive, because in a subtle way, she had
         taken control of the situation.

Pauley   So he sat there at your kitchen table drinking beers
         with his mask on. And what did he tell you about
         himself?

Frake   How bad of a childhood he had, how he's always
         been down on his luck, how he was an outlaw.

Pauley   (Voiceover) He talked for a couple of hours. Then
         she said it was time for him to go, and he did.
         Police arrived within minutes of her call, but he'd
         vanished into the Florida night. Police had no leads.
         The trail went cold. Then five years later, Sarasota
         police detective Robert Gorevan, following a hunch,
         finally put all the pieces together, using DNA to
         link her rape and a horrible crime spree just two
         weeks later. Gorevan asked Janet to come down to
         the station.

Gorevan We just kind of broke it to her that we had, you
         know, reason to believe that we had identified her
         attacker.

(TV broadcast) In Gainesville, Florida, police are still looking
for a suspect in a series of gruesome murders.

Pauley   (Voiceover) It was an awful revelation--the man who
         invaded her apartment, tied her up, raped her at
         knife point, and drank beer at her kitchen table,
         was Danny Rolling. The same man who later that
         month had gone up to Gainesville, to the campus of

the University of Florida. In late August of 1990, a
serial killer held this college community under
siege, breaking into these student apartments. And
in a frenzy of rape and murder, he killed four
women and a man. The media dubbed him the
Gainesville Ripper, because he literally carved up
his victims. This college community was utterly
traumatized. Parents were taking their sons and
daughters home. Some never returned.

(Police at crime scene; police cars; building on University of
Florida campus; students on campus; students crying; police
carrying body out of building; police entering crime scene;
apartment building; photos of young women and young man;
police carrying body in body bag; people hugging and crying;
people packing belongings in cars)

Pauley   (Voiceover) Not even after Danny Rolling was
           arrested and charged with the crimes. And five
           years later, Janet Frake didn't rest easier either.

Frake   I didn't sleep for many nights.

Pauley   Why not?

Frake   Guilt, anger.

Pauley   Guilt?

Frake   Like maybe I could have prevented it.

Pauley   What happened in Gainesville? If only you'd, what?

Frake   Maybe called the police sooner, they would have
           caught him.

Pauley   How long did you wait?

Frake   Well, he told me to wait 15 minutes. And I guess I probably waited 10 and called.

Pauley   And those 10 minutes, you think may have made the difference of what happened in Gainesville?

Frake   Maybe they would have caught him.

(Danny Rolling in court)

Rolling   (Speaking in court) About our world...

Pauley   (Voiceover) In February of 1994, Rolling pleaded guilty to five counts of first degree murder.

Rolling   (Speaking in court) I feel whatever I might have to say at this moment is overshadowed by the suffering I've caused. I regret with all my heart what my hand has done. For I have taken what I cannot return.

Pauley   (Voiceover) The jury was not moved.

(Courtroom scene)

Juror   The majority of the jury advise and recommend to the court that it impose the death penalty.

Pauley   (Voiceover) Rolling was sentenced to death five times over. Today, he's nearly exhausted his appeals.

Pauley   Looking back on it, why didn't he kill you?

Frake   I'll never know that.

Pauley   It's just chilling knowing how close you came.

Frake   Exactly, why didn't he? I'll never know. And that
           bothers me.

Pauley   (Voiceover) At least he's in a place where he can't
           hurt her, or anyone else, again. Or so she thought.
           Then one evening Janet Frake heard a TV news
           report that sent chills up her spine--Danny Rolling
           had written a book.

(Prison interior; book store; *The Making of a Serial Killer*
book cover)

Pauley   Did you know it was available at Barnes & Noble?

Frake   Yes, they said that on TV reports.

Pauley   So you came to look?

Frake   I came to look. Just to see if he had written about
           me.

Pauley   (Voiceover) Now, seven years later, from Death
           Row, Danny Rolling had managed to victimize her
           all over again. Not only was there a book, but with
           the help of another woman, he'd found a loophole in
           cyberspace.

Pauley   Was there anything Janet Frake could do about it?
           When we come back.

Pauley   It sounds too bizarre to be true that a convicted
           serial killer, locked away on Death Row, could
           publish a book that makes his crimes read like pulp
           fiction, and sell it at a mainstream bookstore. But
           that's exactly what Janet Frake would discover. And
           that's not all.

Frake   I started shaking. I was in shock. I couldn't even tell you the words I felt. It was horrifying to see that.

Pauley   (Voiceover) She carried a copy of *The Making of a Serial Killer* to a corner and opened it to find page after page of Rolling's salacious prose and illustrations describing his crimes with lurid grandiosity. Styling himself The Dragon, The Ninja Assassin, The Shadow. Under the title "Attack of the Spider" was Rolling's version of a rape he committed one hot August night in Sarasota.

(Frake in bookstore; book cover; Table Of Contents page; drawings and text from book)

Pauley   It's graphic. It's titillating.

Frake   Oh, yes! It's pornographic, and I couldn't even read it. It just made me nauseous.

Pauley   (Voiceover) Her name is never mentioned, but there's little room for doubt. The victim in the book is Janet Frake. He even talks about the Keystone Gold. "It was really weird," he writes, "almost as though she was entertaining a welcome guest instead of a rapist." If that was bad, maybe this was worse. Rolling was marketing his book on the Internet.

(Frake with cat; glass of beer; text in book; Cyberspace Inmates Web page; Rolling's Web page)

Frake   It's unbelievable that a Death Row inmate can have a home page on the Internet! And you can also get his artwork.

Pauley   (Voiceover) This is the '90s, but how can a serial
           killer have his own Web site? Janet wanted to know.
           And so did we.

Sondra London on NBC Dateline

(Rolling's Web page, Sondra London)

London   Danny Rolling contacted me in 1992 with the
           intention of asking me to help him tell his story.

Pauley   (Voiceover) Meet Sondra London. Through her,
           Rolling has found a way to reach beyond the barbed

wire and steel doors that were meant to keep him from society.

(Sondra London with Jane Pauley; prison guard tower)

Pauley   (Voiceover) Have you basically made a career out of Death Row journalism? Is that fair to say?

London   I suppose you could say that's a fair statement to this point.

Pauley   (Voiceover) Her previous collaborations with murderers and serial killers earned her a dubious distinction as the Death Row Media Queen.

(Book covers)

Pauley   That's an odd thing to be known as, isn't it?

London   It's all pretty odd, Jane.

Pauley   Does it make you uncomfortable?

London   Yes.

Pauley   Does it embarrass you?

London   Yes. I think there's a lot of misperceptions about why I'm doing what I'm doing. Indeed, what am I doing?

Pauley   What do people think that's incorrect? They think you're doing it because what?

London   A lot of people think that I like murder, that I'm attracted to criminals, that I intend to glorify criminals, and that make a million bucks.

Pauley   Are any parts of that true? Do you, in fact, have a fascination with murderers? And have you, in fact, found a meal ticket on Death Row?

London   I don't think either one of those are true. I've had questions that I needed to be answered. And particularly to focus on those who have an uncontrollable compulsion to kill.

Pauley   (Voiceover) But London has helped create what amounts to Danny Rolling Enterprises. Some of the descriptions – killer art, killer letters, killer autographs.

(Rolling's Web page; text on screen)

Pauley   Killer this, killer that. There's something so cold and flip about that. I see no respect for the fact that he earned the title killer by killing a lot of innocent people.

London   Mm-hmm.

Pauley   It's awfully cold.

London   I'm sorry you feel that way, Jane.

Pauley   You don't think it is?

London   I just think that the titles are appropriate.

Pauley   (Voiceover) London is not only Danny Rolling's co-author, architect and keeper of the Danny Rolling Web site until recently, she was his fiancée.

London   No, he doesn't scare me. He trusts me.

Pauley   (Voiceover) That's right. This self-described journalist makes no apologies for falling in love with her subject.

(London surrounded by reporters)

London pursued by reporters: "No comment."

(Rolling at sentencing hearing)

Rolling   Sondra, they can't stamp out the love and affection that I have for you in my heart.

Pauley   (Voiceover) They became engaged in February of 1993, though they only met once, face to face, in prison. And again at this sentencing hearing three years ago when he serenaded her!

(Rolling at sentencing hearing; police officers)

Rolling   (Singing) I recall the day I first saw you. I reached out to say I love you.

Pauley   (Voiceover) Do you believe that either one of them is really in love with the other one?

(London at sentencing hearing)

Frake   No. She's just an opportunist.

Pauley   He's got some weird kind of status going when you can find him at the bookstore, at the mall. And as long as that's going on, even though he's on Death Row, he's got some kind of intellectual freedom, doesn't he?

Frake   Absolutely. It's almost like he has a job.

GAINESVILLE SUN SATURDAY, DECEMBER 6, 1997

LONDON: State law challenged

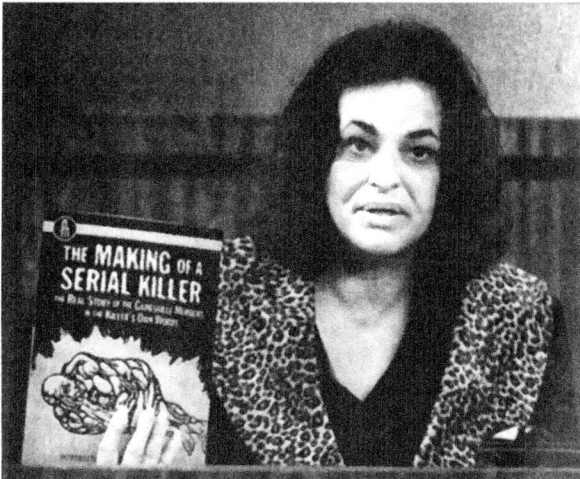

STEPHEN MORTON/The Gainesville Sun
Writer Sondra London, in an Alachua County courtroom Friday, holds a copy of the book she co-wrote with convicted murderer Danny Rolling.

Pauley   (Voiceover) A Florida statute prohibits a convicted felon from profiting from a published account of the crime for which he was convicted. The law also applies to anyone on the felon's behalf. And because the Florida attorney general says that includes

Sondra London, the state has put a lien on her profits from the book.

(Court building; London; Attorney General logo; legal documents: "A lien...on royalties, commissions, proceeds of sale")

Pauley   Do you have a contract together?

London   We have contracts. Multiple contracts. He ceded the rights to all of his writing, his artwork, any form of utterances to me, irrevocably. And indicated that he would never receive any financial remuneration through me or, in any regard, to the projects that we were collaborating on.

Frake   I think that's why they didn't get married, if they truly were going to ever, Sondra and Rolling. Because then they couldn't have written the book and he couldn't have gotten any money.

Pauley   (Voiceover) In June of 1996, the engagement was called off. London says she didn't want to be tied down. London claims her work has been acknowledged as invaluable research on serial killers by the former FBI agent often credited with coining the term. But in a statement for *Dateline*, Robert Ressler said, 'the material is written in an exploitative style and is clearly targeted to the true crime voyeur.'

Pauley   To have a Web site, to have a book with your name on it, when Danny Rolling in his whole life has never done anything worth writing to anybody except to kill people. That's not glorification of the crime?

London   Mm-hmm. I think a lot of serial killers go through a phase when they're first arrested, and their face is in all the papers, and on TV, and in the headlines, where they're going from being a zero to a hero.

Pauley   But whatever you say about the perhaps lofty purposes of your book, that doesn't apply to selling that autograph.

(Voiceover) Yes, Danny Rolling autographs. London hints the price is somewhere between $25 and $75.

(Danny Rolling signature)

Pauley   That autograph is being sold purely for the purposes of the celebrity cult of the serial killer.

London   Uh-huh. Is there a question?

Pauley   How can you do that?

London   How can I do it?

Pauley   Yeah.

London   I have something, and you want it, you need to pay me for it.

Pauley   (Voiceover) And it's legal. Because an autograph could not be described as an account of a crime. Rolling will never be prosecuted for raping Janet Frake. Prosecutors deem it a waste of taxpayers money to try a man on Death Row. So last spring Janet Frake filed a million-dollar civil suit, though it meant surrendering her anonymity.

Pauley   It's possible that your going public with us was a mistake, that you might be feeding his ego, you might be giving him the very thing he needs.

Frake   Possibly.

Pauley   But what choice do you have?

Frake   I don't have any choices.

Pauley   (Voiceover) Danny Rolling does not have $1 million to lose. And even Frake's lawyer concedes she's not likely to win because of the statute of limitations.

(Sketch of Rolling in jail)

Pauley   And you're never going to see a nickel!

Frake   No.

Pauley   You're never going to see a penny. In fact, it might cost you something?

Frake   Well, it already has. Lost work time, driving to the attorney. I mean, yeah, it's cost me time. You know, emotional. I'm tired of it, and he needs to stop!

Pauley   What will it take for you to stop?

Frake   Maybe when he goes to the electric chair.

Pauley   (Voiceover) Incredibly, despite the DNA match, and the similarity of details in her police report, and his book...

Pauley   (Voiceover) Danny Rolling still denies that he raped Janet Frake. We wanted to ask him about that. So, in August, I e-mailed our questions through his Web site.

Frake   What did you say?

Pauley   (Reading e-mail message) Were you the man who attacked Janet Frake in August of 1990. If not, can you explain the coincidences between her attack and your story, "Attack of the Spider"? Two questions. Do you think I'll get an answer?

London   I have no idea, Jane.

Pauley   (Voiceover) We have no idea if Danny Rolling even got the message. We never heard from him. And while he's never had direct access to the Internet, in October, Sondra London was officially notified that the e-mail messages she had been sending via the post office were now considered contraband. The home page does not advise visitors that e-mail messages to Danny Rolling will no longer be delivered. However, a message from Janet Frake was. After seven years of silence, seven years of keeping her attack a secret from almost everyone, including her parents, Frake does not want Rolling to be the only one doing the talking. She shared with *Dateline* a videotaped message she sent to him in prison.

Frake   (On videotape) You're less than a man, you're less than a human. And mostly, you didn't have the power, or the control. I saved my own life that night. I summoned--summoned up every part of my body and my soul to survive. I will close by telling you, that you know what? You will never forget me, for the rest of your life, however brief that may be. You are nothing! And today and every day I can celebrate my life! That is justice.

Pauley   Several other major book chains also sell Rolling's book. Barnes & Noble is not the only one. But in a statement it said, "We do not feel we have the right as a retailer to censor the reading tastes of the public." Janet Frake said she hopes people would buy something for your kids instead.

Janet Frake & Robert Gorevan

Rape Victim Janet Frake's identity was never revealed by Danny Rolling or Sondra London; Frake herself chose to let NBC broadcast her face and name over national TV. Here she poses with the detective who claimed to match DNA to Rolling "on a hunch." But since the statute of limitations for rape had long since run out, no charges could ever be brought. And since no DNA is ever run by the Florida State Lab without an active case number attached, it's evident that NBC's sensational coverage is not only hypocritical and fraudulent, but malicious.

Sondra London on *Ron & Ron*

On November 10, 1994, Sondra London appeared on a radio show called *Ron & Ron,* nationally syndicated out of Tampa, Florida. Ron Bennington & Ron Diaz were the hosts. There were callers on the line and an assortment of visitors in the control room who spoke up, including Hulk Hogan's manager Jimmy Hart and a standup act called the Disciples of Comedy, comprising Mitchell Walters and Jimmy Shubert. The transcript does not distinguish who said what, but Ron Diaz played the heavy, Ron Bennington played the gentleman, and the others played the clowns.

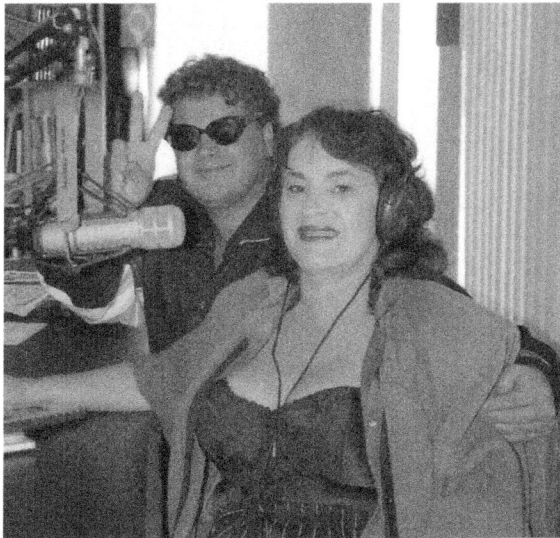

Sondra London with Ron Bennington

Ron Diaz

Ron: All right, Sondra is here. Sondra, welcome. (Applause)

Ron: Welcome to the show. Congratulations on your song.

Sondra: Thank you. *All the Fallen Angels.*

Ron: Did you have any help from Danny writing this? Or did you write it yourself?

London   I wrote it myself, but it was written from real life. The imagery of the fallen angel is taken from a drawing Danny did.

Ron   We were asking this question off the air. When you met Danny, he had already been arrested?

London   That's right. He contacted me in June of 1992 and asked me to help him tell his story.

Ron   His side of it?

London   Yes.

Ron   Do you believe he's guilty of the murders?

London   Yes, look. This is his drawing of a Fallen Angel.

Ron   Ah, look. He's talented.

Danny Rolling :- 1-5-96 ★ ☾⁞-

London It's really not so much that he's talented, but that he uses his talent to probe within his mind.

Ron   Now, they let him draw, paint in prison?

London Yes.

Ron   And right now he's listening?

London I hope so, yes.

Ron   What do you want to say to him?

London Danny, this one's dedicated to you.

Ron   We're gonna listen to the song, but we're gonna go to a break right now. Sondra's gonna remain with us. You comfortable, everything okay?

London   Yes, everything's fine.

Ron   Want some coffee or anything?

London   Yes, I sure do.

Ron   All right. If you like, we have wine or beer.

London   Greeeeeeat. (Laughter)

Ron   Whatever you like.

London   I haven't even had my coffee yet, you know, that's kind of moving right along, isn't it?

Ron   Yes, it is. (Break) Sondra London is here with us this morning. She's the girlfriend of convicted serial killer Danny Rolling who is on Death Row right now.

Ron   We were just posing for some pictures for Danny. So he can see what the whole gang looks like.

Ron   You and Danny have never had a physical relationship, right, Sondra?

London   A physical relationship?

Ron   Uh-huh.

London   Well, we met personally, and we talked behind glass.

Ron   So you've never even kissed him or touched him?

London   I've never kissed or touched him.

Ron   You never will be able to.

London   I don't know about that.

Ron   You think he's gonna be let out?

London   No.

Ron   Okay, so you realize he is one day gonna be executed.

London   Yes, I do.

Ron   How does that make you feel?

London   Not good. How must it make anyone feel?

Ron   True. Now that is what your song, you were describing to me off the air, Ronnie didn't even know this, but she wrote the song while coming to visit us in May to arrange the rights to *Mystery Rider.*

Ron   That's when you wrote this song?

London   Yeah, riding down the road. That's where I got the melody. But the words, part of them, were released as a press release on the last day of the trial, because this song really came out of my experiences of sitting through the trial, where someone that I love was sentenced to die. I was an observer, I was also a participant. I was also very touched by the victims' families...

Ron   Did you talk to the victims' families?

London   Well, they talked to me, they hurled death threats at me, but...

Ron   But can you understand their rage?

London   Yes. I think that came out in the song, because I think a lot of people have cast me as a dragon lady, the enemy, saying that I'm callous, I love murder, or whatever, but it's not true.

Ron   Well, how did you fall in love with this man?

London   I was trying to tell you about the song, I'll be glad to tell you about Danny, but...

Ron   Okay, tell us about the song.

Ron   Don't badger her.

London   It's okay, I'll tell you why I love Danny, let's just try and finish this one first.

Ron   Okay.

London   So, sitting there through the trial, seeing the victims' families and what they were going through, it's a torment. And I think people don't realize that the offender goes through quite a lot of torment as well, particularly if he is guilty. I think a lot of people believe they are getting away with something, and they're happy...

Ron   Yes.

London   Or they're getting over, they're 100% behind what they've done, but with Danny, that's not the case.

Ron   He's sorry.

London   He's *real* sorry. And I felt, on my own behalf, that I love him. And everyone is trying to make this very hard for both of us, come between us, tell us that we're insincere about each other, and so forth, it's very difficult. So going through this trial and all, I lost my voice because of the stress that was coming from every direction. I couldn't raise my voice to a normal level. And out of that came this song. Because I just could not express the complete combination of things that were going on there except through this song.

Ron   All right. *All the Fallen Angels.* (Plays song.)

ALL THE FALLEN ANGELS
by Sondra London ©1994-2021

Between the land of the living & the land of the dead
Is a place they call Death Row
Where all the fallen angels slowly go insane
Looking in a mirror & seeing the Grim Reaper
In their own... eyes.

The undead memories of the lives you have taken
They won't let you rest, every night you awaken.
They're dancing on your grave, demanding nothing less
Than your whole life.
Cause you've been dancing with the Reaper
Now every day you see him
In your own... eyes.

You talk to yourself, you whistle in the dark
Your dreams become real... as reality just slips away
Like some long-forgotten dream
& you don't know what it means
When you look into a mirror & see that old Grim Reaper
In your own... eyes.

But what of Love, sweet Love?
Can it cross into that doomed domain
Where all the fallen angels slowly go... insane
From seeing the Grim Reaper, & every day they see him
In their own... eyes?

Questions may be asked
But the answers come back in their own way
As we look into a mirror & see that old Grim Reaper
In our own... eyes

SPOKEN:
*This is for all the fallen angels
On Death Row all over the world.
Some are guilty of terrible crimes
But all are part of humankind.
With bloodstained hands & haunted eyes
They live with death, they'd die for life.
Execution makes us killers too.
I know, I'm a killer, and so are you.
Vengeance demands the killer die.
When will we stop and wonder... why?
God help us all.*

Ron   (Applause) Sondra London. Now, Eddie, I noticed on the cart you put together you put "Sondra Locke." That's Clint Eastwood you're thinking about there.

Eddie   I'm sorry, I was so captivated by the music, I wasn't even thinking about the name.

Ron   That's a nice voice you have, I'll say that. Now in the song you're saying we're all murderers. How do you figure that?

London   Well, so long as we are citizens of a state that espouses execution, so long as we're in a courtroom dancing up & down with *joy*, that someone is gonna be *killed...* that makes us the same.

Ron   So you're saying we're as guilty as Danny.

252

Cheering the Death of Danny Rolling

London   I'm not gonna really, you know, this is not a political campaign, it's not a polemic, it's just a song.

Ron   All right.

London   And like I say, we can ask these questions, hopefully sooner or later, someone will look into the mirror and see in their own eyes the same lust to kill that they are so upset about in the killer.

Ron   You were saying earlier that Danny is very sorry. He's told you this?

London   Yes.

Ron   Was it because he had some kind of a bad childhood? Or... what got him to this point?

London   Well, I think that reduces the situation to simplicities, and certainly there are many contributing factors to any violent act that erupts, and it goes back for years in the offender's life. The Danny Rolling case illustrates some very important issues regarding the kinds of things that go into the making of a serial killer. We certainly had the child abuse. And then further, which I think is more important to what I'm trying to say, is that when the abuse was reported, they refused to take the reports. And in that sense, that means all of us are involved here. We all made him.

Ron   Who abused him?

London   It was within the family, domestic abuse. What I'm saying the domestic abuse could have been isolated right there, it could have been stopped. But when the family turned for help, it was refused. So then the problem got worse. In Danny's case we also had a situation of prison abuse, and this is another question I'm interested in exploring, the fact that we completely discard those who have failed in our society. We start when they're kids, and they may just be high-spirited kids who just have no direction, not evil people in their heart...

Ron   So you don't think he was evil? At that time?

London   Not just Danny, but a lot of kids. What happens to them when they fool around and get messed up with the juvenile justice system? Sooner or later we put them in prison. You know, it's really a monster factory. You take a kid that's just looking for kicks, you put him in there and send him to crime college, he learns more and better ways of committing crime, you pack all the hatred into him, all the rejection, all the failure, and you can't execute all of them, you know, you can't kill them all.

Ron   Although that would be a good idea.

London   Most of them are going to be coming out. Well, they're you.

Ron   No, they're not me.

London   They are your sons, they are your brothers...

Ron   But at one time this was a little baby, right?

London   At one time, this person, like I say, it's a fallen angel. This is a person, any offender, please try and broaden this.

Ron   Okay.

London   I think what's wrong with us that keeps us breeding more Danny Rollings, and certainly this is getting worse, is that we are in denial about those of us who fail, and we have this knee-jerk reaction of lock-em-up, throw-away-the-key, burn-em, that'll solve the problem.

Ron   What do you think you should do with a Danny Rolling?

London   I think that when you have a troubled family or a troubled juvenile situation, it should be part our thinking that we immediately provide help, rather than trying to isolate one offender and decide whether or not to punish them.

Ron   Okay, we gotta do a break right now... (Break) I'm looking at the lyric sheets here, *Songs by Sondra London,* and there's a little note here: "This song is for Death Row inmates all over the world and for those who have not forgotten them. It was composed by Sondra London for Danny Rolling after he was given five death sentences in Gainesville Florida on April 20, 1994." You say as you sat in court, there were victims' family members that were talking to you.

London   They threatened to kill me.

Ron   Did you speak back to them?

London   I don't think so, no.

Ron   One thing Sondra asked before she did our show is
           that we wouldn't do any surprise victims' family
           members on her, you know.

Ron   What about phone calls? From just listeners? You
           can handle that?

London   Yes, I've had one cup now, so I guess I'm about up
           to running speed.

Ron   Coffee we got, Sondra.

London   Hit me, hit me. (Laughter)

Ron   Bring the pot in here, Denise.

Ron   I notice this is not just one song you have here, *All
           the Fallen Angels,* there's an actual, there's a whole
           album.

London   There's one song in there, *Dangerous Pussycat,*
           which Danny Rolling is particularly fond of.

Ron   Why's that?

London   Because he's my dangerous pussycat, and I love to
           make him *yowl.* (Laughter)

Ron   So at this point all you do is send pictures to him?

London   Send pictures? No, we write letters.

Ron   Oh yeah, write letters, but I mean there's no visits?

London   That's right.

Ron   Is that *Dangerous Pussycat,* kinda like "Dangerous
           pussycat, whoa-a-woe-a-woe" (sung like the song
           "What's New Pussycat")?

London No, no, no, that's someone else's song. That's stupid.

Ron It's not a parody, right?

London You do parody, Ron. I'm not Weird Al Yankovic.

Ron (Laughter) That's what I do.

Ron All right, let's take some calls here. Carlos?

Caller Yeah.

Ron Go ahead.

Caller I'm calling from Miami. First of all I want to say "Maha bone."

Ron "Maha bone" to you too, brother.

Ron "Maha bone" to all our friends.

Caller First of all, I'd like to say, I can understand you meet somebody, in the course of work, whatever, but I mean, just, you can't say, I know he killed somebody, but outside of that he really is a good person. No, because he's a killer, he's a serial killer, that's part of his personality, that's who he is. And I can't see how anybody, how could she?

Ron Al Capone had a family.

Caller How could she fall in love with this guy?

Ron How did you fall in love with him? I asked that question earlier.

London That's right, I appreciate the opportunity to...

Caller   You know, I saw her yesterday on I don't know whether it's Geraldo, or one of these talk shows, and she's playing how she fell in love with him, he was writing to her, because he was getting a lot of fan mail, and he wanted everyone to know how he felt, this and that, I don't know, it's inconceivable.

Ron   So you started writing to him?

London   No.

Ron   How did it happen?

London   He contacted me, he had seen a screenplay I wrote, he contacted me and wanted me to help him tell his story. So we began corresponding. First of all, a lot of people don't realize I've been working with inmates for six years.

Ron   Oh, okay.

London   And I have extensive contact not just with killers but with serial killers and so forth. So the fact that Danny is a killer, or a serial killer, isn't really as unusual to me as it might be to someone who did not have this background.

Ron   Have you had relationships with other prisoners?

London   Well, relationships, not in terms of being in love or being engaged to be married, no. I've had working relationships with them, yes.

Ron   But you've never been in love with another inmate then?

London   That's right. But there's quite a difference in personality with Danny.

Ron   What is it about Danny?

London   Okay. What is it about Danny? Well, first of all, what people don't realize is that it's not that he committed the crimes, it's how he is about it. And what at this point of time, as I met him, what he wanted me to work with him to DO about it. And that is, he wants me to study him to help explain what I see there, to him and to the world, to at least offer up his life, or the tragedy of his life, so that possibly some understanding can be gained, as to how his life went wrong. And if somebody else is coming along, struggling with the same kinds of compulsive urges to commit violence or whatever, possibly his story will help. Now I find that very engaging, or disarming, or attractive per se, because most serial killers are very defensive, play games, do not want to be known...

Ron   Ted Bundy. I mean I hate to call people names, but I mean, right up the last second he lied.

Ron   Well, look at John Gacy.

London   I worked with Gacy.

Ron   Did you?

London   Yes. And Gacy and I went round and round on his autobiography, and Gacy was in total denial, and he wanted to propagate lies about his case, and about the FBI in particular. I couldn't deal with that. Danny Rolling is completely different. He has been very cooperative.

Ron   Stand-up?

London   Stand up?

Ron   You know, like a stand-up guy? In terms of convicts...

London   Oh yeah, yeah. I think he qualifies for that.

Ron   So he's always admitted it to you.

London   Prior to his being tried, if he had admitted to me that he had committed the murders, they would have had to make me a witness against him.

Ron   How did you get involved in working with prisoners, working with inmates?

London   Well, this kinda goes back a long way. When I was very young, about 17, I had a boyfriend who is now at Florida State Prison.

Ron   Is he on Death Row?

London   No, he's doing double lifes. He was convicted of killing two young women, and connected with the disappearances of approximately 32 others.

Ron   And you were his girlfriend then?

London   Yes. For a year. I was very close to him and he was a very nice boy, and I knew him very well. When I found out nine years later, when it was all over the news, it was a shock to me, and it was a mystery to me, that I wanted to research and understand, how can this be possible for you to know someone so well, and for them to have a secret life at the same time.

Ron   So for nine years you had no idea this man was a murderer.

London   No, he was out of my life. Then my family brought me the headlines. So at that point that began to be a kind of a puzzle. Then in 1989 I contacted him and we worked on a book at that time.

Ron   What's his name?

London   His name is Schaefer.

Ron   And he's at the same prison as Danny?

London   Yeah.

Ron   Do they know each other?

London   Well, Schaefer knows about Danny.

Ron   Of course.

London   And he's a little bit unhappy.

Ron   A little jealous?

London   I guess.

Ron   Cause he feels abandoned.

Ron   Sorry, Schaef!

London   Oh well.

Ron   Well, Schaef ain't gettin' out either.

Ron   You know? Easy come easy go, baby!

Ron   Best man wins!

Ron   That's right!

London   Well, Danny's younger, better looking.

Ron   He's got it all over him.

London   You want to know what his qualities are that I see in him?

Ron   What are they?

London   Danny's tough, he's very rugged, he's also sensitive and creative, and he loves me like a *maniac*.

Ron   Like a maniac, Ronnie.

Ron   I know Danny's listening, I hope Schaefer isn't.

London   I don't care if he is.

Ron   Cause he's gettin' his heart broken all over again.

London   Oh well. His whole life is gonna be a heartbreak, you know, because this is reality.

Ron   If Schaefer's listening, he's probably got that steel cup, rippin' it along the bars right now, "Lemme outta here!" (Laughter)

Ron   Now wouldn't you be afraid if you had a chance to be alone with Danny, that he would commit an act like he did to the Gainesville women?

London   No.

Ron   Why do you think he wouldn't?

London   Well, if you know anything about his case, you'd know that's not typical of his behavior.

Ron   He's changed.

Ron   What is typical of his behavior?

London   These murders were not committed against
         someone he knew. He had a social life. He had girls
         that he dated. Even after committing the
         Gainesville murders, he went to Tampa and spent
         the night with a girl, and he slept on her sofa.

Ron   You know, we talked to a girl that he dated, and she
         had no idea he was the Gainesville murderer.

London   Well, that's typical of a serial killer. It's a very
         unusual condition, I think the media makes it seem
         like it's very common because they focus on it in so
         many stories. In truth, it's a very unusual type of
         personality or case.

Ron   Mike, you have a question for Sondra?

Mike   Yeah, it's actually a statement. I'm not real sure
         she's part retarded or just a hell of an entrepreneur.
         She's a little on the loose side, I mean.

Ron   You gotta admit, it's a good song.

Mike   Well, yeah, she's gonna make some money. That's
         the important thing.

Ron   Is it, Sondra, is it the important thing?

London   You know, that's all anyone ever talks about is
         money.

Ron   Have you made any money off the Danny Rolling
         case?

London   Absolutely not. I'll be glad to give the state all the
         money I've made off of this.

Ron   Isn't there a ruling in the past that someone who
         has committed a crime cannot benefit?

Ron   But Ronnie, we're not talking about money here, we're talking about art.

London   Yes. That law is unconstitutional.

Ron   But it has passed.

London   Hold on. Hold your horses, let's go real slow here.

Ron   The law has passed.

Ron   Slow down, Ronnie.

Sondra London in Bradford County Courthouse with her attorneys, Lloyd Vipperman and Mary Day Coker.

London   The Son of Sam law was overturned by the United States Supreme Court in December of 1992, before I started with Danny Rolling, Okay, well-advised by counsel that I reside within the Constitution of the United States. Florida has a Son of Sam law which had never been applied to anyone. They have unconstitutionally applied it to me. And wrongfully so. I am not a felon. I am a journalist.

Ron   But you cannot benefit.

London   The lien that the state took out against me was overturned in the First District Court of Appeals, the panel of judges using such words as "dismayed" and "appalled" at the state for bringing this suit and for the trial judge ruling the way that he did. Now they've brought it back again, I have the ACLU behind me, this is a First Amendment case, I am a journalist.

Ron   So it's not over.

London   Of course it's not over.

Ron   Okay, we're going to a break... (Break) Okay, we've got Jimmy Hart (Hulk Hogan's manager) *and* Sondra London. Is there a possible management situation here, Jimmy?

Jimmy   You know, it could be. She looks pretty hot, she looks pretty good, man, she's definitely got, uh... about maybe... what's the weight, sweetheart?

London   Don't get into that.

Jimmy   Oh, *scuse me!*

London   That was so rude of you. That is so tacky, I mean, we have serious issues we can discuss, and here you...

Jimmy   And you don't think weight is one of them.

London   I certainly wouldn't make any comment about *your* weight.

Jimmy   I know, I know, now we're friends.

London   Which I *could.*

Jimmy   But we're friends!

London   Let me ask you, who looks better, me or him?

All   (Clapping & chanting) *SON-DRA! SON-DRA! SON-DRA!*

London   Yes! Yes! Yes!

Ron   Sondra, I've been nothing but on your side today.

London   You're right. You're a sweetie.

Ron   And I've been nothing but against you. All day. (Laughter)

London   You're a pussycat.

Ron   I'm your *dangerous* pussycat.

London   Yes, yes, yes. Mercy mercy me.

Ron   Now Jimmy, isn't it odd that you would come to the studio on this day, when Sondra, the girlfriend of Danny Rolling, is here?

Jimmy   You know, I can't believe this, this place has gone wild and crazy. I come in here, you've got the Dead German Tourists laying out all over the living room out here, the front room, they want to challenge Hulk Hogan and the Rassling Boot Band to a battle of the bands, can you believe this?

Ron   Yeah, I'd love to see that.

Ron   It's unreal. But are you guys gonna be able to make it to Orlando? (segue into Hulk Hogan infomercial)

Ron   Now Jimmy, you know music. Did you hear Sondra's song?

Jimmy   Yeah, I did.

Ron   Did you like it?

Jimmy   Yeah I did, really. But someone said, "You know it's gonna be a hit. It's gonna hit every trashcan in Florida." But I said, "Are you crazy?" I didn't say it, Sondra, I'm telling you that right now, sweetheart, but this is what one of the Dead German Tourists said a while ago. But I'd kinda like to listen to it again maybe later on.

Ron   Okay, you got it, Jimmy.

Jimmy   I'd love to listen to it again.

Ron   The name of it is *All the Fallen Angels.* Here's a cassette copy of it.

Jimmy   Ah, can I have a cassette?

Ron   Sondra?

London   Sure.

Jimmy   Beautiful! Thank you very much.

Jimmy   This is actually a beautiful song, Ronnie. And Ronnie, I don't wanna tell you how to live your life. But sometimes I wish you'd look for that old grim reaper in your own eyes.

Ron   When I hear those lyrics, I personally want to choke Danny. This is the way I feel, for what he did. And I don't see how you've fallen in love with this man.

Jimmy   But that's her point.

Ron   I don't understand that.

London   That's all part of it, that's what I'm hoping that you will see, Ron.

Ron   What?

London   That you have that same feeling in your own heart.

Ron   I've never murdered anyone.

London   No. But you wanted to.

Ron   But I haven't.

London   I know, but that's not the point.

Ron   There's a big big difference between wanting to and doing it.

London   Sure there is, sure there is. Sure there is a difference. And that accounts in a big way for why we're so fascinated with tales of violence.

Ron   Right.

London   Because most of us don't ever commit the violence. But we think about it. But certainly we are not so different from the violent offenders as we would like to think.

Ron   We're not that far removed from the apes.

London   Wasn't Jimmy Carter talking about lusting in your heart?

Ron   Right.

London   There's some truth there.

Ron   And Jimmy, you'll back me up on that, the last time
             you refereed a bout, where Henry Aaron attacked
             Ron Diaz with a cane...

Jimmy   It wasn't Henry Aaron. It was you.

Ron   ... here's a guy that you consider to be a champion
             role model of children, you know, a home run
             leader of all time...

Ron   Jimmy, did you witness Henry Aaron hitting me?

Jimmy   Can I tell you the truth?

Ron   Yeah.

Jimmy   I was a referee that night, and you know referees
             never see anything, man. So I'd love take sides, but
             you guys are my favorite tag team, you know that,
             and I like Ron, and I like Ron, and I'm just happy to
             be here, brother.

Ron   Way to straddle it.

Jimmy   (Singing) When you see that old grim reaper in
             your own eyes...

Ron   Do any of the other songs on this album, Sondra,
             have that same feel? That same, almost a calypso, a
             Caribbean-type thing?

London   Yes, a lot of my music has that same feel.

Ron   Do you have any that are hard rockers on the
             album?

London   Yes, there's *My Sexual Connection.*

Ron   Whooooo.

London   That's a pretty hard rocker.

Ron   Cue that one up. Check it out.

London   I had my own reggae band for seven years.

Ron   Oh really?

London   Yes.

Ron   Reggae, that's where that's coming from.

London   Yes.

Ron   We said it was an island sound.

Ron   Kind of a Mediterranean feeling. Or Caribbean actually.

London   Yeah.

Ron   So when you and Danny, if you and Danny ever get a chance to get together, is it gonna be very romantic, I mean are you going to be like animals together?

London   You know, I've imagined that moment a million times, and I've imagined it a million different ways. I just don't know. When we were actually... I mean we both kind of took turns saying to the other one to just chill, you know, it's Okay, kind of an overcome by emotion feeling, and you really don't know how to act.

Ron   And you were separated by glass?

London   Yeah. But they have rules, you know, about your demeanor and your physical contact. So you can't really just throw each other down and rip your clothes off, you know.

Ron   Did you wear something sexy when you went to see him?

London   No, you better not, not in a prison.

Ron   Right.

Ron   Well, this morning you have an excellent bustier.

London   Yes, thank you.

Ron   Even BL said during the break, "Nice pups."

London   What a rude... there you go again.

Ron   Who said it?

Ron   BL said it, I'm just telling you what...

BL   Don't look at me.

London   You know, I mean, that is so tacky, Ron...

Ron   I think it's more tacky to fall in love with a serial killer actually.

Ron   Ronnie, now you're nit-picking, now you're nit-picking.

Ron   Hey I'm making a comment, actually repeating a comment that BL made about your pups, and you're offended by that.

London   Do we have to hear this?

Ron   And yet you're not offended...

London   This is the third time now. Do we have to hear this?

Ron	And yet you're not offended by the fact that this guy has been convicted of killing...
London	Allegedly.
Ron	...not allegedly, he's been convicted of killing four women and a man.
London	Yeah.
Ron	That doesn't offend you?
London	Sure it does.
Ron	Then how can you be in love with him?
London	It's a very complicated situation.
Ron	Well, try to explain it.
London	Here, Ron, here's a mirror. Look for the old grim reaper in your own eyes.
Ron	I've never killed anybody, Sondra.
All	(Singing) In your own eyes, in your own eyes, in your own eyes.
Ron	Only love can kill the demon.
Ron	That's right. Only love, Ronnie.
Ron	Yeah. Rebecca?
Caller	Yes.
Ron	Go ahead, you're on.
Caller	Thank God. Ron Diaz, I want to give you a hand. Danny Rolling is not worth the dynamite it would

take to blow him to hell. Y'all are running a vigil for that man up there.

Ron   (Singing) When you see that old grim reaper...

All   (Singing)... in your own eyes, in your own eyes, in your own eyes.

Caller   That's sick.

Ron   You see, Ronnie.

Ron   No, I don't see. I don't see at all, at all.

Ron   Ron, we're all sick.

Ron   No, we're not.

Ron   We're all sick. (Laughter)

Ron   We're not sick. We didn't kill people.

Ron   No, no we didn't.

Ron   So we're not all sick. He is sick, he's a murderer. I'm not a murderer.

London   But when we start in with the "burn-em, blast-em"—

Ron   Kill-em...

London   —then we are killers in our own hearts. I'm just hoping that sooner or later it will dawn on people that there's a certain sense of irony there, when you want to kill someone because they have killed, and you feel you are better than them—

Ron   Right.

London   —you can say, "I want to kill," you know, but he can't.

Ron   Right.

Ron   Saying it and doing it are a little bit different. Hello, Chrissie?

Caller   Yeah.

Ron   What's happening?

Caller   I'm totally on your side, Ron Diaz, Okay, love is great and everything, and I think she should reevaluate that, but I don't wish her any harm or anything, but I don't think she's been a victim of a murder. I mean, I have. My whole family wanted to kill this guy at one point. But I mean come on. We're human beings, we're God-abiding citizens, and I just don't feel, I don't know. I just think that the man upstairs is going to take care of the person who did this. He is sick. He is totally sick.

Ron   Thanks for the call, Chrissy.

Ron   Well, you know, we can all sit here and name-call.

London   Just because I sing in a soft voice and just because I'm in love, please don't get the idea that I'm excusing Danny Rolling for the crimes, or any offender for the crimes they have committed.

Ron   Okay.

London   My song portrays what it's like to sit on Death Row having done terrible things, and having to contemplate that. My song just depicts and puts the focus on the fact that Death Row is a place to be.

Ron   When I heard the song, I was literally picturing that. It's eerie.

London   It's a state of mind that a lot of us are in, it's a place... and I don't think it says, "Yea, killers," or anything like that.

Ron   Have you written a song or thought about writing a song about the execution itself?

London   No.

Ron   Okay, we're going to a break... (Break) Sondra, during the break you got a chance to meet a couple of the Disciples of Comedy, Mitchell Walters and Jimmy Shubert.

Jimmy   Hello, Sondra, how are you?

London   We're well acquainted.

Mitchell   We've put together the Top Ten Reasons Danny "Rollins" is on Death Row.

London   "*ROW*-ling."

Mitchell   "*ROW*-ling."

Ron   Why can't you get it right?

Jimmy   Number ten. He was his Uncle Larry's boy toy.

Mitchell   Nine. He didn't have cable.

Jimmy   Number eight. He loves the idea of visitors by appointment only.

Mitchell   He needed some time to catch up on his reading.

Jimmy   Number six. He got caught.

Mitchell   Number five. He wanted to retire to Gainesville at an early age.

Jimmy   Number four. He wanted to test the court system.

Mitchell   Number three. Needed a good long look at himself.

Jimmy   Number two. Loves the idea of having to wear one outfit only.

Mitchell   Number one reason Danny Rahlins is on Death Row. It's a great way to meet chicks. (Laughter, applause, cheering)

Jimmy   She's looking at you like a serial killer's old lady.

London   He won't say his name right.

Jimmy   Say his name right. Danny Rolling.

London   See, that's what I mean—

Jimmy   (Singing) Rolling, Rolling, Rolling...

London   —you people must be inbred or something.

Jimmy   (Singing) Here comes Danny Rolling, Rawhide... move-em up, head-em out, fry-em down, *kkkkkkxxx...*

Mitchell   Jimmy, be nice.

Jimmy   I'm sorry.

Mitchell   I saw your show last night. You oughta see the big grim reaper in your own eyes. It's time for an intervention with you, my friend.

Jimmy   Ronnie, I was in denial, but no longer. I'm gonna face, I'm gonna take a meeting...

Mitchell Were you hammered last night?

Jimmy   No, I wasn't hammered last night. I mean, you know. Okay, I was a little hammered.

Mitchell He was drunk.

Jimmy   But after the show, after the show.

Mitchell That's denial.

Ron   No, but BL was at the show and she said it was during and before the show when the drinking was taking place.

Jimmy   No, absolutely not true. I only got hammered after I finished work.

Mitchell I saw him at the hotel. He was trashed. Don't listen to him.

Ron   Was he really?

Mitchell He was trashed.

Ron   Oh you met them last night?

Mitchell Forget it.

Ron   And Sondra is a good judge of people.

Jimmy   Yeah. Obviously. I'd like to say good morning to Veronica.

Ron   Who's Veronica?

Jimmy	She's a girl I met about four years ago, we were involved in a relationship.
Ron	Is she on Death Row?
Jimmy	She was almost last night if I would have stayed at her house.
Ron	What happened?
Jimmy	The weirdest thing happened. I met her four years ago, and we hit it off really good but she was going out with someone else. And I'm not like, you know, that other guy in our group.
Ron	You're not moving in on her.
Jimmy	Exactly.
Ron	Danger Wolf.
Jimmy	Yeah. Whatever. Nothin. Hello goodbye, we called a few times. Now four years later she's working for a company selling musical whatever...
Ron	Could you be a little more vague?
Jimmy	Muzak, she's selling Muzak.
Ron	She's selling kazoos door to door. (Kazoo imitations) Hey!
Jimmy	So she goes to Bonkers in Orlando where I was at Universal for Fright Week, and comes and sees me. But she's living with this guy. Now I find out during dinner that the guy wanted to go to the show, and she said, well I'm just going with all the girls. She did go with all the girls, she came and saw the show. Now I find out over dinner last night, she's telling me the guy wanted to know who I was.

Ron   There's a guy after you now?

Jimmy   I had no idea. He came to Bonkers looking for me Saturday night.

Ron   Let me tell you something. He wants you, he's gotta go through Danny Rolling first.

Jimmy   All right.

London And to get to Danny Rolling, he's gotta go through me, honey.

Jimmy   Ouch!

All   Whoooooah!

Jimmy   (Singing) When you see that old grim reaper in your own eyes...

All   (Singing)... in your own eyes, in your own eyes.

Ron   What about falling in love with somebody who's not on Death Row? Just, what if you met somebody...

London I think I'm falling in love with you right now, Ron.

All   Whoooooah!

London I mean, I could be wrong. It is very tempting.

Jimmy   Yeah, Ronnie D, he's got that look.

Mitchell He's got the look, I don't think he's got the feel, though.

Ron   No, I don't have the feel. You're absolutely right. I can't understand your song, your attitude, I can't understand your being in love with Danny Rolling.

London   Get a grip.

Ron   I am. You get a grip. You're in love with a
         murderer. Get a grip. He ain't gettin' out.

London   Yeah, that's how it works.

Ron   Ronnie, would you listen to the song? You're nit-
         picking.

Ron   Hello, Ryan, you're on.

Caller   Yeah, I just want to address that ah, woman?

Ron   Yes, her name is Sondra.

Caller   Sondra, I think you need some real serious help,
         honey.

London   Thank you.

Ron   I think you need some serious help. You've fallen in
         love with a coward murderer that deserves to be
         burned at the stake, if not put back in general
         population so he can be raped and murdered just
         like he did to them young people.

London   So you're a killer too, aren't you?

Ron   He's not a killer.

Caller   I would never hurt anybody. I think you're sick to
         be in love with this animal that should be removed
         from the face of the earth.

London   You'd like to kill him, wouldn't you?

Caller   No honey, I wouldn't kill him, he's not worth my
         time.

London   You'd love to get your hands on him.

Caller   If I got my hands on him, honey, he wouldn't go far.

Jimmy   (Singing) When you see that old grim reaper...

All   (Singing)... in your own eyes, in your own eyes, in your own eyes.

Ron   Joe. Go ahead, you're on.

Caller   Good morning. I got two questions for Sondra. One, is there any chance she's gonna release a version in Spanish?

London   *Sí, yo hablo español como nativo.*

Caller   Oh good. And number two. Any chance of getting her to come back for Body Shop Friday?

Ron   Nah. Can't drink that much. See ya, Joe.

All   (Singing)... *en sus ojos, en sus ojos, en sus ojos...*

Ron   Bruce. Go ahead, buddy.

Caller   I've been holding for awhile. Look, I'm pretty outraged. Let me say one thing. I'm not a killer. You see a cockroach, you step on it, you are not a killer, you're merely exterminating a pest. Now of all the names I've heard, the five most important I have not heard: Powell, Hoyt, Taboada, Larson & Paules. Five young lives that were brutally snuffed out by a scumbag who does not deserve the title man at all. He has proven he cannot function in society, he is not a member of the human race, he does not deserve anything. And as for you, you profiteering, blood-sucking wench, you don't deserve any of the air time you're getting, I hope

Florida takes all of the money you get, and I'd like to see you broke and homeless out of this state. You've shown again and again that all's you do is thrive off of serial killers by writing books. Oh, you want to know about them. I hope some day you get to find out about one of them, in the middle of the night when they come into your house, tie you up with duct tape, brutally rape you and stab you in the back...

London   You mean somebody like you?

Caller   Somebody like me? No, I am not...

London   Someone with the kind of ideas you have? The kind of urges you are telling us about?

Ron   These are not his ideas. He's repeating, he's telling you what Danny did.

London   These are his own urges, these are his own words.

Caller   This is what Danny did.

London   And this is what he wants to do.

Ron   He didn't do it.

London   That's what this man here wants to do.

Ron   No, that's not what he wants to do.

London   That's what he just said.

Ron   No, he's repeating what Danny did.

London   He said he hopes that happens.

Ron   So he's as guilty as Danny, you're gonna stick with that.

London   That's the only point I'm trying to make—

Ron   It's no point.

London   —is when you start jumping up and down—

Ron   Right.

London   —whooping with delight that someone is going to be killed—

Ron   Whoooo! Whooooo! Whoooo!

London   —that makes you a killer too.

Ron   That is so stupid.

Caller   I am not a killer.

Ron   Neither am I, Bruce, thanks for the call.

Larry   (Singing) When you see that old grim reaper...

All   (Singing)... in your own eyes, in your own eyes, in your own eyes.

Ron   God, that song sucks, and I'm so sick of hearing it.

Mitchell I wish people would stop sugar-coating how they really feel when they call in.

Ron   How many other books of serial killers have you written?

London   Well, I had *Knockin' on Joe* come out in England last year, it's gonna come out again here in America, St. Martin's is bringing it out. Actually, I'm not focusing on the Danny Rolling story, so much as a whole series of stories. Do you know the movie *The Thin Blue Line?*

Ron   Yes.

London   Errol Morris?

Ron   Yes, yes, yes.

London   He's working with me now, I'm doing a movie based on me and the stories I've developed.

Ron   I can't wait for that to come out. Who do you think will play you?

London   Me.

Ron   Oh, you'll play yourself?

London   Yeah. Don't you think I can do it?

All   (Applause, whistles)

London   Can't I be myself?

Ron   Yeah, sure. Just act naturally.

Ron   That's not the way it happens in Hollywood though, you know. They'll probably get like Roseanne Arnold to come in.

London   I just came back from Hollywood. It worked out fine.

Ron   You know who I see playing you, Sondra?

London   Who?

Ron   Goldie Hawn.

London   Yeah, right.

Mike   I was thinking Nipsey Russell.

Ron   Mike?

Mike   Yeah, Sondra, I could easily say that you're wacked out totally crazy but I think we all are a little bit crazy and we all know that line we step across. Danny stepped over that line, not once, not twice, not three times, not four times, but five times. I can understand someone killing somebody, just flipping out, you know, real quick. I mean, like OJ or somebody. But geez, how can you see anything in this guy after he did it more than one time. The guy was camped out in the woods. He'd creep out in the middle of the night and kill these people, skin-em, take their heads off. Can you honestly look yourself in the mirror and say you're right for being with this guy or for being in love with this guy?

London   Once again, it's the way he is about what he did. He's very sorry, and—

Mike   He's sorry.

London   —he wants to work with me to try to help understand—

Mike   It's a little bit too late. Maybe after the first time, but—

London   Of course it's too late for Danny Rolling. The idea is, maybe it's not too late for someone else, who's dealing with the same condition coming on.

Mike   Maybe if I hear the story and can learn more about him it will keep me from skinning people.

London   Maybe if we can contribute some research of these kind of criminals, and accumulate a body of literature about their lives and what went into it, when we begin to identify some of these patterns, perhaps we can stop some of the violence from erupting.

Mike   You know, I actually saved someone's life last week.

Ron   Who's that?

Mike   Jimmy Shubert.

Ron   How's that?

Mike   He shot a pistol at me and missed.

Jimmy   Well, actually... thanks for stepping on my *line*.

Ron   It's fifty-five after and this is the Ron & Ron Radio Network. (Break) Here's someone else who has worked with Danny Rolling, it's Flipper, the singer with the Dead German Tourists band. How did Danny and you collaborate on this song?

Flipper   Well, it's his words and it's our music. We made up the music for it, and that's how the whole collaboration started.

Ron   Like a Bernie Taupin/Elton John thing?

Flipper   Kinda, yeah. (Laughter)

Ron   Okay. Mystery Rider. And the video is out?

Flipper   It's coming out this week. It premiered in Gainesville, the original cut, a week ago.

Ron   Right. When you did the show with the Genitorturers?

Flipper   Right. Okay, you're familiar with the band, Sondra. You like the band?

London   Yessss, they're greeeaaaat.

Ron   All right. The Dead German Tourists with *Mystery Rider.*

(Spoken over guitar & bongos) Jingling spurs, rolling into town, oh black stallion, you've met the grim reaper, dressed in snake hide, worn black leather. Mystery rider, what's your game, you're a killer, no one could tame. Mystery rider, what's your name, you're a drifter, a drifter gone insane. (All singing) Mystery rider, mystery rider, mystery rider, mystery rider, mystery rider (Fade) (Applause)

Ron   Sondra, did you help Danny write that song?

London   No, he wrote that before I met him.

Flipper   That was the in-studio acoustic version, we do it differently every time we play it, but that's basically...

Ron   It was really moody.

Flipper   They can never remember any two songs the same way, so it's always a little different.

Ron   Steve, you're on the air.

Caller   I just want to know how come Sondra don't pose for like a men's magazine or sumpn like maybe jazz, an article like take my wife or the slut next door?

Ron   Okay, have you ever posed nude?

London   That's not my line.

Ron   That's not her style.

Ron   That's not her thing, Ronnie.

Ron   No, not at all. I don't know what that guy's talking about.

Ron   Brian.

Caller   Hello, I just have a question for Sondra. Okay, Sondra.

London   Hi.

Caller   How ya doin'.

London   Fine.

Caller   I'm not gonna call up and call you names and everything, because it doesn't seem like you really care about that. But you had mentioned something earlier about you know, you write these books and Danny wants to help people. How are you going to help somebody that's criminally insane?

London   Like I said, it's too late for Danny. This is not about helping Danny.

Caller   No, I understand that. But if someone else is criminally insane so they haven't killed somebody, how are you gonna stop them from killing somebody?

London   You know, that's a really good point. And I think it's a shame that we haven't even completed enough research into these types of conditions to have developed a successful therapy. We're a long way, folks.

Ron   Well, you're doing a lot of good work in trying to
           get a lot of help for us to get in that direction,
           Sondra. Other than a lot of these other people, who
           just complain *after* the fact.

Ron   How do you figure she's doing good work, Ron?

Ron   The song. And bringing it to the light...

London   Let me just put it this way. I'm gathering data. I
           work very closely with the FBI—

Ron   You do? Doing what?

London   With the research that I've been doing for six years.
           In other words, Robert Ressler is the man who
           invented the term serial killer—

Ron   Right.

London   —and he's the man who started the Behavioral
           Science Unit for the FBI. They no longer have the
           Behavioral Science Unit I don't know if you're
           aware of that.

Ron   I wasn't.

London   The outfit that *The Silence of the Lambs* is based
           on?

Ron   Uh-huh.

London   That kind of research? The funding has been
           slashed, but that research is going on in the private
           sector. And the work that I do has a serious intent
           in terms of working with law enforcement...

Sketch by Sondra London

Ron   So they come to you for tips?

London   We share our insights, put it that way.

Ron   When they're looking for a suspect, do they contact you?

London   No, no. No.

Ron   Can I ask one more question?

London   Go ahead, man.

Ron   Gee whiz, I forgot it.

London   That's one of the first signs. You're beginning to be a serial killer.

Ron   What about the cases in Louisiana? Are they ever gonna take those to court?

London   Those cases have been closed.

Ron   How many victims were there in Louisiana that may have been linked to Danny?

London   Three.

Ron   I thought it was in the double digits.

Ron   Did he definitely do them or do you know?

London   The case has been closed, in other words, it's probably more of a financial matter than anything else, the state doesn't want to really bring charges and then have to follow through with the prosecution. So they consider the case closed.

Ron   Now does Danny sit around thinking about escape?

London   I really couldn't answer that, you know. I only know what I know. And I'm very careful about going beyond that and saying, you know, oh I know this and I know that, when I don't.

Ron   True.

London   I have to have my sources.

Ron   You're an honest person.

London   Thank you.

Ron   Honestly ugly.

Ron   Lisa. Hello.

Caller   Hi, Ronnie D. I want to ask you a question. So what do you think of this Sandra?

Ron   Um, profiteering, no remorse...

Ron   I think that she's an artist.

Caller   I've seen her on *A Current Affair* and honestly?

Ron   Uh-huh?

Caller   It's definitely a man with a sex change. She's a beast.

Ron   You see that, Sondra? That's what you're gonna get when you put your heart out there.

Ron   Mitchell, you're in here, we've all been heckled before.

Mitchell There's really no way to respond to this type of comment.

Caller   Well, honestly, she looks like a man.

Ron   Okay, Lisa.

Mitchell   See, people can't even have an intelligent conversation.

Ron   Hello, Jeff.

Caller   Yeah, Ron & Ron, how ya doin'? I just gotta tell you, waking up this morning and hearing that song of hers really uh... set the day off.

Ron   Did you lose wood or did you get wood?

Caller   I lost wood. (Laughter) I just couldn't picture it. I'm sorry, Sandra, that you've fallen for this guy, but the punishment has to fit the crime, and when you slaughter five people, you deserve to be slaughtered.

London   I'm not saying that you don't. That's a fact.

Caller   And if they can make room for you, you ought to join him in the chair.

Ron   No, she hasn't committed any crime.

London   Oh, you're a killer too?

Caller   Yes, I am.

London   I see. In your own eyes, baby.

All   (Singing)... in your own eyes, in your own eyes, in your own eyes.

Ron   See ya, Jeff. Hello, Matt?

Caller   I got a question for Sondra.

Ron   Go ahead.

Caller   Sondra, you've got fifteen minutes of fame right
          now, so you better start milkin' it. This is just
          marketing. All you're doing is you're jumping on
          some controversy, they just said you were on *A
          Current Affair,* how long do you think you can ride
          this out? Working with the FBI and the police
          department, that doesn't sound right. I can't
          understand the FBI or police department coming to
          you, a reggae singer, for fifteen or however how
          many years, and then coming to you for advice?
          What's going on with that?

London   It's a long story. Wait for the movie, I guess.

Caller   You say you've been doing this research since you
          found out that the guy you've been dating when you
          were 17, he ended up being a serial killer...

London   Right.

Caller   And when you found that out, that's when you
          started doing research.

London   No, not quite. When I found it out, I just left it
          alone. I started in 1989.

Caller   You know, just like a lot of girls date rock bands, or
          comics all have groupies, jokies, waitresses, you
          have your serialies.

London   There's a lot of groupies that contact people like
          Danny Rolling...

Caller   John Wayne Gacy had a lot of fan mail.

London   They all do.

Caller   That make you jealous though?

London	No, I handle it. I have a newsletter called *Dan's Fans.* Danny does not respond personally to anyone but me.
Caller	How many Dan's fans do you think there are?
London	Well, I don't know. All I know is that the fan mail that comes in is directed to me, and if they have asked Danny something interesting that he wants to respond to, I will publish that correspondence in *Dan's Fans.*
Caller	Sherry, how did Danny feel about proposition 8?
London	My name's Sondra.
Caller	Oh, I'm sorry.
London	And I don't read his mind, I only know what he tells me.
Caller	What do you think of proposition 8?
London	I don't get involved in politics.
Caller	How do you get the newsletter?
London	How do you get it? I think, normally, that if you wrote Danny a letter that was interesting enough that he wanted to answer it?
Ron	That's why Flipper's never gets through. It's not interesting enough.
Caller	You can't subscribe?
London	Well, there's only been one issue so far. I don't know if Danny wants to write any more of these letters.

Caller   Cause I think my Christmas shopping may be done right here. (Break)

Ron   The Disciples and Sondra were having a heavy discussion off the air during the break about Danny Rolling's artwork.

Ron   Shubert thinks he knows everything.

Mitchell   He knows a lot except how to work straight.

Jimmy   Yeah, but we were thinking about playing the song and having her sing it live with the Disciples kind of backing her up a little bit, which would be kinda fun.

Mitchell   I don't wanna be involved in any of that kind of stuff.

Jimmy   Why?

Mitchell   It's a bad omen.

Jimmy   It's not a bad omen.

Mitchell   It's a horrible omen.

Jimmy   We're keeping people from getting skinned!

Mitchell   Yeah but look at those pictures, Jimmy.

Jimmy   I was saying I noticed in a lot of his pictures, Danny Rolling has a Godlike complex. And he gets power, you can see, he feels like he gets power from killing people, is his thing.

Ron   Do you believe that, Sondra?

London   The God complex you are talking about, I don't think you have sat down and studied this for very long.

Jimmy   How do you know? Why do you judge me? Maybe I like to read in my off hours.

London   You just walked in and I know you haven't...

Jimmy   How do you know what research I've done in my life up until this point?

London   I mean into his art.

Jimmy   You're judging.

Mitchell You just sobered up fifteen minutes ago.

London   His artwork is what we're talking about.

Mitchell You're not ready for this.

London   And what I was trying to say was yes, Danny Rolling is a born-again Christian, and...

Jimmy   Excuse me for not getting it right the first time. Sorry.

London   ...the imagery he uses in his art consists a great deal of the struggle between good and evil. A lot of angels, a lot of demons...

Ron   It seems like a lot of these killers or these criminals as they hit bottom, then they do become born-again Christians. Do you see that a lot in serial killers?

Mitchell Like OJ.

Ron	Sort of a hypocritical situation where people would be put in prison and then would claim to be born again to get sympathy?
Jimmy	Oh, but in Danny's case, it's different.
London	Danny was a Christian for years before this. For years he was very active in the church, going five, six, seven times a week.
Ron	Maybe he was going to church too much.
London	Maybe so, I don't know.
Jimmy	So because he was going to church and he's a Christian, he should be forgiven?
Ron	I mean, he is forgiven...
Jimmy	That's up to God.
London	Well, he's not forgiven, he's on Death Row. He's gonna be electrocuted.
Jimmy	We're talking about religion, it's kind of a heavy subject.
Ron	I'm talking about reality.
London	And we were talking about his religious background. He didn't find his religion after going to prison. It was a lifelong situation.
Jimmy	He was a born-again Christian who happened to be a murderer.
London	Well, he was a born-again Christian for years before he...
Ron	He was both.

Caricature courtesy of a street artisan

Mitchell   It didn't stick, Ronnie.

Jimmy   Sometimes you feel like a nut, sometimes you don't.

Ron   Now Ronnie, we do have just the music only cued up here, if Sondra would like to sing live along with the music.

London   You mean the whole song?

Ron   Yeah!

London   Okay, sure!

Ron   Ready? (Applause)

(Sondra sings *All the Fallen Angels* live over instrumental track. All join in on the chorus "In our own eyes..." (Applause)

Mitchell   Very very nice.

Eddie   She's got a beautiful voice. Very nice.

Ron   Go ahead, Sid.

Caller   I don't condone what Danny did, and I think he's getting what he deserves, but for Sandy...

London   Sondra.

Caller   Sorry. I believe she's unique the way she could love somebody that's so evil. I kind of admire that. Beauty and the Beast kind of thing.

Ron   No, the Beast and the Beast.

London   Let me just say that Danny Rolling is strange and fascinating, and I do find him beautiful in his own way.

Caller   So is my uncle Harry, but I wouldn't write a song about him.

London   I think somebody probably loves him too.

Jimmy   (Singing) I'm just wild about Harry.

Ron   David, go ahead.

Caller   Yeah, I want to talk to her about the remorse of the family. She undoubtedly don't have any. Her song should only be sang by Retard Eddie and her personal research is on the same lines as the Clinton's on health reform and tax reform.

Ron   Okay. Thanks for the call.

Mitchell   That one stunk.

Ron   Sharon?

Caller   Yes. I have two questions for Sondra. One, if he was so sorry, why did he try to deny he did it in the very beginning?

London   He had an attorney who advised him how to plead.

Caller   Okay, well, second question. How can she be so compassionate? What if she was related to the family, if it was her own daughter or mother, would she have the same compassion for him?

London   You know, this is a very serious and sensitive issue. I realize this is an entertainment show, and you guys are getting off making a lot of jokes, in an inappropriate situation. But people were killed here. And I am not insensitive to that at all.

Caller   And you don't think it's inappropriate what you're doing?

London   No. I came into this to do a story. I had no idea what was going to develop out of it.

Caller   Right?

London   When I found myself personally involved, I said Okay, look, let's be real, let's be serious. People want to know how I feel, people want to know what's going on, and this is true. If I tried to clean it up or make it something else, I would be less than honest. Yes, of course I am very moved by what happens to anyone who is a victim of violent crime. I have been a victim of violent crime myself.

Caller   What kind of violent crime?

London   I don't want to talk about it, but I am a victim of violent crime. I have a daughter the same age as these victims, Danny Rolling has a daughter the same age as these victims, and I think it's oversimplifying to assume that I don't have these feelings, or even that Danny doesn't have these feelings.

Caller   Can I ask a question? Would you be as compassionate if it was your daughter he raped and murdered?

London   Like I said, I have the same feelings as anyone else, and I am a mother.

Mitchell   That's the whole point of your song.

London   That's the whole point of my song. I'm not trying to convey that the killer is right. I'm trying to convey the complexity of the situation.

Caller   That's what some people are afraid to see.

Ron   Now you're saying some people are making inappropriate jokes. You're talking about Shubert?

Jimmy   I apologize if I did that, I was just making a couple of jokes. I realize people have lost lives, I just think it's a little crazy. However, if I had just killed six people, it would be all right, and you could try to understand me at that point.

Mitchell You see, Jimmy...

Ron   No, Jimmy's right. How can you? I mean his jokes are inappropriate. This guy's a murderer but it's okay.

Mitchell I just wish Jimmy woulda made the jokes last night at the Comedy Scene. (Laughter) When people actually paid to see his humor.

Jimmy   I mean, if you take it a hundred percent serious, you're gonna go out and kill somebody. My life, the way I look at life is, there has to be a little joke somewhere within the system.

Mitchell Right.

London   I feel the same way too. It's just like someone who works in an emergency room, or works in a funeral home, it's a terribly grim situation, and certainly sometimes you have a sense of humor, but...

Ron   You pulled up in a limousine yesterday in front of a Howard Johnson's Motel. You didn't drive up in your own car. You didn't drive from point A to point B to be on this show.

London   So what's your point?

Ron   Financial angle.

London   No. Can I tell you guys something?

Ron   Of course it's a financial angle. That's why you wrote the song, that's why you're showing this artwork.

London   Let me correct you on that. I have been working on this story for two and a half years, with no income whatsoever. I'm quite sure, that if your bosses told you...

Ron   I got no bosses, babe.

London   ...or if your syndications told you, come on into work, but we can't guarantee you a paycheck, you would not be here.

Ron   You're absolutely right.

London   And all of you who do your work expect to be paid.

Ron   True.

London   And I as a freelancer have been doing this work without being paid, and it's been two and a half years.

Ron   Is that because it's still in court? The Son of Sam law?

London   No , it's not.

Ron   It's not still in court?

London   It's not why.

Ron   This is the Ron & Ron Network. (Break) Sondra, wanna take some more calls here?

London   Sure.

Ron	Lisa. Go ahead.
Caller	I just have two things to say. One I have to say about the comment about him being a Christian? If he was a Christian, he wouldn't do something like that.
Ron	Okay.
London	He's a fallen angel.
Caller	It doesn't matter, if he's a true Christian, he wouldn't do something like that.
London	I appreciate your comment. The reality of Danny Rolling's life is something that is just beyond normal. I think when you're saying that, you're thinking of someone that is normal. Danny deals with multiple realities, and... gosh, it's kind of a deep subject to go into right here.
Caller	I think it's pretty simple. He's just a murderer. A scumbag murderer.
London	If it were that simple, I don't think there would be any value in studying him.
Ron	I don't think there is any value in studying him. Okay, what's your other point?
Caller	My other point is that I lived in Gainesville when all this was going on, and she doesn't seem to understand what it's like to be terrified for your life, to be afraid to leave your apartment, because you don't know if you're gonna come home that night, or if you do come home, there's gonna be somebody there. I lived in the development where one of the murders happened. I was so scared.

Ron   Hey, you should try to be married to me. You never know what mood I'm gonna come home in.

London I did have some of that same feeling. During the Danny Rolling trial, you might recall that Meissner was escaped at that time, and I did stay in a room very close to the scenes of the crimes, I had a sliding glass door, you know, I spent more than one evening...

Ron   How long were you there though?

London I think it was about six weeks, during the trial.

Ron   Who escaped?

London Meissner, Richard Meissner. He was a kind of a Gainesville Slasher. He had killed one girl and attempted to kill another girl, left her hanging by her hands from a balcony.

Ron   Did you study him, research him?

London No, no.

Ron   No songs about him?

London No, she was just saying I didn't know what that was like, I guess I know a little bit.

Caller That's a gray area.

Ron   All right, John.

Caller I got a buddy, he just got out of Starke for a while.

Ron   What was he doing time for?

Caller A little blowzinski.

Ron   That doesn't make you a bad person.

Caller   No. But anyway, he said everybody that goes in there that's gonna serve a pretty good amount of time picks up the Bible and tries to act like they're reborn and everything, hoping to get some mercy from the judge.

Ron   That is common.

Caller   Another thing is, I think Ren Hillock said it best, "You sick little monkey."

Ron   "You sick little monkey. Monkey hate cling."

Caller   When is going to be the next time you visit Danny? Is there gonna be a next time?

London   I don't know when it's gonna be.

Caller   Have you asked?

London   We're taking it through channels.

Caller   Has he proposed?

London   Yes.

Caller   When are you gonna get married?

London   We're taking it through channels.

Caller   I wouldn't mind getting a nice little apartment right outside Death Row, not right in it, close enough where you could be to Death Row but also you could be on your own.

London   Like in lovely downtown Starke? Mm-hm.

Caller   Does he have a window?

London   Yeah, he has a window.

Caller   Could you camp outside his window and wave, would he see you?

London   You mean like that song *Come to My Window?*

Caller   Yeah, just like that.

Ron   Hello, Jesse.

Caller   Yeah, I'd like to ask her how do you guys feel about the victims' families, right now?

Ron   How do you feel, Sondra?

London   It's hideous. Anyone who loses a child, I can't think of anything worse.

Caller   Losing a watch. Lost a beautiful watch, it was worth like twelve hundred dollars.

Ron   So don't you feel sympathy for the victims? Don't you think that...

London   Yeah, really.

Caller   You do?

London   It's sickening dealing with what Danny Rolling actually did, I'm hard-pressed to imagine more horrible crimes.

Caller   Did you read in the *Globe* where for two hundred bucks he did a series of articles? Sondra was involved in this.

London   It was twenty thousand dollars.

Caller   Twenty thousand dollars?

London   Yeah. Not two hundred bucks.

Caller   It sure wasn't worth twenty thousand bucks.

London   Well, you know people are so interested in the accounts of the crime, but I'm more interested in the Making of the Serial Killer, which is the title of our book. And I think it's more important to put the crimes into the context out of which they arose.

Caller   And what context would that be, Sondra?

London   In the whole life of the offender. It's a short question with a long answer.

Mitchell   You see, Ronnie?

Ron   No, I don't see. Because of the abuse early on?

London   I mentioned the abuse. There are other factors. The situation in prison.

Ron   I think there was probably some genetic predisposition in that case.

Mitchell   I think seafood can do it to ya too, at a young age.

Ron   Hello, who's this?

Caller   Dr. Geiger here. I'd like to speak with your guest on the program?

Ron   Sure, Sondra is right here. Go ahead.

Caller   Good morning, Sondra.

London   Good morning, sir.

Caller	What I want to remind you and everybody was about another serial killer from when I was a youth, who was patronized over the years, and now is making a resurgence in the United States. I'm talking of course about Adolf Hitler.
London	Yes.
Caller	I don't feel, I feel however your guest is like the modern-day Eva Braun. One day perhaps Sondra we are going to find you waking up with your head cut off in a bunker.
London	I don't think Eva Braun's head was cut off. I think she was shot in the head. What is your point, doctor?
Caller	My point is, is not Sondra in fear for her life?
London	If so, it's not from Danny Rolling.
Caller	Perhaps you could look at Mary in the church.
London	Yes.
Ron	Thank you. We'll see you. Is this Lisa?
Caller	Yes.
Ron	It says here you testified in the trial?
Caller	Yes, I'm a personal friend of Tracy Paules, and I testified at the trial, I'm also on the line with Tom Carroll.
Caller2	I testified as well.
Caller	Okay, Tom found Tracy, all right, and Sondra London was actually there when we were there, and I just don't understand the point of exploiting this

whole situation. And you talk about the victim's families and friends, I mean we're still victims. We're still alive and we live each day. And this is sick that I mean you guys even have her on the air. She's a sick person. She should be in the cell with Danny Rolling.

Caller2   She should.

Ron   Did you talk to her during the trial?

Caller   If you could have seen her during the trial, it was a joke. The media at the trial looked at her as a joke. If you could have seen her parading herself around and waving to Danny...

Caller2   ...and blowing kisses to Danny, it was absolutely pathetic...

Caller   ...it got to the point where she would leave the courtroom, trying to get the media to follow her, the media didn't even follow her. Nobody cared.

Ron   Were you blowing kisses and trying to get the media's attention, Sondra?

London   I did blow one kiss to Danny at the beginning, but his lawyers said no more personal gestures, so that was that. Regarding trying to get the media to follow me? No. I was actually at the trial doing a job. The reporters followed me for their own reasons, no matter what I did, and all I ever said to them was, "No comment."

Caller2   We saw you at the trial, we followed you outside one day, I mean Lisa was ready to smack your stupid face.

Caller Who were you covering it for? You say you were covering the trial?

London I did cover the trial for the *National Examiner.*

Ron Did you get paid?

London Do you get paid?

Ron No, I do this for charity, you idiot. Forty after, this is the Ron & Ron Radio Network. (Break) Eddie, did you give Sondra her tape back?

Eddie Yeah, I gave her her tape and her DAT tape.

All (Singing) In your own eyes, in your own eyes...

Ron Eddie this is perfect for you, you're almost obsessed with serial killers, John Wayne Gacy, Bundy, and now you can get together with Sondra and study Danny.

Eddie I'm looking at the artwork by Danny, I'm listening to Sondra's voice, absolutely beautiful, and I can't believe, what a waste of talent.

Ron Neil Mirsky just told me that he is gonna put this on as an ad, it's gonna be in major rotation, and I believe the rest of the country will follow very quickly, Ronnie.

Eddie Ah, it's a beautiful song.

Ron You say you're a reggae singer, or had a reggae band for years, so you have stage experience obviously, you have these new songs, have you thought about going out on the road?

London   I've thought about it, but I don't have any plans. Like I said, I'll probably be working on this movie project.

Ron   What's the name of the movie?

London   We don't have a name for it yet, it's just a project in the works with Errol Morris.

Ron   Hello, Austin?

Caller   Yeah. She mentioned that one of the qualities she liked in Rolling was he's a rugged man. What exactly is her, my impression of a rugged man wouldn't be a spineless jellyfish like he is.

Ron   I'm thinking more of a Grizzly Adams as a rugged man, not a Danny Rolling.

Caller   Not a spiny little wall-climbing flea that creeped in in the middle of the night on innocent women.

Ron   Yeah, that's not exactly rugged.

Caller   I mean somebody who'd go fisticuffs with somebody and let the chips fall where they may.

Ron   Hello, Dave.

Caller   Ronnie D, thank you for being the voice of reason.

Ron   Thank you very much, sir.

Caller   This makes my heart hurt. You know, I listen to you guys to laugh and stuff, and you put this lady on and this lady says she's got feelings just like everybody else? I almost threw up when she told me she's got a fan letter called *Dan's Fans.*

Jimmy   Actually I thought it was about Dan Marino. (Laughter)

Ron   Marino killed somebody?

Caller   I got a name for the movie. The Idiot Bitch And The Scumbag Killer.

Ron   Nobody would go see that. Hello, James.

Caller   Got a couple things I want to say. She's milking this for good money. She's pretty smart actually. She's doing a good job there. But being a Naval Flight Officer, we go through a little prisoner of war camp training. And I tell you the real issue here is we need to reform this Death Row thing. They ought to cut all those cells in about five pieces, put em in a 2x3 room with a big stake down on the ground and chain em up if they gotta wait, just give em a piece of bread and water every day. Make these people not wanna go killing people just for that reason.

Ron   What is his cell like?

London   Just a standard issue. You know, Danny Rolling's not the only one on Death Row.

Ron   What's Death Row like, how's it different from the rest of the prison?

London   Sorry, I've never been there.

Ron   I know, but you correspond with him, does he ever describe it?

London   I don't ever extend what I say beyond what I know myself.

Ron   Okay.

Caller   Diaz, you know my dad used to tell me something that kinda makes sense. And really has been brought to light today. He said we don't cultivate weeds in our garden, so why do we keep these guys around? I say, get rid of em, throw em in the garbage.

Ron   I know it does seem like a waste, the ten years between the time they are sentenced and the time they are executed.

London   They're not just waiting. They're spending their time looking in the mirror and seeing the grim reaper in their own eyes. Now I don't care how premeditated a murder you commit. There is no one on Death Row in the state of Florida who has spent seven years planning to kill someone and advising them of when they're gonna die—

Caller   What does that have to do with it?

London   That's the whole point I'm trying to make.

Caller   You're making no point.

London   This is premeditated murder. Execution is killing.

Caller   And we oughta kill this guy—

London   So you're a killer too.

Caller   Yeah, I'm a killer.

All   (Singing)... in your own eyes, in your own eyes, in your own eyes.

Ron   I'm glad it's over, Sondra.

Jimmy   I'm glad my tax money goes for three squares for this guy.

Mitchell   You don't pay taxes. As far as the U.S. government is concerned, you don't even exist.

Ron   Well, fifty-five after, that's it for now. See ya.

Sondra London on WGST Radio

Talk radio host Kim Petersen invited Sondra London to
appear on WGST Radio, Atlanta, Georgia, on April 6, 1995,
the day before British citizen Nicholas Ingram was executed
in Old Sparky, Georgia's electric chair.

Sondra London with Kim Peterson on WGST

Before his execution, Ingram thanked Clive Stafford Smith
and the other attorneys who defended him, and stated: "If I
die, I hope it is not for nothing. I hope people will see that a
ritualistic killing in the electric chair solves nothing." He
declined a final meal, but when relatives bought him some
chips from a prison vending machine, he ate them.

When the warden asked if the condemned man had any last
words, Ingram spat at him: "Let's get on with it."

Sondra had no personal connection with Ingram, but the setup was just a pretext anyway. It turned out to be a Gotcha, in which only adverse callers were put on air to attack her personally over Danny Rolling. Instead of engaging in an even-handed discussion of the legal and moral issues involved in Ingram's case and capital punishment, London was ambushed by the sister of one of Danny Rolling's victims, who proceeded not only to insult her with impunity and encouragement, but to lie repeatedly about taking money for movie rights to the story, which was disingenuous because it had already been revealed nationally on ABC *Turning Point*. The talk-show host berated London for daring to call the woman on her lies. And all the while, Nicholas Ingram was lost in the fog of this war, his name only mentioned in mean-spirited jest.

Kim   This is the Kimmer, look out, we have a special treat for you today. We have an actual guest in the actual studio, something which as you know, almost never happens here at the News Monster. What a treat, what an enjoyment—her name is Sondra London, and you are a writer, and I guess a singer, that's you on the song, right?

London   That's me.

Kim   And you're almost a professional guest on the death penalty. You've been all over the world, you've been on TV shows, you've been on what, *A Current Affair*, and some of the real sleazoid magazine shows, right? I mean you've been everywhere.

London   I've been on some of the nicer shows too.

Kim   Some of the nice ones, but there aren't that many nice ones left, so it's kind of hard to single them out.

London   Well, there's your show.

Kim   That's true. And we should add two things, one, you
            have never heard me or this program before so you
            have absolutely no idea what we do here or
            anything else. It's a news talk but it's a little kinky,
            a little crazy.

London   So I'm like a virgin, yes.

Kim   Kinda like a virgin. You know, you walked in and I
            said she looks like a virgin to me. It was just first
            sight thing. And you live in Atlanta.

London   Yes, I do.

Kim   For a long time, or you've been here a long time?

London   I'm a native of Florida.

Kim   Okay. And the reason you are here, among other
            things, is Nicky Ingram, who is the guy who was
            born in Britain who is an American citizen also,
            who murdered one person and tried to murder the
            second person, is on death row and is supposed get
            the Old Sparky tonight at seven o'clock. Two
            possible appeals left, unlikely, chances are he'll be
            executed tonight at seven o'clock. And did you
            contact Mikey? I don't even know how this started. I
            think you contacted us because you wanted to talk
            about the issue of the death penalty and death row
            and stuff like that, and then it turns out, as I find
            out more about you, that you are, are you actually
            engaged to the guy who butchered those coeds
            down in Florida in 1991? Is he your fiancé – or your
            husband or what's the deal on him? Danny.

London   Danny Rolling?

Kim   Yeah.

London   I was brought into Danny's life to help him tell the story of his life and the murders, and in the process of working with him, we developed a personal relationship that went a little bit further than just the journalist and the murderer.

Kim   Now how did that work out? Because he was in jail and you were like behind a glass partition, right, so did you just like, did you hug up against the window? Or how did you work that? I mean, you must have had a kind of a personal thing going there, I mean you're in love with the man, right?

London   We're not talking so much about the physical relationship. It's really the work that we have done with his mind, and bringing out what it is about him, and really the experience of I suppose you say empathy that I developed with him, and so it made it easier for him to tell me his story. In that case, we became more sympathetic, as I got to know him more.

Kim   And you know John Wayne Gacy?

London   Yes.

Kim   And are you like in love with him too?

London   No way.

Kim   You're not engaged to John Wayne Gacy?

London   No way.

Kim   But he's a friend, or you communicate with him, or?

London   I've worked with probably at least two dozen convicted killers.

Kim   How about Ted Bundy? Did you know Ted Bundy?

London   No, I didn't start working on this subject until the Ted Bundy execution. It generated so much interest that it really drew my interest.

Kim   Okay, so— and I should tell you this right up front too. It was a few weeks ago when Rolling was, when was Rolling convicted, it wasn't that long ago, all right, when they came out with the death penalty sentence for him, it was what, about a month ago maybe?

London   A year ago. April 20th, a year ago.

Kim   No, that can't be right. When did we talk to his sister?

London   It's right. No, it's true. He doesn't have a sister.

Kim   No, no, we talked to the sister of one of the coeds that was murdered by Danny Rolling—

London   Yes, she lives here.

Kim   She lives here, and she called me on the air and we talked about this, it wasn't that long ago.

London   It was a year ago. April 20th, 1994. I was there.

Kim   Wow. Well, there was another reason then. I forget what it was. But there was something else about him in the news about him. Anyway she called, and I just wanted you to know that, well I guess you do know that she lives here, and in fact, don't be surprised if she's calling, because this is the man who butchered her sister, so this could be really interesting today. Now, is it fair to say that you are a professional death row what, enthusiast?

London   No, it's not.

Kim   You are really on the, well, tell me, how do you describe what you do?

London   I'm a writer.

Kim   Okay, but—

London   I'm a journalist—

Kim   Yeah, but, oh, let's do the song.

London   Why don't we do the song?

Kim   In fact, I am now told that when you came in here you told me you actually got a message, tell me about the message that you hope is going down to Jackson today.

London   Well, I know Clive Stafford-Smith, who is Nicky's attorney, and I advised them that we would be playing this song, which is dedicated to everyone on death row all over the world, and in particular, we'd like to send it out today to Nicky.

Kim   So we have a song that, you wrote this, right?

London   Yes.

Kim   And recorded it. And in fact it's one of many songs, are these all songs, or are they poems? I guess they're all songs.

London   They're songs.

Kim   That you've written.

London   Yes.

Kim   And you're dedicating this to all the people on
             death row all around the world, or America, or?

London   Yes.

Kim   Okay, well, let's listen to it, shall we? Shall we play
             this? This is Sondra London, and the song is called
             All the Fallen Angels.

(Plays song)

Kim   (Over song): Kinda got a nice beat to it, I like it—
             say what?

London   You're not on the air?

Kim   Yeah. Yeah— Sondra, stop that!— No dancing,
             Sondra, no dancing— Okay, one little waltz.

(After song ends)

Kim   Kind of a ballad. Kind of a dancing ballad thing.
             Sondra London's our guest. She wrote and sang the
             song. And you are in love with Danny Rolling, who
             is the guy who butchered those girls down in
             Florida, and you're hoping that Nicholas Ingram is
             listening right now to the Kimmer program today,
             because it looks like he's gonna meet Old Sparky
             tonight, I mean that's the deal. Is there anything
             that you wanted to say? Before we— a lot of people
             wanna talk to you today. Cause this is a very— I
             mean, it's not often that we get a woman in here
             who is in love with a brutal, mutilating killer, and
             is, uh, do you condemn the death penalty in all
             cases, do you think there is ever a time when the
             death penalty is appropriate? Or do you think we
             should never have it? Your song says it makes us all
             killers.

London   Well, I'd just like to raise the level of awareness of what we are doing. If this state, and the good people of this state, believe that in the name of the state, that we should all commit murder, then I think it's a good idea to at least understand that's what's going on, face it, cop to it, don't stand up on your lonely pinnacle of perfection and look down on someone who has killed, while you are filled with vengeance and rage and the desire to kill.

Kim   Hm. Exactly.

London   As I sat in the trial where Danny Rolling was sentenced to death five times over, and watched the people dancing, jumping up and down with joy—

Kim   High-fives, cheering— I mean it was an unbelievable—

London   Exactly. I would just like raise the awareness—

Kim   — party, kind of a courtroom party is what it was.

London   That's what I saw when I went there. And this is what my song expresses. When someone is convicted of murder and they go to death row, it isn't just like that. They sit for years and contemplate the grim reaper.

Kim   We should do it fast, don't you agree? If they're gonna be sentenced to death, wham, like a week, boom, that's it? Fifteen years is silly.

London   It takes that long for an innocent person to prove that they are innocent. Are you aware that there are people that are—

Kim   (Laughing) I don't think that happens that often.

London   Are you aware that there are people that are convicted wrongfully and that later prove that they are innocent?

Kim   (Laughing) Once in a while you make a mistake, you know, I mean sure, one or two are gonna get it, just outta, but that's you know, to satisfy the masses, you know we're talking democracy here.

London   Where does the killing stop?

Kim   With the killers. If we kill all the killers, then there won't be anybody to kill any more.

London   Because you'll be a killer. You'll have blood on your hands too.

Kim   Well, ahhhh—

London   Remember that.

Kim   Okay, all right, I tell you what, let's take a quick cowabonga here, we have lots of calls, and you're gonna be here for a while yet, right? Okay, we'll do that. Our guest is Sondra London, who is a writer, singer, uh, a guest, and an anti-death penalty aficionado, what's the matter, that's not right?

London   I haven't said that, have I?

Kim   You mean it's unfair to call you an anti-death penalty aficionado? I mean that's what you do, right?

London   I don't think you based that on anything that I gave you.

Kim   Are you in favor of the death penalty?

London   No.

Kim   Are you ever in favor of any kind of death penalty forever no matter what the case is ever?

London No.

Kim   You think we should not have any death penalty, it should all be life in prison?

London Oh, I didn't say that. I am not gonna take on the position of saying I am against the death penalty and argue with people about whether they are going to have the death penalty or not. The fact that they have it—

Kim   Okay, I won't argue with you, I just want to make sure whether you are or not—

London — the fact that I live in a state where the majority of the people believe this—

Kim   — Right. But you're against it.

London I would like to get people to *think*. Just *think*.

Kim   Okay, we'll do that. We'll do thinking. Sondra, we'll have so much thinking in here, it's going to be unbelievable. But the fact is, you don't like the death penalty, you think it's wrong, you think we should not have a death penalty, correct?

London I think killing is wrong.

Kim   Okay, is it a hard question? Let's just do the one question. Are you against the death penalty?

London (Pause)

Kim   Go ahead, try it, come on, yes or no, come on—

London   I'm against the death penalty.

Kim   (Shouting and cheering) Oh, that's it! I took her! You know, sometimes there's a stronghold, but you know, by golly, we just, now we're together, now we're on the same wavelength.

London   No, Kimmer, we're not on the same wavelength—

Kim   All right, well, well—

London   — because I'd really like to talk not about whether or not we should have a death penalty—

Kim   We do have a death penalty.

London   — but what does it mean?

Kim   It means that they die. They don't get to kill anybody else. But that's the short version.

London   But what does it do to us? To us?

Kim   It makes us a people who are, who are—

London   Bloodthirsty—

Kim   — horrified by the—

(Newscaster's Voice over:) The parole board chairman sees a condemned man. "Chairman wants to go down and look the man in the eye." And five young men accused of gang-raping two teenagers. "These are the types of cases that really make no sense." (Break)

Kim   And we're gonna continue this conversation. Our guest is Sondra London, who is in love with Danny Rolling, or is engaged I guess, well, anyway, you're having a loving, romantic relationship between the bars.

London   You know, I think the important part about my relationship with Danny Rolling is that I am his biographer, and we are working on trying to explain what's wrong with him. And that's the—

Kim   Okay, but you fell in love with the guy.

London   Yes but—

Kim   Okay, Okay.

London   — the important part is that we are doing a book, and that we are trying to get to the root of the violence that exploded there.

Kim   Okay, talk to Laurie Lahey. Laurie, hi, it's the Kimmer, you're on the News Monster.

Laurie   Hello.

Kim   Hi. Would you tell our guest Sondra London, who you are, Laurie?

Laurie   I'm Tracy's sister, Sondra. And I approached you in the courtroom? When we were there? When they sentenced Mister Rolling for murdering, brutally murdering my sister? And you had sympathy for this man? And you're trying to, you're trying to explain why he did this? And you're humanizing him? You're just trying to get money, lady, you're at it again. Just trying to make money off the pain and suffering of our family. And I don't appreciate it. And Kimmer, I don't believe you're having her on the show. I just lost a bit of respect for you right then and there. Cause that's all she's trying to do. Is get money. And make money. And that's what she's been trying to do. From day one.

Kim	Sondra?
London	Number one, I have no product on the market. Number two—
Laurie	You tried! That's cause we're trying to stop you from it, lady.
London	No, that's not correct. I do have a book coming out in a year.
Kim	Mmm-hmmm.
London	And of course, as you know, the story of the murders was already published. Okay. So there is nothing for me to profit from my making this appearance.
Laurie	That's because we put a stop to it.
Kim	Tell you what, Laurie, can you—
London	No, the stop has not been put.
Kim	All right, all right. Laurie—
London	That is an—
Kim	— ALL RIGHT, ALL RIGHT—
London	UNCONSTITUTIONAL law—
Kim	HOLD ON HOLD ON HOLD ON HERE! Can you hold on, Laurie, can you hold on for me, I don't want to, but break's coming up. (Break)
Kim	Okay, Sondra London is a writer and singer, and a woman who has been very involved with the death penalty, and in fact is in love with and very close to

Danny Rolling in Florida, who butchered the
students there, one of whose sister is Laurie, and
we've talked to Laurie before, and had I think a very
powerful conversation with Laurie, and I was
hoping you were out there, Laurie, because I know
that you are closer than any of us will ever be to
this case. Welcome back on, you're on with Sondra
London.

Laurie   Mmm-hm.

Kim   Okay, Sondra did you want to reply or something?
Okay you go ahead, and we'll continue this. Go
ahead, Sondra.

London   Yes, I'm very sorry that the victims in this case have
been manipulated by the state's attorney's office so
that their hurt feelings regarding the loss of their
loved ones have been turned around against me, as
a focus of the fact that stories are told about crimes
that occur. I'm a journalist and I tell a story. And if
I tell a story, just like anyone else who shows up for
work to broadcast or write a story, I do expect to be
paid, and I will be paid. I'm sorry if that offends
Laurie. But I have a question for Laurie. How much
money did you make, Laurie, from selling your
story and the story of your dead sister?

Laurie   Not a penny, lady.

Kim   Sondra, that is a vicious thing for you to say.

London   Excuse me? No, no.

Laurie   This woman is—

London   Excuse me? All of the victims' families have
received payment—

Laurie   We haven't received a penny.

London   —for the rights of the movie script—

Laurie   My family has not received a penny.

London   —Excuse me? I talked to your lawyer, ma'm.

Laurie   Listen, I'm telling you this right now—and I'm
          telling you the truth—

London   I talked to your lawyer.

Laurie   I don't like being accused—I don't lie—I'm telling
          you we have not received *a penny*!

London   Well, that's not what your lawyer told me.

Laurie   Well, you've got wrong information. And that's not
          the point.

London   From your lawyer?

Laurie   I'm not misrepresenting myself as you are. And I
          don't know who you think you are—

London   Have you not sold the rights to your story?

Laurie   No we have not.

London   I see.

Laurie   We have a movie right that is out, we had like 29
          offers and what not, and we have not received a
          penny and that's none of your business—

London   That's not what Diana Hoyt told *Turning Point*
          either. She showed the check on TV, Laurie.

Laurie   Well, that's Diana Hoyt then. That is Diana Hoyt.
          And that is her business.

London And she did speak for your whole group.

Laurie No she did not speak for our whole group and neither do I.

London And your lawyer also speaks for your whole group.

Kim Okay, hold on a second, I think the difference here is, this is the victim's family that we're talking about as opposed to Danny Rolling and you in sympathy with the guy who butchered them and tortured them and cut off a head and stuck it on a shelf.

Laurie Innocent children they were, by the way.

London And what are we talking about? We're talking about selling a story, we're not talking about doing a deed.

Kim Well, I could interview him and sell the story, but I didn't fall in love with him, you know, I mean you're in love with the guy.

London We're not talking about that either—

Laurie Yes we are talking about that—

London —we're talking about money, I believe—

Laurie —and once again you're on the air, you're trying to promote—

London —that was her particular subject—

Laurie —and trying to make money off of—

London —see, she's talking about *money.*

Laurie	—what happened to my little sister.
London	Right.
Laurie	—and that's what infuriates me—
London	I am not making any money off your sister. Okay, did I get paid for this appearance?
Kim	Oh no. Not for here, but you are writing a book with Danny Rolling.
London	The book is not out.
Kim	But you wrote it, I see it right there.
London	If I do a talk show today, in other words, how am I going to make any money off that?
Kim	Well, when the book comes out, they'll remember your name and—
London	But that's a year from now.
Kim	Well, but still you hope to make money from the book, right?
London	So. Any time I ever do an appearance or any time I ever publish a statement of any kind then this is going to grossly offend Laurie and her group?
Laurie	My group is my family.
Kim	What I heard Laurie say is that she is offended that you are glorifying or trying to get sympathy for a butcher, a madman, a killer who deserves to die. And I think that's a perfectly reasonable stand for her to take. Don't you understand why she feels that way?

Laurie   Sir, what you said, now let me say one thing, and I was unable to read it. I had someone read it for me because I could not. She went and took excerpts from this book which were in detail, what he did, what he said, not only to my little sister but to the other children that were involved in this, and detailed exactly what he did to them, each and every one. He raped my sister twice and he brutally stabbed her in the back. She was at home, she was on the phone with me, she was in the safety of her home, with Manny in the other room, her friend from high school, feeling safe and calm, but this man went in there to act out his fantasies, whatever they may be, his sick fantasies, not just to rape my sister, but to kill her. He went in there with the intent to kill her. So what Sondra has done, is gone and gotten this information, printed it, and in such detail that it's just horrifying. And you don't think I'm going to be offended by that? My sister is dead. I can't do anything about that any more. I spent all her life protecting her. And looking after her. I can't do it any more. But then this woman comes on and continues to damage my sister after she's dead, and she's innocent. She's just a beautiful young girl who was killed by a sick man. And this woman claims to be in love with her (sic) and then tries to make money? And tries to glorify what he did to these kids? It infuriates me. She should not be on your show. She should not be on any show.

Kim   Sondra? I mean I think she's got a great point.

London   If that were the case, you know it has the right sound.

Kim   What's wrong?

London   Any time you write about a subject that does not mean you are glorifying it, Okay? What happened there was a tragedy. What happened there was hideous.

Kim   Well, Okay, but let me—

London   Wait just a second. Let me finish, please. To describe what has gone on in any murder or any tragic event naturally is not going to be a pleasant, uplifting subject. This was an excerpt that was taken from a book. The title of the book is *The Making of a Serial Killer.* And the emphasis of the work that we are doing, and that we are continuing to do, is to try to find out how these kinds of violent acts erupt in lives? What goes into this? What makes this happen? In other words, we are continuing on a path as a society so that more and more of these types of crimes are arising. Why is this? Is there being any research done to talk to these offenders to find out what happened in their lives that brought this about?

Kim   I think the criminal justice system and the FBI have whole departments dedicated to this, but here—

London   Oh, excuse me. The funding has been slashed.

Kim   (Laughs) Oh, Okay. So you're picking up the slack, I guess. Listen to this. "I approached my meeting with Danny," these are your words, "thinking I was prepared for anything. But there was one thing I was not prepared for. I had no idea what a fine-looking man he is today. Instead of the broken and dejected loser I'd seen on TV, standing before my hungry eyes was one gorgeous hunk of man." Now, doesn't that sound a little kinky that you're whacked out about this serial killer, this brutal butcher, that murdered Laurie's little sister? I mean don't you think she has a right to be upset? My God! I mean what kind of a kinky deal is this?

London   I want to make sure you understand—

Kim   You're in love at first sight with a guy that's gonna be dancing with the Devil in a period of months?

London   I want to make sure that you understand what there is that I see there in Danny—

Kim   What difference does it make?

London   —and it's not a matter of the murders—

Kim   What redeeming value could there be in a butcher like this?

London   May I answer?

Kim   Please.

London   The redeeming value in this particular case is that he wants to understand what is wrong with him, he wants it to be made a matter of study, so that possibly if he can put himself together enough to reveal what went wrong with him, if someone else can read it and see the warning signs along the way, if someone can see, this is what's happening with my life, and if I continue on with this, someone's gonna lose control, there's gonna be a tragedy.

Laurie   You know, I don't believe that for a minute.

London   There are so many killers that you could talk to—

Laurie   I don't know who you could talk to and let them fall for that line of bull.

London   I have talked to numerous killers—

Laurie   No intelligent person could possibly believe that he
          wants to redeem or whatever you're just trying to
          say. He told the detective that went in there that
          interviewed him and got the details of what he had
          done and how he confessed to all this, and he said
          he wanted to be bigger and badder than Bundy. And
          I believe that over what you're trying to pull here.

London   Excuse me, that was a quote from Bobby Lewis.

Laurie   He wanted to be glorified, he wanted to be bigger
          and better, he wanted to put fear into Gainesville.

London   Laurie, you are believing what the state's attorney
          has told you.

Laurie   I believe that more than what you told me, lady.

London   It's not true. Bobby Lewis is the source of that. And
          Bobby Lewis is someone that I know very well.

Kim   What is he, the prosecutor?

London   No, he's another killer.

Kim   Ahhhh. Another killer!

London   He's the one that snitched on Danny. And I know
          Bobby Lewis at least as well as I know Danny.
          Bobby Lewis is a compulsive liar and this is one of
          the lies that Bobby told.

Kim   Okay, I gotta go to a break, Laurie, do you want to
          hold on for me? Or have you gotta go?

Laurie   (Sighs) I'll see, we'll see. (Break)

Kim   The older sister of one of the victims of Danny
          Rolling, the butcher from Gainesville, Florida, and
          my guest in the studio is Sondra London, who is in

love with him and has written a book with him that hasn't come out yet, but you've got the manuscript, and you've written many articles, Okay, Laurie, I know how difficult this is, if you want to say one last thing, or whatever you want to do—

Laurie   Yeah, I do, it's just a little point about the movie. As I'm sitting here calming down a little bit and thinking about it, we have signed with ABC to do a movie that is coming out—

London   Thank you, thank you—

Laurie   —Hush, Sondra—

Kim   HOLD IT, HOLD IT, HOLD IT!

London   Hush, Laurie.

Laurie   —that we don't know when this is going to come out. We haven't heard anything. We've seen one script, and didn't approve it, and that was over a year ago, and we haven't seen or heard anything since then. Now, the only reason we did this as a family, well, all the families got together, and we had to, we were forced into signing this because if we did not sign a contract, anybody and their mother, meaning Sondra London, a brother, this journalist, this so-called journalist, will go ahead, and make a movie based on what happened to my sister and these other children. When we signed this, this alleviated that. So that other people could not make a movie without our consent. Now. One of the clauses in the contract that we had was to say that we have control over what appears in this movie. This movie will not depict Danny Rahlins (sic) whatsoever. It's gonna show you these kids from their childhood, on up to their teenhood, through aspiring college students, going through college, and then what tragedy came upon them because of this sick man. He's barely going to be part of this, but we support that because we want these kids to be remembered as beautiful young children, athletes as they are, scholars that they are. That is it. The money we are getting is so minimal, it doesn't even do a thing. I won't even be able to put one child through college! And my parents get it. And you know something? I was against it before, but I support it now when I see the pain that my mom and dad go through today over the loss of Tracy. I want them to get anything. They deserve it. They are going through so much pain and so much sorrow every single day. They deserve that little measly money that they're getting from this movie. We're not gonna watch it, we don't care about it, we don't approve of it, but we did it so that nobody else could go ahead and make a movie based on these people, which everybody else is hungry to do. 29 production companies tried to get us to make a movie, and all wanted to glorify Mister Rahlins (sic), and we refused to do it. And this is the only company we went with that will not do that. To my sister. And if that's the only way I can continue to protect my sister, I'll do it. And I'll fight you on anything, lady. If you ever try to deface my sister, and-and-and hurt her any further, and hurt my family any further. You're lucky I don't go on these talk shows with you, because I don't think I could control myself.

Kim   Laurie, I know you want to go, I'm glad you called. I was almost hoping you weren't listening. I didn't know about this until late yesterday and the first thing I thought was oh God, if Laurie's listening, I know how painful this is going to be.

Laurie   It's gonna take a while to get over this woman. She just has no clue that she does this to us, that she brings this all back up to us, when we try to recover every day, going through this.

Kim   Let me just ask you this one thing while you're still on, and ask Sondra. Sondra, you are obviously angry, you're feuding, you're making faces at Laurie. Why don't you understand that they're going through a terrible ordeal and they are suffering. Don't you feel any sympathy or empathy for the victims at all?

London   Sure I do. I think they should—

Kim   You do for the butcher—

London   —no, they should—

Kim   —but you're yelling at her, you're calling her names—

London   —they should do their story—

Kim   —how could you possibly do that?

London   I think they should do their story. I think America should be more interested in the stories of the victims. We should put them on prime time. We should have stories about victims every night. We should not have stories about killers.

Kim   But don't you understand what Laurie's family is going through because of the man you're in love with?

London   That's what I just said.

Kim   Okay.

Laurie   Then why are you doing it? Why do you continue to do it and then go into such detail as to what happened to them? Why do you continue to do that? I don't believe a word you say.

London   The story of his life would be incomplete without the account of the murders.

Laurie   I don't believe it.

Kim   Laurie, thanks for calling.

Laurie   Thank you, goodbye.

Kim   Okay, bye. I'll take a quick call. This guy's been on for an hour and a half. Rick in Marietta. You're on with Sondra London, sir. Thanks for waiting, man.

Caller   I can't believe what I'm hearing with this guest you've got. She's just absolutely unbelievable. I was sitting here the whole time listening to the last conversation, of an analogy and I'd like to hear her reply to it.

Kim   Okay.

Caller   Ma'm, do you have any children?

London   Yes, I do.

Caller   Okay, how old?

London   I have a daughter very close in age to the age of Danny's victims, and so does Danny.

Caller   What age?

Kim   Teenager.

London   Eighteen.

Caller   Okay. Let's say a murderer is put in prison and
          paroled, in the average what, seven to nine years,
          and then murders your daughter. What is your—

Kim   No, they have to rape her first. Rape and then
          murder and then cut off her head.

Caller   Hey. What can I say, I'm sorry.

Kim   Let's be accurate.

Caller   Yeah, exactly.

Kim   We'll have her react to that, keep listening, buddy.
          Can we hold this over? Can you stay? (Break)

(Newscaster's voice-over) Meanwhile the death watch
continues at the state prison in Jackson. Nicholas Ingram
this afternoon has been visiting with family members and his
spiritual adviser Randy Loney, who is described only as "a
non-Christian." In the hours prior to execution and right
about now, Ingram is being placed in a cell adjacent to the
electric chair, his head will be shaved, and he will be offered a
final meal. "He has indicated that he doesn't feel that he will
be very hungry this evening, so he has not asked for anything
special for his last meal." Ingram's mood is described as
"copacetic."

Kim   Who's this?

(Canned joke track, sounds like Rodney Dangerfield)

Caller   Good afternoon, Kimmer, this is Rodney, for cryin'
          out loud.

Kim   Rodney Dangerfield, the respect man!

Caller   Someone asked your guest, Sondra London, how she felt about OJ? And she said OJ? Oh, he'd have to kill a lot more people before I'd be attracted to him!

Kim   Ho-ho-ho!

Caller   I mean right now he's a rank beginna! Ah you kiddin'?

Kim   I don't know, Sondra, does OJ turn you on? That's a whole other issue, I'm guessing, right? She's batting her eyes at me, refusing to answer! Vell, ve haff vays to mek you talk! Ha-ha-ha! Let's get back to the program here. This is the Kimmer and I'll tell ya what. I really do feel terrible about poor Laurie. And every time we talk about executions and killers and mass murder and stuff like that, and I talk to Laurie, and my heart just breaks. I just, I mean what these families have gone through, and I don't blame her a bit for being steamed about anybody who would in any way glorify or try to get sympathy for a brutal butcher who has Satan in him, who is going to be dancing with the devil. I know exactly how she feels. I don't even like the idea of this whole thing. The reason we're doing this today in fact, is the issue of the day is capital punishment and the death penalty, because this British guy is gonna get it tonight, apparently, we believe, and so this is one way of doing the program, and we wanted to give you an opportunity to take some calls and talk about the issue.

London   If someone has been through a tragic life and they are totally out of control with the violence within them, and they have committed a crime, or a series of crimes, a number of crimes, there is something wrong there, Okay? For them to tell you what's wrong, so you can find out, you have to approach them in a sympathetic way. You cannot walk in there confrontationally and shake them down and

343

find out what is wrong, what has gone wrong for them in their whole life.

Kim   I don't think you had to fall in love with him, though, maybe—

London   No, I didn't. And as I said—

Kim   —you know, I love you, tell me your story kind of a thing—

London   —I've worked with over two dozen killers, and I didn't fall in love with any of them—

Kim   —In fact you were telling me—

London   —It's not necessary—

Kim   —your first boyfriend was a serial killer when you were seventeen—

London   —Okay, it's really not necessary to stress that emotional relationship—

Kim   (Laughs) Wait a minute, your first boyfriend at 17 was a—

London   —because that is not what's going on—

Kim   —wait a second, was a serial killer?

London   Yes.

Kim   Sondra, do you have a, isn't it like the bad boy thing?

London   You're not telling your audience the rest of the story.

Kim   I don't know the rest of the story.

London   Right. See, so they think that's all that's going on
          here.

Kim   Ahhhh! What *is* going on here, that's the question!
          Let's find out, and the answer is with Steve in Stone
          Mountain. Steve, hi, you're on the air with Sondra
          London.

Caller   I wanted to ask Sondra a couple of questions.
          Sondra, do you believe Danny Rolling is innocent or
          guilty of the crimes he's committed?

London   No sir, he's guilty, and he's very repentant about it.

Caller   And what attracted you to him initially?

London   The attitude he has about what he did and what he
          wants to do about it.

Caller   Okay.

London   Which is completely different from any of the other
          killers I have ever dealt with.

Caller   True.

London   Typically, someone this disturbed that goes so far
          as to become a serial killer, or a serial rapist or
          whatever, has such severe problems that they can't
          face, and they are in denial about, and when you
          deal with these people you hear a lot of lies, a lot of
          self-justification, and Danny Rolling was the first,
          and so far the only offender I have worked with,
          who was willing to be honest about what is wrong
          with him, his weaknesses, his failures, and his
          inadequacies.

Caller   So you're attracted to what you perceive as his
          honesty about what he did?

London   When you get to know someone, there are many personal qualities that they have, and I'm not trying to say Danny's great, or glorify Danny, or make anyone like him. That was the cost that was paid—

Caller   Do you have any qualms about what he has done, not just to his victims, but to his victims' families?

London   Qualms? Yes, of course. It's horrifying. But here's the point, folks. It doesn't just happen out of a clear blue sky. If that's all it was— Okay, my book is not called "The Killing of the Victims." It doesn't just go into, then I stabbed her and then I raped her, it goes into what was put into that person over years, that eventually erupted into violence. If we don't look into the roots of the violence itself, then we're never going to figure out—

Caller   So you don't look so much—

London   —what we can do.

Caller   —at what he did, you look at why he did it—

London   Yes.

Caller   —what caused him to do it.

London   But I don't *not* look at what he did, I think that's why it's important because it did go that far.

Caller   Well, Sondra, you seem to be attracted to the sort of person that would go out, and to be blunt about it, slaughter and butcher and rape people. Is there something within you that causes people—

London   I'm sure that's how it appears on the surface.

Kim   But I saw an article where you admitted that you get turned on by bad guys.

London   I did not.

Kim   You did too, it's right here.

London   Find it.

Kim   Okay.

London   Let me talk to your caller here while you're looking for that incriminating quote.

Kim   All right. Go ahead.

London   Let me just put it this way. This is my work. I am a writer, a producer, and a researcher. And in the process of doing my work, I happened to find someone that I have a personal relationship with. I want you to understand that I have worked with many, many offenders, and there is no personal relationship, and I am not attracted to people who commit violence. The violence is a tragedy. The fact that they can't control themselves, that this happens, is not a happy thing.

Caller   Do you think that it's not his fault—

London   Not at all.

Caller   —or do you think it's caused by external forces?

London   There's an element of will, and he does take responsibility for what he has done. He does not blame anyone but himself. He squarely takes responsibility.

Caller	How do you feel about that? Do you think he did it, he put the knife in these people, he raped these women?
London	He did. Here's what I think. I think that in a case like this, everything has to go wrong. There has to be a number of factors involved. The factor of the offender at some point taking it into his own will and doing it, that really is not blood on our hands. But the blood is on our hands when there are things that are under our control.
Caller	But now wait a minute—
London	Such as the conditions that went into his life.
Caller	—You say the blood's on our hands, he's the one who's committed the murders, now this collective guilt, I'm sorry, I'm just can't find that.
London	That's what we're talking about today. It is us as a society.
Caller	Now Sondra, I've been listening to you speak and talking to you, and I've come to the conclusion, and I'm sure a lot of Kim Petersen's listeners have, that you are a severely disturbed person, you're an, I'll go ahead and be blunt here—
Kim	She's a Gemini, you're a Gemini, right? All Gemini's are goofy, man.
Caller	—you're very disturbed and you have a lot of problems yourself, and you're working them out, and you more or less sound like a groupie to killers and butchers and murderers.
London	I'm sorry that—
Kim	But only honest butchers and murderers.

London   I'm sorry this appearance has given you that
         impression.

Caller   I'm trying to control my emotions because my
         family has been touched by crime, and I'm trying to
         keep a rein on my emotions—

London   I'm sorry this appearance has given you that
         impression—

Caller   —there's a part of me that's trying to understand
         you but—

London   —because only part of what I have done has been
         brought out here today. And I can understand that
         based on what you have been allowed to know about
         me that this is what you would conclude. Perhaps
         you when you read some of the books I have written
         and find out a little bit more about what I have
         done, maybe you will change your opinion.

Caller   Well, if first impressions count for anything, you
         sound like a real sick puppy.

London   Okay. Thank you so much.

Kim   Thanks for your call, man. I gotta rush. Coming up,
         (Laughs) Sarah and Rick and Doug. All right. You
         aren't armed, are you, Sondra? I believe in guns.
         Everybody should have a gun. Do you believe that?

London   I'm just armed with my wit.

Kim   Armed with wit! Incredible! And what a better place
         to bring it than the News Monster! Back with
         Sondra, but first— (Break)

Kim   Would-be wife, lover, fiancée of the butcher from
         Florida, who is here, and actually you're hoping

that the killer from Britain, Ingram, is listening to
the program this afternoon. Did you have a
message for him, or did you want to talk to him, or
I wasn't clear about that.

London   No, I just wanted him to hear the song really. It's
dedicated to anyone on death row.

Kim   In fact, it could be that the last music he ever hears
will be Sondra's music. On the Kimmer program. So
that would be fairly special. I guess. To you.

London   Yes.

Kim   Okay. To the phones, to the phones. It's Doug in
Marietta.

Caller   Kinda sorry to hear that she's only armed with her
wit. I really don't believe in an unfair fight.
(Laughter)

Kim   You're a hard man, Doug, a funny man but a hard
man. Sock it to her, buddy, she's here to take you
on, man.

Caller   I don't know if you saw that *Turning Point* piece. I
saw it and I taped it. I've seen it several times. I
lived in Jacksonville when that whole thing
happened. I was in college, and we had—

London   So you saw the check that Diana Hoyt held up for
the cameras—

Caller   — yes I saw the—

London   — of the money that they received for their story—

Caller   — but you're not telling the whole story—

Sondra London in WGST Studio

Kim   Sondra, Sondra, Sondra, why are you so angry at the families of the victims? What is your problem?

London   Because they are trying to cast aspersions on me because I am a writer and I do work—

Kim   But you don't believe in the death penalty and you want to save the life of the guy who butchered their families.

London   I didn't say that.

Kim   Yes you do, you want him to live.

London   I didn't say that.

Kim   You don't believe in the death penalty.

London   I know that he's going to be executed and I have
          said nothing about that.

Kim   But you don't believe in the death penalty, do you?

London   (Silence)

Kim   Do you believe in the death penalty?

London   My comment was about the money for the story.

Kim   You want to try to save the life, you don't want this
          guy to die. You don't want Danny Rolling, your
          lover, to die. The man who butchered their family.
          You want him to live. You're in love with him. Come
          on. Admit it, say it, it's true.

London   (Silence)

Kim   Go ahead, Doug.

Caller   She's not really telling the whole story, because the
          check that was held up, that was one of the checks
          that was sent to the families in advance of all the
          offers. They said here's the check, and they're
          saying if you cash this check, we know you accept
          our offer. And the woman that held up the check
          said I'm not cashing the check. The point that was
          made in the story that they weren't going to accept
          that offer.

London   Not that offer. They did accept another one, and I
          did talk to their lawyer and confirmed that.

Kim   You're the one that mentioned the check on TV and they didn't accept the check, so that was a lie.

London   They did accept a check for the movie rights to the story.

Kim   You said you saw the check on TV and that was a lie.

Caller   A blatant lie.

London   They all did. And if you did live in Jacksonville that Florida Times-Union story did cover that and I did talk to the attorney, and it's true.

Kim   Okay but the check they showed they did not take.

London   And she did admit it. When she got herself together and started thinking about it and even though she'd like to deny that she has accepted money for the story of her dead sister, it's true.

Kim   You make it sound like the family is trying to get rich off the brutal, terrible tragedy of their family, and the fact is it's actually the other way around. Do you really think they're trying to get rich off the brutal butchering of their daughter?

London   The story.

Kim   Do you really think they're trying to get rich off the brutal butchering of their daughter?

London   They sold the story.

Kim   Okay. Doug, I gotta run, man. (Break)

Kim   Nah-nah-na-nah-nahhh! QUOTE! QUOTE! "Like many women," says Sondra London, "I've had a weakness for good-for-nothing men." I rest my case! Nah-nah-na-nah-nahhh! Ha-ha-ha!

London   Good-for-nothing men is not necessarily—

Kim   Bad guys?

London   — criminal.

Kim   I didn't say criminal, I said bad guys. Well, your first love was a serial killer, I mean come on. (Laughs)

London   My husband was a musician.

Kim   A musician?

London   Mm-hmm.

Kim   Well, those guys are all killers anyway. Same thing.

London   Good for nothing, I think is the operative term.

Kim   Exactly. Back to the phone. Rick, Suwannee. How ya doing, man?

Caller   You know, they need to double -em up tonight, don't they?

Kim   We could do two at once.

Caller   I think we could. Because every breath you're taking is one breath too long. Am I wrong?

Kim   (Laughs) No, you're not wrong. The man took a life, tried to take two lives, he deserves to die. That's it. And it's great deterrence because he'll never kill again.

Caller   I'm talking about this bonehead down in Florida she's in love with. You know, this guy that has already breathed too many breaths.

Kim   Danny. Hunk man. Okay, see ya, man.

London   I'd just like to point out that the deterrence, that's a myth, you know, it doesn't.

Kim   No, if we kill him, then he will not be able to kill anybody else. So we're deterring him.

London   That's an argument that is—

Kim   That's a fact.

London   No it's not a fact.

Kim   Sondra, do you think he's gonna, he's coming back from the dead (laughs).

London   Excuse me, the countries where they do not have capital punishment the crime rate is lower. The states where they put capital punishment in, the crime rate elevates.

Kim   In Britain when they eliminated capital punishment the crime rate went up. (Singing) Da-dant-ta-da-da-*DANT!* Thank you.

London   When you have an execution, generally the crime rate goes up around the time of the execution.

Kim   Well, that's from peaceniks who are angry about the guy being killed, and they go out and kill people, it's unbelievable, the facts in this case are—

London   The deterrence factor is not true.

Kim	It is true. I'm sorry, Sondra, I'm very late on time, but let's get back to the phones with Sarah in Buckhead.
Caller	Well, I just think it's really sad that she can even sit up there and talk about this guy that killed all these people has any right for anyone to feel sorry for him or even try to understand what he did. Lots of people have things go wrong in their lives, there's a lot of tragedy going on in the world, but it's sick to torture the families of these people by acting like somehow it can be mentally all better if he can explain to us all what's wrong.
Kim	Why should we care about Danny Rolling?
London	The families, when the murders first started, every interview they gave, all they said was, "We just want to know why." There's only one way to find out why. And that's to get close up and personal with someone and find out why they've done what they've done.
Kim	I think the answer's almost unanimous with all of them. They're just crazy and rotten and mean and vicious and filled with the devil and they killed people and didn't give a damn about the sanctity of life. There's your answer.
London	That's what we'd like to think, isn't it?
Kim	Why write the book? I mean, the shortest book in history. One-sentence book.
London	If that was all that was wrong, then it wouldn't be happening more and more. It has something to do with us, and our attitudes.
Caller	I don't think it has to do with us, it's because people like you write these books.

London   Not necessarily toward killers, not necessarily toward capital punishment, but perhaps toward children. We're talking about child abuse, Okay—

Caller   I think it's happening more and more because people think they can do this, get away with it, and write a book. (Break)

Kim   It's Debbie, Doraville.

Caller   I thought your previous caller made some great points and I was just thinking about the young lady that called who lost her sister. I'm sure she'd give back all the money she ever made on any movie plus then some to get that girl back again and that will never happen. And I think anything she gets from the movie is justified. And they should be the only money that should be allowed to make money off another person's death.

Kim   I think you're right and Sondra, it sounds as though you're trying to say they're getting blood money. And I think if anybody's going to make money off this horrible crime, then damn it, the money ought to go to the families, as opposed to any other reason.

London   The families are not writers.

Kim   It doesn't matter.

London   Yes it does.

Kim   They're the ones that went through it.

London   Yes it does. For you to put it on the air, to come in here today, you've got to have a paycheck. For anyone to do any story, that is a profession. People want to know about the crimes that occur in a society, and the people who convey that information, that is their job and that is their profession. I am not—

Kim   Well, I don't see anything wrong with them getting ten thousand dollars or something for—

London   — I am not asking for some kind of gift or reward or money, Okay, this is a product. It's a book, it's a story, it's a TV show, it's work, and it's just like everybody else who's covering this story.

Caller   She was just very critical of the young lady because of the movie deal and there's no reason to be critical of her. If anyone should be critical of anyone, we should be critical of an outsider coming it to make money off of it.

Kim   Debbie, I'm glad you called. Greg, you're on, buddy.

Caller   This gal here, she's crazy. I think this English boy, what's his name, Danny? He needs to fry. I'll be singing Oh Danny Boy about seven o'clock, I'll tell ya.

Kim   It's the extra-crispy Brit tonight. Nicky.

Caller   Really. We'll be listening for the snap crackle and pop, and I'm not talking about Rice Krispies.

Kim   (Laughter) Get your marshmallows. Thanks, man. We've gotta say goodbye to Sondra. Thank you, thank you for coming in. This guy's gonna die and he deserves it. Last word, quick.

London   It's a state responsibility—

Kim   — to kill these killers, exactly—

London   — that they are going to be killing this man in the
          name of—

Kim   — right, for a very good reason—

London   — it is a murder—

Kim   — no, no, no, it's an execution—

London   — and the blood is on our own hands.

Kim   No, we're saving humanity by getting rid of this
          scumbag. (Laughs) And I'm sorry, but your fiancé is
          taking it in the neck too in a little while. I gotta
          run, thank you for coming in.

London   Thank you.

Sondra London Hails Eris in Court

This courtroom scene is reminiscent of *Through the Looking Glass* as rendered by Franz Kafka. It's a perfect example of what is meant by "Reality Jumps The Shark." Arguably the only time Eris Discordia has been hailed under oath and broadcast live nationally, is this brief excerpt from *State of Florida v. Sondra London, Danny Rolling, et al.* I'm just glad it was caught on camera; otherwise nobody would believe it. This is no Discordian prank; it's the Awesome Power & Dignity of our Entire Judicial System brought to bear on the avatar of absurdity itself. Our incredulous defendant is required to explain the Shor-Dur-Mar: a vintage SubGenius web-toy for declaring a "Short Duration Marriage."

Thus the Awesome Dignity of the Law has produced, for the edification of the People of the State of Florida, a sworn & witnessed testimony, reading into the record a reply from a prisoner who received a printout of a gag email generated when you fill out the form on the SubGenius website. This absurd contrivance was actually construed by the State as a real wedding – well, real enough to take my profits from publishing confessions, if not real enough to be recognized for visitation.

Florida's Assistant Attorney General George Waas examines the Defendant, Sondra London, on trial for committing journalism by publishing *The Making of a Serial Killer*.

The entire testimony is posted to Sondra London's YouTube channel. This is just the most bizarre part.

Waas   Exhibit A talks about a cyber wedding does it not?

London   Yes, it does.

Waas   Are you married in cyberspace?

London   What we have here is a document called a "Shor-Dur-Mar."

SHOR-DUR-MAR!!!

STEP RIGHT UP! Test your mettle and win your little Sweetie a Sacred Certificate of Short Duration Marriage(tm).
GUARANTEED to Absolve and Sanctify ALL otherwise "illicit" Couplings!

FREE SHORT DURATION DIVORCE(tm) IF NOT COMPLETELY SATISFIED!

Simply fill out this EASY TO SWALLOW Shor-Dur-Mar License and the Ceremonies will begin.

What is your Good Name?

And your e-mail address?

And you are a:

Subgenius
Man
Woman

What is the Name of your Beloved?

And your Beloved's e-mail address?

Your sweetie is a:

Subgenius
Man
Woman

What is your preferred Short Duration Personal Savior for this Marriage?
JHVH-1

How long do you wish for this Period of Sanctified Coupling to last?
nanoseconds

Tie the Shor-Dur Knot!   I Screwed Up - Reset

Waas   Are you married in cyberspace?

London   If you want to read this document and draw that conclusion, you may.

Waas   I'm not asking you to impart my conclusion. I'm asking you whether you are married in cyberspace. It is either yes or no.

London   I don't think it is yes or no. I don't think that there's a jurisdiction that would recognize this facetious article as constituting a marriage.

Waas   Your characterization of the article as facetious, is that true?

London   It is palpably so.

Waas   Did you write it?

London   No.

Waas   Who wrote it?

London   It is the result of a computer software program which is on another website.

Waas   Is it your position that everything in Exhibit A is facetious in nature?

London   No.

Waas   Okay then, let's eliminate the facetious stuff and go to the non-facetious stuff. The non-facetious stuff also talks about being married in cyberspace.

London   It does? I don't see anything of that nature.

Waas   You see Danny Rolling's writings in there, do you recognize them as Danny Rolling's writings?

London   This part right here?

Waas   And what is he saying about it?

London   You want me to read it?

Waas   Yeah, go ahead.

(Nancy Grace voice-over)

Grace   Miss London is what's normally termed a *hostile witness.*

Nancy Grace Calling a Defendant a Hostile Witness

London   (Reading Exhibit A) I-Net Wedding. Just a few close friends at the Ceremony. Reception at Disney Online two dash NY at CO at mp3. Sondra, the Movie Star Erisian Elestria, and I, the Hallucinated Alien, the Gainesville Slasher. Danny, do you take this Princess Supreme Erisian Elestria as your SubGenius wife in spiritual matrimony. Quote. I do. And Sondra, do you take this Hallucinated Alien, as your Caged Knight, for better or for worse? And the lady says I—I think so. Then, so be it. You may kiss now. Mmmm-wah! Good Sugar! The Movie Star and the Hallucinated Alien forever. Amen. Bonsoir, Mon Chéri, Love always, Your Danny.

Waas   Is that also done in humor and facetiousness?

London	It's hard to tell.
Waas	You don't consider yourself married in cyberspace, do you?
London	No.
Waas	Why'd you put that on the webpage, on the Internet?
London	I'm a Discordian.
Waas	What history does that tell?
London	You see, I don't understand your question.
Waas	You said you're a historian.
London	I didn't say that.
Waas	What did you say?
London	I am a Discordian.
Waas	What does a Discordian do about putting items like that on the internet? How does that relate?
London	It's a kind of a deep subject, do you really want me to discuss this here?
Waas	As briefly as you can.
London	All right, I'll tell you about Eris Discordia, who is the Greco-Roman goddess who tossed the provocative item into the fête of the gods, and then left the name-brand gods and goddesses to fight over who deserved the designation of "The Prettiest One." Then as you know, Paris intervened to declare the rightful winner. He was offered different bribes by the top three goddesses: Hera,

Athena and Aphrodite. And the one that offered the
winning bribe was Athena. She guaranteed Paris
the hand of the most beautiful woman in world, who
turned out to be Helen of Troy, and that's what
started the Trojan War. So therefore when I say I
am a Discordian, I'd say that a lot of my
philosophical background would emanate from the
model of the Greco-Roman goddess Eris Discordia.

Waas   So there's nothing there that explains to the world
        why Danny Rolling is a serial killer, is there?

London   No.

Waas   These other things, Valentines, love letters... (Long Pause)

London   Okay?

Waas   I assume you put those on the Internet as well?

London   Yes.

Waas   And I suppose you did that because you are a Discordian?

London   No.

Waas   What purpose do those letters serve to inform the public as to why Danny Rolling is a serial killer?

London   Oh, that's a very good question.

Waas   That's why I asked it. Now answer it.

London   As you know, the crimes he committed were ostensibly sexually motivated and I think that there has been quite a lot of discussion about this offender's relationship with women, and how he sees women. I find it very enlightening to examine the way he sees the woman in his life, which would be me. If there were any changes in his expression, that would be equally relevant. Which I would expect any time.

Waas   And all those explanations are on the web page as well, are they not?

London   Excuse me, all what?

Waas   Those explanations you just testified to.

London   No. They are not.

Waas   So the public has no idea why you put those on the web page.

London   Like Eric Discordia, I just tossed the provocative item into the fray and let them argue about it.

Sondra London Live in Court

One wag on the internet called this one of the most bizarre moments ever to air on Court TV. "Somewhere out there, there's somebody who stumbled on that while channel-surfing and still hasn't quite recovered." And that's just some rando watching it! Imagine being the one in the hot seat.

Printed in Great Britain
by Amazon

43726476R00215